Now when it rains

Now when it rains

A WRITER'S MEMOIR

Jeffrey Paparoa Holman

STEELE ROBERTS
AOTEAROA

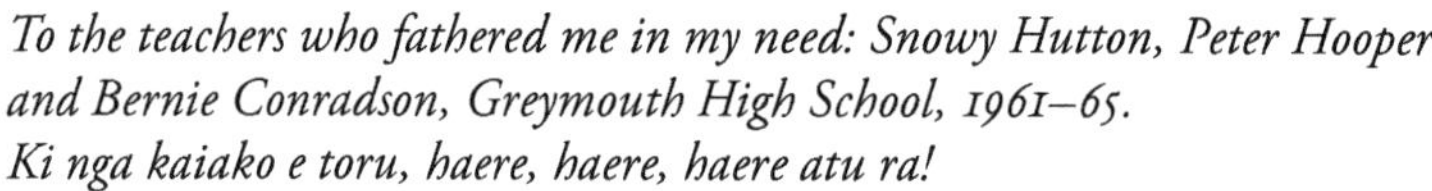
To the teachers who fathered me in my need: Snowy Hutton, Peter Hooper and Bernie Conradson, Greymouth High School, 1961–65.
Ki nga kaiako e toru, haere, haere, haere atu ra!

Author photograph (front cover): Romain Fiasson (2013).
Il est mort 2018; haere ra e taku hoa no Wiwi.

Editorial & production assistance: Simon Garrett, Krysana Hanley, Richa Kohli.

ATL: Alexander Turnbull Library

ISBN 978-0-947493-77-6

Steele Roberts Aotearoa
Box 33555 Petone 5046 Aotearoa New Zealand
info@SteeleRoberts.co.nz • www.SteeleRoberts.co.nz

Contents

PART III IN BED WITH THE MUSE

Ehara taku toa i te toa takitahi — engari he toa takitini.
My strength is not that of one person, but comes from many.

Now when it rains I hear my life in flood.
The purr of gas burns blue from anthracite.

Now when it rains how near is my ferry.
The light from the hall, playing 45s.

Now when it rains I know I was there.
There rang a bell for an epoch, tolling.

Now when it rains I think of the women.
Mothers who bred seven sons for the pit.

Now when it rains I'm ripe to surrender.
Give in to all that was always to be.

When it rains now we're what's left of Blackball:
all that the mine was is somebody's dream

fading away at the mouth of the tunnel
where light's absolution and fresh air is sweet.

The late great Blackball Bridge Sonnets, Steele Roberts 2004

Prologue

Is there a particular childhood sound, heard again, that can trigger who you were? Where you were? What something felt like? When I hear the rain these days, it's not the same music of the rain that fell on our tarred, corrugated iron roof in my Blackball mining town home: drumming, receding, advancing, calling somehow.

My rain today falls on the Perspex roof of an urban verandah in Christchurch: restrained, muted, timid. It's not the same rain, even when it teems. Still, my memory senses those West Coast moments and back it flows: in rivulets, in tides that swirl with people, talk and faces, music and voices, night birds, cicadas. Is it similar for you?

Where do poems come from, if not in these early primal sounds: as vibrations we absorb in the words of parents, siblings, friends and neighbours as we grow, like tuning forks, instruments in a divine orchestra that learns to play in the everyday world?

Just as music has high and low notes, life too is seldom without joy and despair, success and failure for us all. What follows in my story is like yours, with the faces of those who blessed and encouraged us, and others who wounded and did their worst.

As a kid I broke my leg and broke my arm in quick succession; as a teenager I broke my arm again. As a dreamy boy I saw great silver planes pass over in the Christchurch sky; at high school, I got to fly a joyride in an Auster that once landed on skis in the Antarctic.

I wanted to soar in Spitfires; I ended up sweating in a sawmill, a high school dropout. I yearned for one girl after another to love me; I managed to lose one wife through divorce and another in a road death.

I loved writing at school and was good too, my teachers told me; I had at least one career in the shearing sheds and another pounding the streets, picking up people's rubbish bins. I did social work. I did drugs. Everything, but what I am doing right now in the middle of this sentence. Writing.

I found God. God found me. I went back to the place of my English birth and had a mental breakdown. I became a bookseller. I started writing again. I came back to New Zealand and finished an abandoned English degree. I learned te reo Maori, or at least I made a start. Tihei mauri ora! The breath of life!

I started breathing deeply, breathing out the poems I'd begun to write after I gave up being somebody I wasn't. All those roads, all those masks, all those stumbles, may not have been poetry on the page, but bodily, physically, just like the rain that drummed its fingers on the roof of my childhood, they taught me to make my own music, to be my own person — now, when it rains, and now, when it ceases to fall.

Rapahoe, West Coast.
Logan Baty

I

The sap is rising

How lonely a small boy poet, dressed in black, feels on the vast and terrifying frontier wilderness! Little by little, life and books give me glimpses of overwhelming mysteries.

Perhaps I didn't live just in myself, perhaps I lived the lives of others? … My life is a life put together from all those other lives: the lives of the poet.

— Pablo Neruda, *Memoirs*, Farrar, Straus & Giroux, New York 1977

I

Little Pommie

I was born — inauspiciously — in spite of a medical prohibition: that my mother should never again fall pregnant, after a near-death experience carrying and birthing my older brother Eric. He was born in February 1946, with Mum in the full grip of that most often fatal condition, eclampsia — pregnancy toxaemia — at a time when either mother, or baby, or both would die. My father, coming as he did from a family of four and not relishing the prospect of raising an only child, persuaded my mother they should try again — there being little obvious risk to himself. I'm not sure to be grateful or chastened by the threat I may have posed to my mother's prospects of survival, but happily all went well. In the November winter of 1947 — after the earlier disastrous deep freeze March winter of the same year — I emerged to face reality a month before Christmas.

London,
Winter 1947.
Wikipedia Commons

None of this of course I knew, in the sense I now have of my history. We are told the story of our beginnings in retrospect; I had a powerful storyteller waiting behind my parents to include me in hers and shape mine: Nanny Airey. Much later, a world away in New Zealand where she would join us, she wrote in me through her reminiscences a family history I am carrying on here. Well into her 80s, my grandmother would retreat into the vanished worlds of her Victorian childhood, right up to the end of World War Two, taking me — often unwillingly — along with her. Had she not called me to her bedside, I would have known far less about who she was. What that had to do with who I was and would become is less clear; reclaiming her seems more necessary than ever now, and as I write her, she returns.

Her courage: she faced down a bull in a country lane around West Derby in Lancashire. Her daring: she and her two brothers practised target shooting in the basement with pearl-handled Derringer revolvers, brought back to Liverpool from America by her adventurous father. Her excitement: that same father, Peter Daniel Bywater stopping Buffalo Bill in the streets of Liverpool in the 1890s by calling his name, whereupon William Cody jumped down from his horse and embraced him, shouting, "Peter!" — so proving great-grandfather's tale, told earlier to his unbelieving children, that he had ridden on the Pony Express with Buffalo Bill. In danger: the bombs that fell on and around her house in Wavertree, Liverpool, during the Liverpool Blitz of May 1941, when she was a local air raid warden and my mum was a Wren — a member of the Women's Royal Naval Service — in Western Approaches Command. The terror: their poor crazed foxy, chewing a block of wood to shreds under the kitchen table as sirens wailed, searchlights swept the night skies and anti-aircraft guns broke all hell loose.

Nanny's stories were told to me up to eighty years after the event, ripples in the flow of history sweeping me along with her. By then I was living in New Zealand with New Zealanders, growing up as one of them. The family stories I was hearing came not just from another time but another world, another country: England, the England of the past. This was true for more than just me in the coal mining culture of the West Coast where I grew up. My two closest friends had one or both parents born in Scotland or the Midlands, and still with the accents to prove it. Their family culture too was that of recent arrivals (however forcefully we, as Kiwis now, differentiated ourselves from the Poms, as I was learning to call, and despise, the English).

Scots and Irish were a high percentage of our grandparental ranks in the 1960s on the Coast; it was not surprising to find antipathy to the English. And my parents were English, certainly (although my mother had been born in Wanganui in 1921, returning to the UK before she was ten years old). I'm sure I never thought of myself as a Pom, imbibing later with all my schoolmates the same sense of superiority to those arrogant oppressors of the Celts and the Gaels.

The problem for me in my early teens was the suppression of memory, scenes I could no longer access in the life of a two-year-old self born in Kingston upon Thames, London. I had sailed via Panama to New Zealand in April 1950 on the RMS *Rangitiki*, meeting King Neptune on the voyage as we 'crossed The Line' — the equator, landing in Wellington with a crystal-clear English accent imparted to me by my mother's naval training, a process that had knocked any vestige of Liverpool from her soundscape and rendered her pretty much RP — 'received pronunciation'. Yet deep

Dog without a name, my mother Mary and me, Howick, 1951.

inside, I was English: a little Pommie immigrant who would have to forget all those early speech patterns and learn to be one of the boys.

It would be delicious to have some of those lost memories now: the ship passing through the massive locks of the Panama Canal, high above the surrounding landscape; the squadrons of magical flying fish I was told could land on the decks of ships; seeing adult voyagers covered in shaving foam and tossed by King Neptune's henchmen into the *Rangitiki*'s swimming pool; waking in the four-berth cabin with my mother, my older brother and three other women, causing a mid-ocean panic by sneaking outside and wandering the ship as our poor mother slumbered on, waking to find us gone. Yes, even the arrival in Wellington and seeing for the first time the place that would become my home, my country of identity. This landfall turned my fate from that of an English boy growing up in London in the 1950s and transformed me into a Kiwified immigrant with not a care in the world about where I came from — or where I might be going.

My waka RMS *Rangitiki*, that carried me here in 1950, aged two and a half.
All About Ships and Shipping, Faber & Faber, 1952

M.S. Rangitiki ('29), Tw.-scr., 16,984, 16 **kts.**

2

Navy kid

My father had sailed from England in May 1949, twelve months ahead of us on HMNZS *Tutira*. The ship docked in Malta with another war surplus Royal Navy frigate, HMNZS *Rotoiti*, Loch-class vessels acquired from England as New Zealand re-equipped her post-war navy. After joining in exercises with the Mediterranean Fleet, *Rotoiti* sailed on to Crete to take part in a memorial service for our war dead, while *Tutira* made an unusual detour to the ancient Greek island of Cythera, at the south-eastern end of the Peloponnesian peninsula. Dad was now a yeoman of signals in the service of New Zealand, en route to a tiny island the ship's captain just so happened to have liberated at the end of the war. The skipper was "feted like a hero", runs the account of another crew member, Arthur Venus, and "He had a street named after him."[1]

My dad's naval service began again, with a Mediterranean booze-cruise, as the crew were showered with ouzo-fuelled hospitality by the Greeks grateful for their liberation from German occupation. This navy would be a little different to the one he had left in 1947; my father was back at sea, a decade after he had joined the Royal Navy as a teenager in 1938. Sailors are sailors, after all; it's hardly a surprise that he went back to Father Neptune after four years ashore. With my mother's serious health problems, he'd had to buy himself out of his last two years of naval service; the sea was in him and wanted him back — and so we became New Zealanders.

After we arrived in Auckland and found temporary shelter in the prefabs at Narrow Neck on navy property, we waited for him as he came and went on his voyages around the Tasman and the Pacific, on tours of duty to Korea after New Zealand joined in the Allied campaign to buttress the south against a communist takeover. Dad was now a Cold War warrior and my brother and I were navy kids. There was a brief spell in a seaside bach at Bucklands Beach near Howick, the area having been since 1847 the home of an earlier generation of English military migrants. These were the Royal New Zealand Fencible Corps, established by Governor George Grey as a territorial army, newly arrived smallholders to be available in times of war. We were now part of an established pattern of colonial

At the bach: Eric at left with a gun, me and our mum, Bucklands Beach, Howick, 1951.

history — warriors and their families who travelled the world to fight imperial wars and reap the spoils.

Whatever the poets may tell you about childhood, it's as true and as false as the unreliable nature of memory. No reports ever come from those experiencing their preschool days as it happens; it's always after the fact. I can look at photographs now and only imagine what I was like: my brother and I in the surf in our bib overalls with Rangitoto smudging the horizon; an older girl we were both in love with, guiding us down a hillside track to the beach; my mother at a set table on the verandah of the bach, we boys seated with her, half-obscured by long-necked beer bottles open for business. I'm guessing from the evidence of the booze that my father took the picture, along with the one of my mother and me, with the dog.

His arrivals home from the base at Devonport on his pop-popping Francis-Barnett motorbike down the dusty metal road were filmic: a white-capped sailor on two wheels. The journey was a mission in those days, considering that he had to catch a ferry once he got down to the end of Queen Street. There was no harbour bridge in 1951; that year would become infamous for the paralysing nationwide wharfies lockout going on all around us. The navy had to act as strike-breakers. Whether Dad was one of those manpowered onto the wharfs to oversee this scab action I would never discover; his left-wing sympathies would have been offended, but an order was an order. He may well have been at sea or up in Korea at the time. We had left Britain behind in our wake, but the tentacles of the big British shipping companies and the old-world struggle of capital and labour had followed us all the way.

Pre-school children we were, ignorant that our new country was experiencing government and police actions reminiscent of the fascists. Everything my father and his compatriots here and in Britain had supposedly fought to keep from these shores was now being visited upon them and their families. We were the sons of a naval petty officer, soon to add two New Zealand-born daughters to the family in quick succession. There was no shortage of work for the country's military in Farmer Sid Holland's Red-beating economy. My father was now in the pay of a government that was out to destroy human freedoms and appease their American Cold War allies.

It was years later when he was a miner and a trade union secretary in Blackball that I — influenced by a magnificently drawn serialised *Boy's Own* version of the life of Winston Churchill in the *Eagle* magazine — would try to tell him what a great man the indomitable cigar-chomping Winnie was. "That bastard!" was his bitter reply — unfathomable to me at the time. My father, it seems, came from the same school as Jock Barnes, the man who led the wharfies to their historic defeat. As the drama unfolded, we happily paddled in the warm and friendly Auckland surf, while once-idle ships were unloaded by scab labour.

Our next move was across the harbour to the North Shore, into a brand-new state house at 6 Plymouth Crescent, Bayswater, a new subdivision full of naval families, many like us newly arrived from the UK. In the following year, back across the same stretch of water, Maori of Ngati Whatua on Orakei marae were to be unceremoniously ethnically cleansed, most of their last acres taken, all the buildings demolished and burned save for the chapel and the urupa.[2] After all, the Queen was on her way, and these "unsightly dwellings" were near the royal route.

1952: Burning the buildings at the Orakei pa, after the eviction.

Sir George Grey Special Collections, Auckland Libraries ID: 7-A14286A

In Plymouth Crescent we played on, ready to welcome our first-born Kiwi, my sister Jill. Having settled his family into their new quarters, leaving my mother with a new tenant due for delivery nine months later, Dad sailed away again to Korea. To placate the Americans and save us from Reds under Beds, my father was going back to war. By June of 1951 my grandmother was also on the high seas, sailing out to join us in Auckland. Her presence, however, did not save me and my brother from being sent for a 'holiday' with some friends my mother had met at a local church. She was then free to enter the maternity ward of the navy hospital at Devonport to have my sister.

On a fateful day, my trusting mother put us aboard a Road Services bus and off we rode to Baylys Beach near Dargaville — a three-hour drive today, much longer then. We made our mark by becoming car-sick; who knows what a sight we presented to our strange new carers as we got off the bus in the middle of nowhere, bewildered, deserted and no doubt bolshie. Our hosts were an older couple, from another age of child rearing. We played one day on the concrete water tank beside their bach, floating sticks in the deep black water. That night I wet the bed, only to be hauled out in my sodden pyjamas by the man early next morning, spanked with a stick all the way up the hill, to the scene of the crime at the water tank.

My poor mother had no inkling that she was delivering us into the hands of such abusers. I do have other magical memories of that dark time: of locals, mainly Maori, digging on the beach for the toheroa, the prized shellfish that lives on the tideline and burrows frantically deep if disturbed. Playing on the beach, we would see a procession of ancient vehicles drive down through the high sandhills and park on the expanse of hard wet sand. Families would descend with spades and sugar sacks to hunt the precious kaimoana. We were invited to help, instructed on the need for stealth, fascinated by this ancient food-gathering rite that my Anglo-Saxon forebears on the other side of the world had practised in pursuit of whelks and cockles.

Once returned by our captors, sadder and wiser, we were presented with a brand-new sister and a grandmother in the house. My mother now had five mouths to feed; at least there was another adult to share the domestic load and help keep us boys in check. Mum was still in contact with the man who had saved her life in 1945, Dr Spitzer, who had treated her with caffeine injections to ameliorate the effects of the pregnancy toxaemia. When she died in 2005, among her few treasured documents was a letter from him written in April 1952 on stationery from the Orient Line ship, RMS *Oronsay*. He and his family were on a cruise, expecting to arrive back

My grandmother Eunice, my mother Mary and Jill, 1952.

in England in May. Thanking her for a "lovely long letter", he congratulated my mother on having a daughter, "but I think it is time you stopped."

She must have mentioned that Jill came feet first into the world — "We always put patients right out for breech births" — and there the letter tails off, the next page missing. It shows how much this man meant to her, 'Walter Spitzer, M.D. Prague', whose ground-breaking research on pernicious anaemia in pregnancy had saved her life and my brother's. She told us later that he had fled from Czechoslovakia after the Nazi takeover in 1938 and established himself in England; he continued to practise at Kingston County Hospital and publish scholarly papers on pregnancy issues well into the 1950s. Here was one good thing, among many evils, that Hitler set in motion by declaring war on the world. No Dr Spitzer, no us.

As sailors sail away, so they return to shore; my father was coming home from his first engagement in Korea. Down we all went with a crowd of navy families to the wharf at HMNZS *Philomel* in Devonport to welcome them. The grey ship, the white sailors' uniforms, the beards, the hugs, the reek of tobacco: there we were on the fo'c'sle with these strange giants returned from another world, playing with the tinny wind-up toys they had brought to charm us: jeeps, tanks, seals with balls on their noses that spun for as long as the spring unwound. These magical items were

ing over, bouncing off the anchor chains as men became s how to play with our new Made in Japan ex-beer can down into the galley where the bearded cook served us all be buckets of ice cream and giant slabs of fruitcake. Home eed — but never for long.

Royal New Zealand Navy

CRUISERS

Bellona (1942). Displacement, 5,700 tons.

Black Prince (1942). Displacement, 5,900 tons.
Turbines, S.H.P. 62,000. Speed, 33 knots.
Main Armament : 8 5·25-in. ; 6 21-in. Torpedo Tubes.
(On loan from Royal Navy.)

FRIGATES

Kaniere (1944).
Pukaki (1944).
Hawea (1944).
Rotoiti (1944).
Tutira (1944).
Taupo (1944).

Displacement, 1,435 tons.
Triple Expansion, I.H.P. 5,500. Speed, 19·5 knots.
Main Armament : 1 4-in.

(Also Minesweeping Trawlers, M.L.s and other small craft.)

Some of my father's ships, 1949–1954.
All About Ships and Shipping, Faber & Faber, 1952

3

Bryndwr boy

Globemasters. That's what living in Christchurch as a kid in the 1950s meant to me. We'd moved again. I was just getting settled in my first year at primary school in Bayswater when Dad shifted us all south. One minute you were here, the next there, and that was that. There I was in the living room of our second state house, 151 Aorangi Road, Bryndwr, crammed with plywood tea crates held together with strips of metal on the corners, one of which sliced my leg open as we played between them. The scar is still there. Thousands of new impressions laid down over the Auckland arrival and voyage out from England were fading. If any one thing talks to me now about those years from 1954 until 1957, it was the arrival of those mighty American transport planes, tasked to carry men and matériel south to the Pole as part of Operation Deep Freeze.

"Old Shaky": Operation Deep Freeze C-124 Globemaster, Wigram, 1957.
Courtesy Peter Tremayne

The trip to our new home too had been by air: as a navy family, we'd avoided trains and the ferries and flew south in style in a magical NAC DC-3, all shiny and noisy and wonderful. We landed at Wellington, nagged my mother for a fizzy drink and then spent the Christchurch leg throwing up into brown paper bags. A temporary home in the Oxford Hotel by the River Avon in town was where we waited for the house to become available, a time when my brother and I caused a major plumbing incident by flushing cardboard Jeyes toilet paper holders down the ancient system. We never 'fessed up to the chaos we had created, waiting for the blows to fall that never did come (more would, for other crimes later, so we always paid one way or another for being normal children).

Being more land-based, with Dad as part of Naval Reserve staff at HMNZS *Pegasus*, we got to go out now and then as a family to one or ıg of cinemas that circled the red-bus swarming Square, the Anglican cathedral. The State, Avon, Tivoli, Regent, ; a night out at one of these was a gala occasion. One s going to see *Cockleshell Heroes*, a classic 1956 British war ımmando raid: the red velvet ropes and brass stanchions in the foyer, nolding us back from a rocking cardboard canoe display in which two face-blackened saboteurs paddled towards the enemy. This was as close as I'd ever been to heaven; through it all I was subtly (and not-so-subtly) taught to believe that not only had we won the war, but that heroism and self-sacrifice were the stuff of battles (rather than terror and the destruction of all that humans hold dear).

Once more we became a state house family. No 151 was part of a large state housing area in the suburb of Bryndwr, which in the mid-'50s was not far from the city limits and the farms on the northern edge of Greers Road (just beginning to appear were the new housing subdivisions for private buyers). Here, on the cusp of a rural area about to be swallowed by suburbia, we could roam between the delights of town and the free range of country. What the Square had for us by night, the freedom to roam Mr Royd's dairy farm could amply supply by day.

Not so delightful were the magpies that nested in the macrocarpas along the drive to his house, as we discovered when we visited this kindly farmer. We were dive-bombed regularly by these black and white Aussie banshees, accurate as Stukas. This rural haven became our playground, all the way out to the distant airport at Harewood, stopping by the Birds Eye pea crops to steal our fill. Whether it was the DC-3 flight from Auckland that set me

The four of us at 151: me, Jill, Eric and Elisabeth.
OPPOSITE My Firestone aircraft carrier, 1955.

off, the towering Globemasters parked on the tarmac at the airport, or even the tiny planes on the plastic aircraft carrier my parents gave me at the Firestone Christmas Party in 1955 that began a lifelong love of flight, something was taking off.

Dad was no longer in the navy, having made an unwise withdrawal from the mess fund to pay off the bookies, losing his career as well as the bet. His spell in prison led to a new manifestation as a rubber factory worker. He would return from his toil blackened outwardly, while inwardly besmirched by the loss of honour among his former naval comrades. Seven years later it would happen again: we would find his petty officer's uniform still hanging, stripped of its authority, in the wardrobe. I was eight years old: boys are not noted for their ability to empathise with adults, nor understand the forces and decisions that shuffle the cards they are dealt. If Dad was out of the real navy, I was pretty pleased with my plastic warship.

Next came the Davy Crockett craze: the coonskin hats, T-shirts, buckskin trousers and Winchester rifles. When the film hit the Square in 1956, there I was, squashed in the crowd of excited baby-boom boys ready to believe anything about this hero with the furry hat. The song was on the radio, the products were in the shops; it was my first real taste of pop culture and its derivatives. By the time Davy had seen off all his enemies, save for the wicked Mexicans who killed him at the Alamo, I was entranced and inconsolable. I wept when he died, then went out with my mother and clothed myself in the merchandise. Time would kill off all the illusions and historical distortions I might pick up along the way, but in that cinema, along with millions of other kids worldwide, I was Davy Crockett.

I was transported, back to a mountaintop in Tennessee; not even breaking first my leg and a few months later, my arm, could spoil things. I had tried my hand at flying by stepping backwards off the shed roof, absorbed in trying to get a cardboard propeller — pinned to a wooden clothes-peg — to spin. I fell into a pile of old firewood and was carted off to hospital in my Sunday School best. "Not you again, Jeffrey?" mused the matron as they wheeled me in for the anaesthetic. I replied by obligingly throwing up my breakfast of bacon and eggs on the medical staff as the gas was sending me to wherever it is we go, talked off slowly, mumbling under the ether our fuzzy replies.

In the next year or two, there would be some blowback from my swallowing the Fess Parker version by Disney, when I would see the film again with my newfound playmates on the West Coast. This all came to pass after my restless father left Firestone, got himself a new job on the New Zealand Railways, and dragged us all in his next geographical move — to the middle of nowhere called Ngahere.

(xxiv)

Rain come down, it all comes down to rain:
the great rain, the dark rain, the Rain Father

pissing his worst in the headwaters, Mother-
of-all-Rains squatting, showering blood, mud

rain ricochets back off the clay, the heavens
polluted, the hills collapse, slip rain, sod rain,

the fat tears of God rain, rain so thick and vast
it can drown the prayers of believers from

you back to Jesus! Fear rain, awe rain, rain no
beggared philosopher washed downstream on a

trunk of rata could ever explain: dog rain, cat and
rat rain, the rain that drowns ambition, swallows

towns and smashes bridges, train-eating, brain-
beating, roof-drumming over & over & over. Rain.

The late great Blackball Bridge Sonnets, Steele Roberts 2004

4

Swampland

To get to this new home on the other edge of the island, we had to do what most newcomers to the West Coast did in the 1950s: enter by mountains. Either by tunnel or steep twisty winding passes, you came to that other world in the manner of being born. Barely ten, I was still a creature of the moment: in the taxi to the station, on the railcar, pies and sandwiches at Springfield, over steepling viaducts, entering the mountain at Arthur's Pass, adaze at our reflections in the windows as the lights came on inside the tunnel and we thundered underground towards Otira for what seemed to take years, too fully alive to know or to fear that we were buried beneath unfathomable tons of rock, rattling and roaring on and on, to Stillwater.

We changed trains there at the junction, stepping down into the new world to wait for the Reefton connection. That railcar, when it came, took us all to what was little more than a railway siding a few miles up the swampland valley: Ngahere, or "Nyhairy" as many of the locals twisted the reo. I would discover the name meant forest or bush, but there were not too many trees surrounding us as we walked onto our new home ground. There was the odd scattered kahikatea, white pine on scrappy farms, trees

Ngahere gold dredge, 1940s: Ted Holmes, back row, centre. He and his wife, Ivy, were models for the Palmers — the publican and his family — in Bill Pearson's 1963 novel set in Blackball, *Coal Flat*.
Courtesy Doreen Adams

that years ago had avoided being milled for butter boxes. Ngahere existed for the New Forest timber mill and in recent times, huge hungry dredges gulping up river stones for gold. Now they were gone, leaving massive holes where they had ceased their cacophonous searches, broken up like surplus warships. These dredge ponds became fishponds where we hunted trout and eels.

The settlement was also a railhead for cattle farmers who would whip their bellowing beasts to the stockyards, and a source of employment for the New Zealand Railways families who had come like us to service these needs. We were met by some of Dad's new workmates and, joy of joys, piled onto a tiny jigger, racing the half mile up the track to our new house beside the school. We went in groups, as there was only room for four adults. I can still see the curve of the track as we whizzed along in the chilling air, bubbling over with the newness of it all, bug-eyed at a startled flock of pukeko who burst up in panic from their watery domain, flapping away from the jigger beast with its roaring Briggs & Stratton motor, like clumsy bats. Heaven.

Pukeko whanau, artist, Jan FitzGerald.

I didn't know that these swamp hens were reluctant to take wing; that they were waders who stepped the marshes and paddocks in their luminous blue coats, flicking white rump tails. To me they were halfway between monsters and omens, shrieking heralds of all that was to befall us in this place of oncoming darkness and vast fields of light. When we got to the railway house over the road from the line, Pikey, our neighbour at the other side of the school was there, showing my mother how he'd laid the kindling in the coal range, got in a load of wood and coal and some meat in the safe, too. Mr Pike, his wife Rona, his sons Colin and Snig and their daughter Gillian would become our first friends and the children, at least, partners in crime.

West Coast hospitality — the sharing typical of many small communities in one-horse towns across the country at that time — was welcomed by my mother. She had come from gas and electric cooking: now, running an old Shacklock Orion was an art to master, as was the meat safe which did for a fridge in those days, and the milk delivered nightly in a billy. The butcher would arrive when the pubs closed late in the evening and carve up whatever Mum ordered from the back of his van; he'd be well alight with the cheer of a night's drinking. There was the outside dunny up the path behind the house, complete with candles for night missions, populated with the rats that bred in this draughty outhouse, betraying their presence by chewing the paper placed there for our needs.

This was not all: amid such excitements, there was a school just through the fence (no easy way to fake a day off) and across the railway lines, acres and acres of river flat swamps, much of it turned to a rimu sawdust dump by the mill's discharges after it had finished slicing up the forest into scantling for framing up houses. Sacrilege today, it was all in a day's work then. Always with you, once smelt: the perfume of sawn rimu. Always inside me, once seen: blue smoke columns rising from the fires beside every mill in the valley, burning the offcuts and slabs. Ineradicable: the purple stain of rimu sap as it sank into your hands revealing lifelines, a boy's own tattoo.

Ngahere School was the site of our West Coast initiation rites: we were outsiders and it wasn't long before we were put in our place. My brother Eric was eleven, I was nine; he was sporty and wiry, I was clumsy and on the chubby side. We probably looked available for treatment, which came on a wet day when we tried to join the other kids at playtime in the shelter shed (common in rural schools at the time). Teachers kicked you outside at playtime, to stay there until the bell rang; lunches were eaten in the shed when it was wet (often). We tried to get in; they pushed us out. Eric led the charge and they jumped us. I ended up trapped somewhere inside a knot of Gillmans, Porters, Balderstones and Donaldsons, all keen to give us the bash. We were in our place now: we were in.

In even deeper when we got called up, days after arriving, for one of the junior Ngahere rugby league teams. An adult arrived at the door and

Jimmy Mountford, Blackball Kiwi — painting by Earl Tutty.

declared to my mother, "Mrs Holman, I see you have a couple of boys there, send them up the hill, they can play for us." Boots arrived from somewhere, along with the jerseys, their yellow V and twin yellow hoops around the blue body. I had no more clue of what to do with a football than fly, but no matter.

"Up the hill" was accurate; the footy ground was on a gravel terrace behind us, cut through by the river aeons ago, providing panoramic views of the Paparoa Range across the valley to Blackball over the Grey River. There, Ngahere's footy arch-enemies in their red-and-black armour lay in wait to chase down every intruder on the mining town's domain — and thrash them with a cricket score.

On that first frosty Saturday morning I was thrown into action, the most clueless of neophytes ever to grace the home of Ngahere rugby league. I ran the wrong way, joined the other team, got yelled at, sworn at — given any choice in the matter, I would have burst into tears and run home to mother. That was not about to happen; it was part of the local religion, to be suffered, embraced and lived with until escape was possible (as it was ten years later in Blackball when, as a sixth former at high school, I resigned from the code forever). Who knew or cared about the heroics of class warfare? Who knew of the arrogance of rugger buggers "over the hill", or just why the men played on Sundays instead of going to church, or the tradition of the West Coast teams as giant-killers to the rest of the country, a graveyard for unwary international tourists? This was the way in, the path to acceptance; however unwillingly to begin with, I wanted in.

'Being in' didn't stop the bullying, though. One of the Porter boys — we called him Shorty — took to pushing me around. I told my brother one evening on the way home from some adventure in the swamps, "I've had enough of that Shorty Porter, next time I see him, I'm going to get him!" Cruel fate: Shorty came cycling out of the dusk toward us, on his own. "Here's your chance," Eric observed. Bugger: now I was in the deep end. Oh, well. "Shorty Porter!" I snorted, "I've got a bone to pick with you!" (where did that come from?). Not knowing much about fighting, I leapt on the startled bully and knocked him off his bike, off his balance and found myself sitting on his chest as he struggled beneath me. Having got my man down, I had no idea what to do next.

"My brothers'll get you!" he wailed, well aware there were two of us. I got off him, expecting a counter-attack, but he clambered back on his bike and took off, swearing revenge. It never came. Having learned a secret about bullies, I puffed up my chest and swaggered home. Hardly fearless in the dark Ngahere nights (a radio programme with screaming pterodacytls

Steam locomotive: John Madden, artist.

heard before bedtime gave me nightmares), I was nevertheless becoming a West Coast kid. The trains whose tracks my father and his railways gang serviced night and day, storm or shine, rumbled past our home on tracks parallel to the road, blinding headlights signalling their passage, splashed from one end of the room to the other. We would jump out of our beds at first to watch them coming and see them pass, the fireman and the driver outlined by the glow of flames in the cab — steaming monsters of the night sweeping past on the way north to Reefton and Westport.

This was an entirely physical, hard-edged world: when my youngest sister Elisabeth was baptised in the tiny Anglican church, the minister's cassock draped on the heater and caught fire. "Holy smoke!" quipped my father from the family pew. That was about as spiritual as it got. We lived in our bodies in a way I had not done before, nor since. Ngahere and the Grey Valley, the West Coast and vast tracts of the South Island were brooding dark green wildernesses, barely domesticated, never tamed. We ran over the rimu sawdust swamps and sailed boats in the water race that flowed beneath the mill, sending the tiny grains of native pine out to form a golden desert where only flax could thrive. On its fringes, in the gorse and sappy brushwood, we hunted birds' nests and stole the eggs. We fished for trout and eels and trapped possums; we even panned for gold and got some flakes of colour, there on the edge of a kids' paradise.

There was an internal world to be had within four walls as well, where my growing obsession with war — especially flight — found expression. A trip to the metropolis of Greymouth and Pegleys' toyshop yielded models of Hurricanes and Gladiators, the Supermarine S6B floatplane that won the Schneider Trophy in 1931. In Blackball the following year and over

Airfix model, late 1950s — my first biplane.

the next decade I would fill my bedroom and parts of the kitchen as well with an aerial fleet that signalled an inner longing to fly. I was hooked. I'd made friends too with another outsider, Larry, the adopted son of the elderly storekeeper and his wife. Invitations to stay over with him opened up another world, between walls that seem now completely divorced from the Wild West culture surrounding us then.

Larry was not part of the in-crowd, so we hung around together and one night I went to stay at his place. We slept in the same double bed, but our friendship did not survive. Was he a Welfare kid, did he disappear? In the midst of it all, I was falling in love with something, even if only the songs pouring out of the family radio: 'Smoke Gets in Your Eyes', 'Red Sails in the Sunset', and of course, 'Young Love'. Was that where I got my first religion? "They say forever boy and girl/There's just one love in this whole world/And I-I-I, I-I-I found mine…" The emotion dripping from Sonny James' crooning love call went straight to my soul, sank in the depths of my small boy marrow and pinned me for good. That horse-walking cowboy rhythm, *tum-te-tum te-tum-te-tum*, is there today and still it hooks me: "Young love, our love, we share with deep emotion."

There were girls in my heart too, and more to come later: Blackball school next stop and the stroppy females of a coal mining culture where kids needed a second skin to survive. Gazing across the valley and up to the hills — to the mountains and streams that would shape my world — a mysterious part of that love, that release of emotion was of the earth itself. This place had claimed me without even trying. The wildness of the world, the muscular presence of the men, the creative power of the often misused and abused wives and mothers: here it was — life and more life. It was the flesh and blood of poetry, though I didn't know it at the time.

Since I was born at the end of the world's worst war, it seemed my father in his wounds and his wisdom took us backwards: from London to Auckland in 1950; from Auckland to Christchurch in 1954; from Christchurch to Ngahere in 1956; and in the next move, to Blackball in 1958. We had gone from England and Europe to a former colony on the cusp of independence; from the warm and Polynesian north to the colder, older south; soon, moving west to what was still almost a pioneer society with tracks for roads and little in the way of high culture or the cosmopolitan heights of an urban century. We had gone backwards not just in space, but in time; the move over the river would complete the process, where we hovered between the 19th and the mid-20th century, everything to live for but no map for the journey.

An abiding image captures some of this: the Hill brothers from Nelson Creek, driving their cattle through the raggedy railway town to the stockyards for transport to the works in Belfast beyond the alps. Here they all were, these very real cowboys, horsemen with whips and barking dogs, cursing the wide-eyed bellowing steers charging barely contained down the road to the railway station and the waiting cattle cars. They had been mustered from far reaches of the Grey Valley and were wild. An earlier drive had seen the beasts break away and stampede into the Ngahere mill, almost wrecking the place as they trampled through, scattering the millhands. One bull charged into a local house, killing the dog as it ploughed into the kitchen, forcing one of the Hill brothers' aunties to leap onto the kitchen table, only to be saved by the chasing pack of slavering dogs that turned the animal and hounded it back outside.[3]

Scary. We had a grassy strip in front of our house and a flimsy white paling fence, and watched from our bedroom window as these angry beasts, streaming strings of snot and blasts of steam, thundered onto the grass and threatened the fence. The Hillbillies cursed some more, whips cracked harder and the cattle blew their fearsome trumpets. For a moment it looked like they would flatten the fence and smash the verandah —

Railways track gang on a jigger, Ngahere, late 1950s.

New Forest Mill, Ngahere, the Heisler 'Lokie', c.1963.
Mike Barnes photo, via Alec Birch

even come through the wall and burst inside! There they are still, wild as forever: Ngahere alive in my bones, the swampland all around me that keeps talking like this, refusing to leave me alone.

Forty years on, it all came back in a poem, 'Ngahere railway lovin' blues, 1958', the first verse kicking off:[4]

> Hate to tell you
> but it's all them coal trains
> hauling my resistance off into the black valley
> that haunt me when they blow
>
> *them horns, them tunes*
> *them long-gone songs:*
> the love smoke of my babylovin'

5

Coal range

"Specsy, Specsy, pass it, pass it!" Walking through the gate of the Blackball primary school in 1958, I see a bunch of boys playing football on the grass, tearing around like animals before the bell rings to herd us all — newbie me and brother Eric — into the long wooden building that loomed huge after the one-room school we had left behind in Ngahere. I must have been nervous. Always a big day for a kid: a new school, new everything and after getting the bash at the playground across the river, what was waiting for me here? I must have played against some of those haring around the schoolyard — would I be treated as an enemy? Blackball versus Ngahere was a local derby, a grudge match from way back, when the red and blacks and the yellow and blues would bowl each other over to cross that line, to earn bragging rights for a week. It was miners versus sawmillers — and now, with Dad leaving the railways to work underground, I was a miner's son.

That skinny kid with the glasses and the wicked sidestep was Frank Pendlebury, son like me of a war veteran with serious issues. He would become one of my two longest-lived Blackball friends. The others I would meet in class, at playtime, on the sports field, or behind the shelter sheds plotting mischief, backed into the Paparoa Ranges that would define my life for the next ten years — huddled around us, sending rain, fog and early winter sunsets. Ken Lee, Peter Fleming, Laurie Rankin, Kevin Williams, Tommie Reynolds, Errol Meikle, Ken Meadowcroft, Gary Murdoch: their names ring now in a roll call inviting the return of a vanished world. Some I would play with, others would bully me; with some I would learn to read, run, swim and fight — but few would ever know me well, nor I them. Only Gary Murdoch remains a close presence in my life, a testimony to

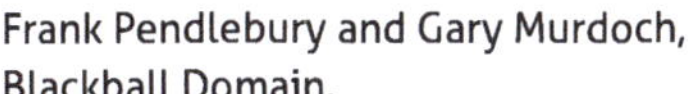

Frank Pendlebury and Gary Murdoch, Blackball Domain.

Blackball kids go fishing, c.1960: Jill Holman; Beryl Pendlebury; Elisabeth, Jeffrey & Eric Holman; Frank Pendlebury.

the fact that schooldays yield few lasting friends, infusing us instead with a radiant experience of good and evil.

There were four classrooms, entered through a doorway into a long wood-panelled corridor hung with coats and schoolbags, a staffroom, and at the end of the building, a few steps away — the murder house. Here a white-garbed woman, a cross between Florence Nightingale and the Angel of Death, would call us into her lair. She would lie us down on a chair, pump us up higher and higher until her white-canopied veil blotted out the lights in the ceiling. Then away she would go, drilling like a miner deep into our teeth. The thought of those dry prickly cotton pads plugging my cheeks to mop up saliva still sets on edge my mined-out molars. Other terrors of the schoolyard paled to nothingness when into the classroom came the call, "Jeffrey Holman, the dental nurse wants you."

I was good at school, which was both help and hindrance: it made the teachers like me and gave cause for some resentment among my fellows (nobody likes a smart-arse). I had found this out in Ngahere when I answered one of Mr Maurice's questions, "What do we call somebody who commands a convoy at sea?" Up shot my hand, me panting for approval. "Jeffrey?" I was right there with the answer. "A commodore, sir!" There were snorts behind me: maybe that display of cleverness set up the need for the shelter shed bash later. Blackball was an advance on this: we didn't get mobbed, but instead were thrown into the gorse by Butch Reynolds, whose place we had to pass to get to school. Through playing league on the weekends and running around the creeks and the hills, I was soon making friends and bedding in.

There never was a time with nothing to do or see, even when we did get bored, trapped inside on a wet weekend, or a wet week in the school holidays. My mother would get us wide white sheets of butchers' paper from Andy Kennedy's shop; Eric and I would create huge dioramas of wartime action, ideas and images gleaned from a steady supply of war comics. Better still, on Friday, Saturday and Sunday nights at the Miners' Hall, the union headquarters so central to the social life of the community — dances, balls, boxing matches, Women's Institute meetings — we could see films. Celluloid dreams arrived in huge metal canisters on the NZR Bedford bus, dropped off at the doors of the hall, picked up later by the projectionist. Nobody would ever dream of stealing them.

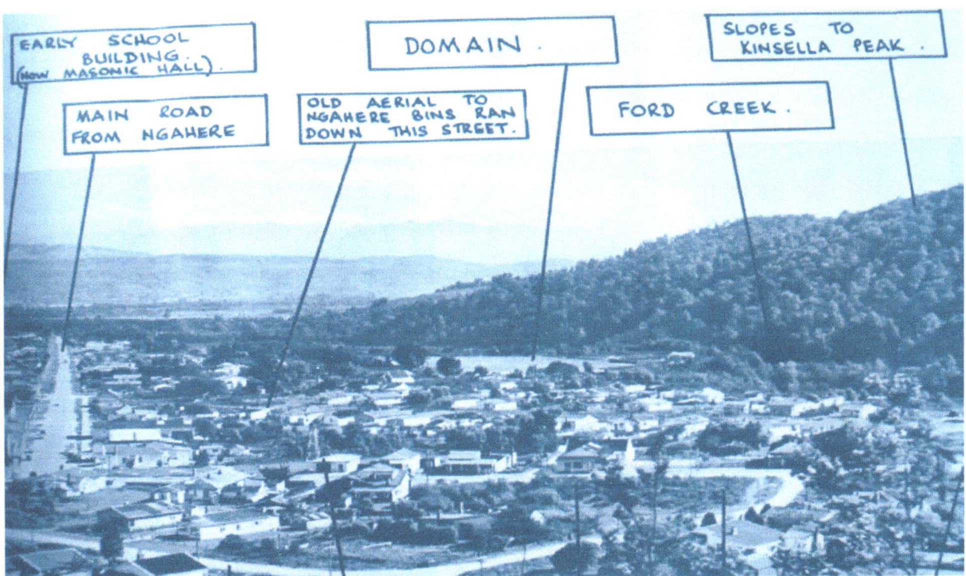

Blackball from Kingstop, 1960s.
West Coast Photo News

It was here that my instinct for telling a good yarn found me out. When it came time for Blackball to see the Davy Crockett film I had seen before in Christchurch (films could take their time reaching us), I was busy at school in the days before the screening telling the other kids what it was all about. I had some cred having already seen it, but that didn't last long. As we sat in the darkness watching Davy kill him a bear and make the West safe, I started to get some feedback. "Hey," they said, "you said X and Y, and Z, and he did this and they did that. You're a liar, that never happened!" I was too quick to get caught like that: "Oh no, the Davy Crockett film I saw was different to this one!" I could tell that they didn't believe me: my conscience must have been waking up at the time. But nothing will get in the way of a good story and in any case, children don't necessarily have total recall. I just wanted to belong. I was a Blackball boy now.

That meant playing league again: I was knock-kneed and podgy in an age when childhood obesity was uncommon. My best friend then — and fellow prop in the scrum — was another large lad, Ken Meadowcroft, who lived just down the Main Road near a cemetery full of miners' bones. After school I would play with Ken until he got called in to chop the silver pine for next morning's kindling, then go for his tea at about 4.30 p.m. when his Dad got home from his shift. I had to go home myself then and wait for our tea and our father — usually an hour later, if he got past the pub that night. These men were a sight, wandering down the road after

Blackball 7th Grade league team, 1960, South Island champions.
I'm third from left, middle row.

Leaving Blackball by railcar to Christchurch, en route to Wellington on a school trip in 1960: Gary Murdoch, Freddie Gear (with the missing tooth), Errol and Barry Meikle.

a day deep in the earth, their sugar sack crib bags over their shoulders, baggy strides, sports coats and battered hats — especially Dad's daily genuflection as he neared the gate of our neighbour, Gladys Mountford.

'Glad' — the mother of a football team of champion Kiwi league men — would stand in her white apron at the Mountford gate, watching the world go by. That was the internet back then: the street and what passed by, to be tweeted as gossip over the next day's cuppa with the other miners' wives. We all did it: who was driving in and who out, who just walked by. I would sit in our lounge at dusk with the coal fire roaring and wait for my father to get home. There he was, passing George Smith's place and there she was too, arms folded over her apron and a womb that had spawned immortals. I could watch the predictable scene from our window. Regular as an alcoholic clock can be, Dad would look over Gladys's way, reach up and tip his hat in salute: "Evening, Glad."

"Evening, Bill."

On a summer's night, you could hear the exchange quite clearly. And that was it — he passed by, and she as the evening cold descended and the coal fire smog gathered about us all, would go indoors to serve tea.

Gladys Mountford, Blackball: Earl Tutty, artist, grandson.

6

Nanny Airey's treadle Singer

When we had lived on the Ngahere side of the river, we had to get to Blackball over the road-rail bridge that led across the moody, dangerous Grey. That was how we went to the films on a Saturday: you caught the pictures' bus at the top pub and rode over the river to the Miners' Hall. It was there on the bridge we saw a stray dog in the bus's lights as we came off on the Blackball side — white, ghostly, dazzled. When we got home after the film, the same dog, an ageing spaniel was at the bus stop at the Ngahere pub and he followed us to the house. "Can we keep him?" we pestered Mum. A former kennel maid, she was agreeable, but only if we couldn't find any owner. The happy dog — promptly christened Sandy — lay in front of the coal range in the kitchen, licking his paws. A notice we placed in the newspaper drew no response; a neighbour who had also seen the dog that same night confirmed they had seen someone dumping him from a car near the bridge and driving off.

Sandy would turn up years later in the opening poem of a series of sonnets I wrote about the bridge, the town and its people. These were prompted by a storytelling impulse, nourished by a woman who lived with us at the time of her arrival in 1951 in Auckland, until our move to Blackball — my grandmother, Nanny Airey. She was with us for sixteen years, making a gradual translation from carer (dressing me in my pyjamas at night, vest off, "skin a rabbit") to story-bearer and live-in historian, a symbol of age and witness to the pastness of the past. If Blackball was a cul-de-sac, so were her memories; once she ventured down that road, it was always a dead end. She had to return to the present to breathe: like a swimmer, she would dive down into the lanes around Liverpool in the 1880s, riding in a pony and trap, off to the shell factory in the Great War, mourning the early death of her dear daughter Lillian in 1934 and the war, the war, the bombs and the war.

As she aged it was my turn, and that of my siblings, to care for Nanny in her 80s. I had to perfect emptying the disgusting commode that sat beside her bed in the sun porch. In the evening, as we kissed her goodnight, her false teeth would bubble and fizz like Alka-Seltzer tablets in their nightly bath of Steradent. Nanny was both the stories and their smells: that old-lady aroma we can recognise but not define, a fragrance of death and persistence. The room had a special collection of objects and devices: her green croupier's eyeshade, the tape recorder that played her books for the blind, and the largest and most active presence — a treadle sewing machine.

Since her arrival those years ago, another of my grandmother's roles had been childcare and the provision of knitting and sewing; the clack-click-clack of her needles and the whirr of a sewing machine orchestrated our growing lives and clothed our bodies. She would hunch over the machine, asking me often to thread needles she was no longer able to sight; teaching my sisters the art of machine sewing, adding to them the experience of the cottage industries killed by the Industrial Revolution in the century of her birth. Being a boy, I was never expected to learn how a pattern became a coat or a shirt, recruited instead to hold out my arms so she could roll the skeins of wool into neat balls.

When Sunday roasts came along, especially the Christmas feasts, consumed in the heat of summer, Nanny was there, shelling peas into a colander and slicing beans. By the fire in the kitchen in the evening she would puff away at her Capstan Cork ciggies, hardly doing the drawback at all. As if a Liverpool docker, she would hoick with various degrees of accuracy into the open fire, her spittle hissing as it hit the grate and coals. She was the inspiration for one of my early sallies at a poem; the first, written at age eleven was a sturdy ballad in honour of the Wright Brothers, jangling along like so: "On a windy day in 1903/At Kittyhawk Sands down

Blackball School, 1960, in front of the murder house: Eric, Nanny, Jeffrey, Jill and Elisabeth.

by the sea…" That 'prentice effort won a prize in the primary school Bring and Buy. She spurred a later poem by wandering through the kitchen one evening, as I was doing my high school homework, musing, "If I had gone to school when I was five and had good eyes, I might have been clever."

I almost said something like, "Cleverness is born, not made, Nanny," being as I was in my teen years and knowing everything. Something stopped me and I wrote a poem instead. Fragments remain: "Age waddles past me on a shaky stick [then the quote from Nanny] … [some reflection on nature and nurture] … [concluding] … "when from where she trembles, we are but a life away."

From primary to secondary school, my interests had moved from the concrete, the narrative, to the philosophical — and moralistic. I like the intuitive grasp of found poetry, a sense of empathy peeping through, seen perhaps in the use of the word 'trembles', as if she was on some kind of brink, fearing to fall. I saw you clear, my dear.

She certainly fed my inner world, the places I could retreat to whatever darkness or light permeated the household. The presence of the physical world, the mountains and the rainforest we had entered like a lost world from the city those years before, were balanced by an active imagination fired by literature and by voice. Whatever I might read about the Luftwaffe, the RAF in the Battle of Britain (I had begun to buy books which detailed the inner workings of Stukas and Spitfires), Nanny could add eyewitness accounts of air raids on Liverpool that came near to killing her and my mother, and of V-1 attacks on London from 1944 onwards. She would mimic the sound of the buzz bombs passing overhead, the heart-stopping moment when the rocket motor died and the weapon fell at random upon the city's streets, suburbs, gardens, schools and hospitals.

My listening, writing, model-making and reading slowly merged into a stream that was to shape a personal history: my view of time and the dark ways of nations, a tactile experience of reality, along with a good deal of hormonal sublimation. For years as kids we had made guns and fought wars in local creeks, along gullies, by the bush-shaded dredge pond where

Doodlebug: V-1 flying bomb chased by a Spitfire over England. I wrote in 'Bombers' in *Fly Boy*: '… Nanny/knew what it meant to be bombed: mines floating down/on parachutes, V-1s putting overhead 'like motorbikes/up in the sky'. She talked bombs to me till the day she died.'

Required reading: *The Dumpy Book of Aircraft and the Air* (back cover).

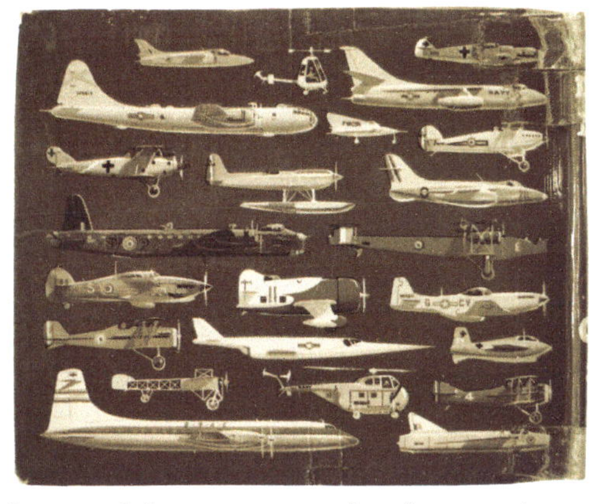

the gold-guzzling monster had long since departed. We created afresh the war games burning in our minds. They flared out in the flesh, too: in the weekend stoush with the Grey Valley league clubs, hard scraps at school, in the physical tests of the axemen at the chops and other testosterone-fuelled challenges. I was fighting old wars in my head: dangers imagined high in the air over the English Channel, dogfighting day after day with the wind-whipped veterans of aerial warfare. I wanted to be a pilot. I wanted to fly. Fly Spitfires.

The films we saw at the pictures continued to grip me, especially *Reach for the Sky*, the Douglas Bader story. Who wouldn't be impressed by the courage of a man who lost his legs in an air crash before the war, learned to walk again and later, to fly with artificial limbs? Someone at the age of thirty — too old by then for combat duties — who fought in the Battle of Britain? He was credited with shooting down twenty enemy planes, before he had to bail out over France in August 1941 and spend the rest of the war as a prisoner of war, most of it in the notorious Colditz Castle after his many attempts to escape.

After the highs of the weekend's wars, it was back to school: assembly lines, school milk, times tables and English composition. I was writing now, rather than drawing: battles on the movie screen and in the bush, as we retold the highlights in our lives since last Friday. Some of the kids struggled with this, but I loved it. A film about highway thieves stealing trucks in Britain featured one week (with a burning lorry, drawn in Lakeland colour pencils). I copied lines from a poem by Babette Deutsch about soldiers marching in the mud through winter cold:

> Plod in the wind with the thrust of a fist.
> Plod plod plod plod.
> Lie on your belly and bed with the damp,
> Rise in the dark. Tramp
> Over streets that are fanged like a shark.
> Tramp tramp tramp tramp.[5]

I faithfully reproduced an image of the men's boots from below knee level: darkness, lines of rain, seas of mud. The idea of a close-up like that must have come from the cinema.

Deutsch's poem, 'Marseillaise', appeared in one of those wonderful *School Journals* that grace our primary schools. It was published in 1925 and found its way to me across the world from America, read aloud in a tiny country school over thirty years later. Here was a seed that would remain after I had left Blackball: that misty, rain-raddled plateau with its profound ghosts, the blood of the workers, broom seeds fired like bullets in the high noon heat of what seemed then to be summers without end, all-day swimming, sunburn and sandflies.

From these early forays into print and reading, I became a book: not a book lover, but an actual book, imprinted with texts of reality in a personal script as unrepeatable as my DNA sequences. I claim no ownership or responsibility for this: we were all like that then, Gary, Frank, Ken, Fitzy and all, written in the body on the footy field and down by the river, graven in the heart by every word that stuck — even some that seemed to miss. *Tabula rasa*, yes and no, but manuscripts nonetheless, with plots fixed and flexible; we grew and grew until we became too large for the once enormous Blackball School. We were fitted out then in uniforms for the school bus ride to Greymouth, to high school — to the Tech and to Marist-St Mary's, to state and Catholic — as long ago decreed by a higher and wider fate.

Sprue and flash

The terrors of high school initiation for third formers ("turds") and the role of school bullying in general has been pretty well painted in literature from *Tom Brown's Schooldays* to Harry Potter at Hogwarts. A litany here would run from capping (being whacked on the arse with cap rims in the school bus) to caning by borderline sociopath teachers who seemed to enjoy giving boys 'six of the best'. You kept your head down and chose companions of the like-minded and like-muscled. Bullies tended to group themselves together, as did victims; I managed to fall mostly in the latter camp. While I was possessed of a swelling adolescent rage, tightly damped down, I had no confidence at all when it came to defending myself.

This came to head in the creaky old NZR Bedford school bus; one of my football teammates, joining in this time with the other bullies, blurting, "Yeah, he's still sucking on his mummy's titty!" However astute his perception of my maternal dependency may have been, that truly was the last straw. I exploded and wrestled him until one of the bigger, stronger Back Seat Boys got a handful of my jersey and pushed us apart. "Sit down and shut up!" As I was still without a guaranteed seat — and had been for most of the first three years on the bus trip to Greymouth, unable to command the respect that got you a reserved place daily — I stayed upright. This flare-up stopped the bullying; shades of Shorty Porter back in Ngahere.

High school was my salvation: I found myself promoted from a 'General' stream to the second-tier Academic class after my entrance tests indicated

ABOVE 1960s NZ Railways Road Services Bedford. If we couldn't get a seat, we would sit in the aisle on our upturned suitcases — made at the Returned Services Association in Christchurch and stamped with their label.
John Le Cren, Archives NZ, AAVK W3493 B8925

OPPOSITE Blackball School prizegiving, 1960: Jeffrey, Jill, Mum and Elisabeth.

I could cope with a syllabus aimed at bringing pupils to a level where they might consider entering the professions. I was a miner's son who wanted to be a fighter pilot, but I went along with this move. Learning French was the price I had to pay for parting company with my Blackball primary school mates. They had mostly gone to Engineering, Woodwork and General (boys) and Commercial, Homecraft or General for the girls. In 1961 this was, after all, a Technical High School and although its name would change while we were there, in a place like the Coast its offerings were pretty well matched to the cohort entering the gates. The ranks of the middle classes were thin in those parts.

That move from General to Academic changed my life: I would be taught by a series of fine teachers and make half a dozen lifelong friends. From 1961 until 1965 — allowing for my elevation with the top students of 4A2 into 5A in 1963 — I was taught geography by one man, Snowy Hutton. Snowy it was who took me by the scruff of my Blackball island mentality and turned me into his kind of continent. Peter Hooper, who taught English in my fifth form year, along with Bernie Conradson fresh from Training College teaching me history, were the other two lynchpins. There were other good teachers in science and maths, doing their best with unpromising material, but I was pretty much a humanities kind of kid (with all due respect to maths masters Jack Flood and David Panckhurst).

I would soon need some de facto fathering: in my fourth form year, Dad got into trouble again with his gambling addiction. He'd stolen money to get out of debt, this time from the school committee's fund. He was sent to prison again; by now, in my early teens, I was well aware of what was happening to us. There was peace in the home with him away, but wounds in our childhood world. My mother took out a separation order but was later persuaded by a well-meaning prison chaplain to take him back: "He's a changed man, Mrs Holman." Dad would return, and they staggered on for another four years as a short-lived attempt at reform eventually succumbed to his alcoholism. I have written of this elsewhere: "From the moment that beer slipped on down my dad's throat, from the instant he put the first bet back on some hopeful nag, he was disappearing from the garden and the church and from us, all over again."[6]

The experience of seeing our father arrested on a Sunday morning and vanishing into the clutches of the justice system was one of those moments when the world collapses. In a series of poems, written years later to capture the experience of growing up in Blackball, I would attempt to freeze this trauma in an act of expiation and deliverance:[7]

The town is not a goldfish bowl, it's a hive
of secrets, the earth above its darkening

mirror underground. Murmuring rumours
hum like cables hauling a jigger of men to

the mouth: "Saw the squad car come and take him.
Flogged the School Committee's money. Bloody

hell! That's robbing babies!" Down they tramp
in a foul old humour. Nobody left to defend my

mother, nobody wants to know my father. Leaving
my heart when my guard is down, a dull grey

Holden is always fading, him in the back, that
chrome rail glistening. We disappear with him:

the clam of shame has swallowed us whole, and
all over town they are sending us packing.

In Dad's absence my male teachers filled a void, becoming far more to me than simply men who stood in front of a class imparting information, that I might gain their approval and pass the tests. They were the difference between my staying within society or running off the rails.

William Barrie Hutton (1894–1965) was born near Timaru and went to Timaru Boys' High School; at twenty when the Great War broke out, he sailed to France and saw action there in 1917 at Passchendaele. In one of the many stories with which he regaled us, striding around the class in his green tweed sports coat and floppy grey flannels, firing chalk at sleepy defaulters, there was the image of an early German bombing raid over the New Zealand trenches. The graceful plane with its black Maltese crosses stooged slowly overhead and suddenly the goggled face of the pilot appeared; producing a hand-held bomb he flung it down at the uplifted faces of the bemused Kiwis. Snowy described the aircraft perfectly; plane-spotty me, I knew this vision with "wings like a swallow" was a Taube. My teacher had seen a real German, face-to-face, high in the sky, trying to kill him. Now here he was, alive to bring me the tale in Greymouth nearly fifty years later.

Taube scout: *New York Times*, 1917.

But it wasn't this rare war story that ensnared me; it was Snowy's radical and passionate teaching style, insisting he had the best pass record in geography for School Certificate in the whole of New Zealand and we, as snotty-nosed Thirds, were starting to build towards passing that exam. He would get us over the line, come hell or high water. In my case — and in many others in that year and thereafter — Snowy did just that. He had developed a system for studying the geography of each country: location, relief, climate, land use, industry, and population. It was broad enough to take in the essentials and could be broken down to specifics; it meant we had a template, he said, to understand our world and describe any part of it systematically. In exams, under pressure, it was a boon.

I thrived under his tutelage and doing well, aiming always to please, became one of the apples of his eye. Three years on, in the last months of 1963 when I stood waiting outside the doors of Coxon Hall to sit the School Certificate Geography exam, Snowy strode up to me with his folded copy of the *Press*, clapped me paternally on the shoulder, booming out to the assembled students, "90%, please!" Then off he shambled, singing a Gilbert & Sullivan ditty most like. Using the knowledge amassed under the years of his teaching — and some sleight of hand when I was faced with a question on Canada I had not prepared for, winging it — I came close. The following January, raspberry picking at Tadmor near Nelson, a telegram came from my parents with my passes: Geography at 89% was the best of my 289 total marks.

In the same year, 1963, I was dealt a sweet hand in English as well: Peter Hooper. Like Bernie Conradson, Peter was quiet and effective, commanding respect without bluster or resort to the cane. A later generation than Snowy, born in England in 1919, he had seen war service as a radar mechanic in the air force in the Pacific. He was a poet and later a novelist and short story writer; when he published his first slim volume, *A Map of Morning*, in my sixth-form year, although I was no longer in his class I was still under his spell. That year he published two of my poems in the school magazine, where I had lovingly reviewed his book. The creative writing lessons he had given us in the fifth form — "Write about the Coast, about what you know," with examples of his own revised drafts handed out in class — had an instant effect on me.

An early fifth form effort still survives and reminds me of the importance of a timely mentor:

> Morepork scolding,
> Night dog howling,
> The wind draws whispers from hidden power lines.

Tree frogs whistling,
Pine trees moaning,
The cloud-cut drifting moon is mute.

In my later adult relationship with this quietly spoken teacher — a surrogate literary father — I would come to know a more rounded and ambiguous figure, but in those final two years of high school, it was pretty much hero worship.

Not quite so with Bernie Conradson. Bernie had arrived as a probationary teacher in his Training College year, assigned to sit in on Snowy's classes and take some of the lessons while the old man retreated to his workroom out the back, singing snatches of operettas as he shuffled his mountain of files and rolls of maps. When Bernie came back in 1963 on staff, he was my history teacher and began to imbue me with a spirit of historical enquiry and a critical pen. Not that I was enthused by the English Corn Laws or the machinations of Metternich, but I faithfully studied the set text and slowly learned to write history essays. I did not shine as brightly as in Snowy's room, but gradually got the feel for what Bernie required and my marks improved. By the sixth form year, after he had nursed me through School Certificate (a respectable 66%), we began to study modern Pacific and Asian history. Standard texts such as Condliffe & Airey painted what would now be considered a rosy version of New Zealand colonial history, but we knew no better than our masters. These writers had been around since Bill Pearson was in school in the 1930s, and their view of our race relations was, to say the least, myopic.

My passion for war stories underlay what became my métier in class — an instinct for modern history. I had parents and a grandparent at home who had lived through Hitler's rise to power and either fought, or survived, as civilians through six years of war. The study of modern Japan and China, the rise of the communists under Mao — I thrived on that. In one of the few visits together my mum and dad made to Parents' Night at the school in 1964, Bernie told them both, "He's my star pupil." I didn't need any more encouragement than that. Alone in my damp bedroom late at night, I read everything I could lay my hands on. I was on my own since my brother departed south in 1962 to work with the Ministry of Works on the Haast Road. Most of my old mates from primary school days were out at work by then: down the mine, into apprenticeships, on the Forestry or in the sawmills. With pocket money and advances from my mother's stretched budget, I was buying hard-back novels and histories at Brislanes Bookshop in Tainui Street, Greymouth. Quite why I shelled out a goodly sum for Christopher Hibbert's biography, *Mussolini*, I'm not sure; the beginnings of bibliophilia most likely. Yet I read it closely and many others at a critical moment of intellectual and physical change. My body was getting leaner and my mind more cynical; I developed the heart of an optimist and the mind of a pessimist. It seems to have shaped itself early, in those high school years. My critical sense was sharper, I know. My brother's largesse, buying me *The Modern World Book of Flying* at Christmas, was warmly received. It wasn't long before I detected a slew of sloppy errors in Chapter Five, 'War in the Air 1939-45'.

On page 63, the photo caption described Lancaster bombers setting out on a night raid (decked out in white, post-war livery); next page, a caption mistaking a B-25 Mitchell for a Liberator and the same again on the facing page. All of these I dutifully corrected, in pencil (just in case). The last straw (which produced a letter to the publishers, Sampson Low, Marston & Co of London, W1) was dramatic series of images spread over pages 76-77, showing a damaged American Hellcat fighter landing onto a US carrier and bursting into flames, as one of the flight deck crew bravely rescued the pilot. The caption read, 'Grumman Martlett' (I knew that Martlett was the Royal Navy's Fleet Air Arm name for the earlier Wildcat). It also dated the crash 'November 27th, 1945' (the Pacific war had ended in September).

The badly damaged plane sweeps in . . . .

careers to the edge of the flight d

On November 27th, 1945, the United States carrier *Enterprise* was carrying out operations off the Marshall Islands. Casualties were heavy. One by one the surviving planes, badly shot up, dragged themselves back to their floating home to make the dangerous landing as best they could. As the Grumman Martlett in these pictures hit the flight deck, its undercarriage crumpled up, it careered to the edge of the deck and burst into flames. Immediately one of the flight crew rushed to the stricken aircraft and ignoring the flames, the exploding petrol and ammunition struggled to free the pilot. The identity of this young American is unknown but his bravery and split second action are recorded for ever.

The unknown hero climbs onto the

Hellcat crashing on USS *Enterprise* in 1943, caption with my corrections.[8]
OPPOSITE 1/144 scale Me-109 model.

Sunderlands, Hobsonville

Blood Ties: new and selected poems 1963–2016 Canterbury University Press, 2017

The sky would dome the harbour, blue with
light; in the air a far-off drone that swelled
till my ears were full, the white weight
of the bird-boat dropping on Hobsonville.
Sunderland: majestic ghosts that spooked
my earthbound life, flew me straight to
that place in the sky where a soul could play
touch the Great Almighty and be
whole; the force inside me broke all rules
as the fleets of flying fish love to do.

Not only was I a rabid plane spotter, but an apprentice critic. My letter to the bemused publisher received a polite, immaculately typed apology with sincere thanks for my having pointed out these errors, mistakes they assured me would certainly be corrected in subsequent editions. Did my pedant's heart swell with schoolboy pride? I'm sure. I know I showed my parents the letter, and others too. I kept that reply for years until it finally disappeared off the face of the earth; the hoarded book, with me still, reveals a smart aleck kid, his writer's eye grown wider. A recent search of Wikipedia — a tool not available to the editors of Sampson Low, Marston & Co, 1893–1969 — has an image of the same crash, dated the tenth of November 1943, as the carrier was in action en route to support the invasion of Makin Atoll in the Gilbert Islands. I can see the bigger picture now: clarified by online searches and sighting the original images, it will never have the magic of the hours I pored over that book, an awkward autodidact pursuing a dream.

The other way I dealt with my obsession with flight was through model-making: plastic air forces that populated my room and my head. I got more skilled through meeting others who made them too. I began painting prior to assembly, taking more time to get the camouflage schemes right as the decals slid wet and warm onto a section of wing or fuselage. Painting some of the smaller parts before removing them from the sprue they were linked to during the moulding process was one trick; removing the flash, the excess flare of plastic, before

1/72 scale Airfix Halifax BIII, with a rake of sprue.

joining cemented sections was another. I was still impatient to get my planes finished, but less so than when I got my first kits and had them cemented together and flying in my hands within the hour. Wedded to static display of my treasures, I refused to let younger visitors near them. Overnight I'd become a museum curator. Stukas, Starfires, Camels, Spads and a string of other historical oddities swelled my collection. Modelling taught me concentration and patience, and gave me some control over my unhappy body, an image misshapen by schoolyard barbs.

Another tongue pierced me in an altogether different way about the same time — the angry, urgent, street-smart voice of Bob Dylan. On most New Zealand radio stations in 1963 to 1964, his songs were heard in covers by the likes of Peter, Paul and Mary, as part of the civil rights movement's use of folk as protest. 'Blowin' in the Wind' sung sweetly by harmonising liberals was never going to strike me as hard and fast as raw Dylan. On a magic night, early in 1965 on Pete Sinclair's Sunset Show from Wellington, 'Subterranean Homesick Blues' poured out of the radio. Sinclair did the whole country a favour; he let the genie out of the bottle, playing Dylan as he was since his fallout with the folkie purists at Newport in July of that year.

Released in March 1965, a Beat-inspired talking blues riff, name checking everything from cooking drugs to civil rights violence, the song was a whirlwind trip gone electric, announcing the arrival of another world. America was sliding away from the middle-class consumerism of the 1950s into the bogged-down bloodbath of Vietnam and the 1960s. It was all there, heralded in this unearthly voice: the polar opposite of Doris Day, Petula Clark, Matt Monro and Cliff Richard. The raw power of the song so shocked John Lennon, he wondered if he could ever compete with it. Yelping and jangling, out of the old Columbus kitchen radio came a rapper's version of the Book of Ecclesiastes: "Ah get born, keep warm/ Short pants, romance, learn to dance/Get dressed, get blessed/Try to be a success ..."[9] Transfixed, I went out and bought the first Dylan album I could find, *Another Side of Bob Dylan*. I don't know what I was expecting, but it wasn't what came next.

II

Jack of all trades

How many Men he hath been in that extent of time.

— Thomas More, Urne-Buriall, 1658.

8

School's out

When I got the Dylan album onto the record player at home, it confused me a little. I was disappointed it wasn't in the style of 'Subterranean Homesick Blues'; this was Dylan solo on acoustic guitar with harmonica, his own original blues material with not a cover in sight. It took a while to get my head around the sound, but the raw voice and cryptic lyrics soon got to me. I didn't know that the record had been released months earlier in the USA (in the previous year in fact, August 1964); what I had on my turntable was a bunch of songs in a style Dylan was already leaving behind.

Today, it would be marketed as 'unplugged'; back then, it was just a niche recording by a backslidden folkie, lucky to sell any copies at all in far-off Greymouth. The black-and-white cover, a lean, scowling Dylan — somewhere between James Dean and an Okie dustbowl farmer, boot up on the rail — was a departure from the standard album art in those days. We were used to bright colour with the shiny happy star smiling out at the buyer. My father hated Dylan, which made him instantly more attractive. I found his obscurities profound, his discordant rejection of anything sweet or sentimental sounded like a rebel yell. A Dylan evangelist in embryo, I played it to my friends, to my teacher Peter Hooper, to anyone who would listen. After reading the Beat-riffing liner notes, Peter wrote a series of poems I later came to think were some of his best: *Notes in the Margin*. *Another Side of Bob Dylan* pushed me further into poetry for its own sake. Dylan was the arrival of a singer-songwriter culture turning popular music on its head. But I was still a regular Top Ten pop junkie too, swept along with the Midlands tide of the Beatles and the Mersey Sound.

When *A Hard Day's Night* was shown at the St James Theatre that year, it amazed my sixth-form schoolfriends when I took my mother along with us. Mum was from Liverpool and she liked their music; I don't think I realised what an emotional wallop hearing the accent had for her. She loved the film and my mates loved her for coming, telling me at school the next day what a great mother I had and how they would never get their mothers to come (would they even have tried?). They didn't know

Elisabeth and Jill with their Beatle dresses, 1964.

how closely tied I was to her, or that going to the pictures as a family was still common in Blackball. The films at the Miners' Hall were communal events: there was no real shame in teenagers walking with their parents to the door, then going off with your mates, girlfriend or boyfriend inside that wooden temple of socialist dreams.

School was now a race to the next hurdle: University Entrance exams, better known as UE. Those of us who had passed School Certificate in the previous year were lined up in Class 6B and told that getting ourselves 'accredited' was the goal for 1964. Those who passed the mid and end-of-year school exams were deemed fit enough to avoid the national examinations, set to determine who would gain entrance to university study. None of us had any real notion of what a university was, or what going there would mean. More study, yes, but if the students who appeared every year on the Coast during Capping Week were anything to go by — party animals selling their naughty Capping Mag on the streets of the town after a booze-sodden trip through the Otira tunnel — university was about breaking the rules and testing the limits.

We knuckled down and got to work; the class was intensely competitive and with my favourite teachers, Snowy and Bernie (Peter Hooper had been swapped in English for Joan Jackson), it was more of the same. I revelled in the process of learning and achieving; whatever was going on at home, school was where I felt I belonged and where my abilities were recognised. My long-time desire to join the air force and fly was whittled away; under the pressure of academic success, my compass turned towards university after high school — but to do what? I was good at English and anything that wasn't maths or science (I had dropped the former and now had the choice of biology alone, without physics and chemistry).

Form 6B, Greymouth High School, 1964 — I'm third from left in the centre row; W. B. 'Snowy' Hutton is at right.

It was assumed that pupils like me were teaching material: off to training college, university study and back into the school system again, with holiday jobs in places like the freezing works to keep us in touch with the world we'd come from — and were expected to leave. I never articulated this to myself but I had no desire to be a teacher; part of me had already started to drift. Whatever it was I wanted, the image on the cover of the Dylan LP was casting a spell on my thinking, as was the music in my ears. For years, we'd been listening on the radio to the Anglo-anarchy of the Goon Show; with the incoming tide of British pop, the recent Cuban crisis, nuclear anxieties, Kennedy's assassination and Vietnam catching fire in the background, it was a heady moment to be changelings possessed of almost-adult bodies.

Along with school came a new social life: parties. We were twenty miles up the valley, but it was easy enough to talk a mate into having you stay over in Greymouth for the weekend, and for them to get the parents' car. Whispered secrets in the school corridors — "You know what that Stones' song 'Satisfaction' is all about, eh?" — were translated into fumbles repelled on somebody's couch with the lights down low, the music egging us on. There was always an older brother, some self-regarding Lothario, boasting of the "easy ones" he'd had, sneering at our innocence. Smoking, sipping awful sherry from the liquor cabinet, that was about my limit; falling for a succession of girls was my secret style, the more troubled the better.

In the course of that year, something else changed: our old headmaster, the formidable Percy Muirhead, was replaced by John Thompson. Greymouth High was not an easy school to manage. The intake of pupils was mainly from working-class areas and rural primary industries. Professionals in the town were few: teaching a cohort of kids who were physically active, hardened by the environment and the culture of a backwoods society had its own challenges. Many of the male staff were ex-servicemen; order was imposed on unruly boys by traditional means — the cane. Any weakness in a teacher was ruthlessly exposed and the classes of those who failed to keep us cowed could be heard in the din from beyond their rooms, as the kids spun out of control.

Percy Muirhead had managed the trick of herding us toward a variety of worthwhile qualifications, and despite its potential volatility the school held its course until his departure. Thompson was a markedly different man and I wasn't the first to get on the wrong side of him. My attempts at rebellion — like folding my socks down until they were hardly up at all — were pretty feeble, but he noticed me one day and hauled me in. That started a slide in my relationship with authority in the school; his manner, a sense that I couldn't trust him, intermingled with domestic issues and deep distrust of my father, set up a dynamic that early in the following year would change my life.

I made it to the end of the year and joined the exalted crew of the accredited who were now free to enter university, or at least leave school

Prefects' dance, 1964: Marcia Russ, Colin Heinz, Anne Thorn, me.

On Mt Davy, overlooking the Grey Valley, 1964.
Colin Heinz

with a better qualification than School Certificate. Mr Thompson had entered the form room and read out the names of those who had passed, leaving the minority — who now must sit the state exam — to lick their wounds in silence. It was hard to celebrate when someone beside you was looking down at the desk, feeling like a failure. But I could feel some pride that the last four years of hard work had paid off, and look forward to the long summer holidays coming up. I went to stay with my friend Colin Heinz, who'd also passed; we went climbing on the Paparoa Range behind Runanga, biking from his place in Cobden and clambering up a track that led off the Rewanui incline. There were still traces of snow and I could see down the other side of the mountain to my mining town home in Blackball. It was a moment to savour as I drew back on my cigarette and posed.

That summer — with *Beatles for Sale* all over the airwaves, soulful crushes on mysterious girls, a feeling that the world of poetry and music was opening up to me — would be a false dawn. I made the most of it. I stayed with friends in town who had cars, driving down the beach among the lupins, sucking on shared warm beer (tasting foul), talking music, talking girls, riffing on favourite Goon Show lines, trying to read the weighty books I thought I should read (Nietzsche and Kafka, for goodness sake, and half the time giving up), going swimming and lazing about. I'd given up my childhood games: I stopped playing rugby league that year. The tackles were just too painful, mowed down by guys my age who'd been out working for a couple of years, hardened in that physical world of work and danger that sustained us — the sawmill, the fishing boat, the coalmine. By January 1965 I was the oldest pupil on the school bus — but at last, I got a seat in the back row every day.

In the seventh form, the teachers treated us more like adults; we were on the top of the tree. Almost the whole class would be automatically made prefects — except for me and my good friend, Maurice Teen. Mr Thompson again: he'd decided we were in need of reminding that insolence did not pay. He proposed that we become deputy prefects (which we instantly renamed Defects) — and we refused. As non-prefects we had no access then to the expected privileges of 6A, so the year was off to a bad start; all the juniors below us would know we'd been passed over. It was not a smart move on Mr Thompson's part — we were potential leaders and needed to be inside the tent. Maurice was also out of favour for playing the despised code of rugby league. He was kicked off the school's rugby First XV. Stupid: he was one of their best players, but that's how the prejudice worked back then.

The next test for my dealings with authority came when the headmaster insisted I continue to study bookkeeping in the seventh form. I'd passed the previous year and it seemed we must take five subjects. I had no ambition to extend my dubious relationship with profit and loss accounts, still bemused at how I had got through last year. I'd taken bookkeeping the previous year as the only other choice was physics. The best part of the class was when we managed to distract Mr Grant (a former WWII Mosquito pilot) and got him talking about the war. A mention of how the Americans coming in had saved our bacon was one good way to get him going, fingering his green hand-knitted ties as he debunked such naïve theories.

I dug my heels in: why not let me study something I was interested in, through the Correspondence School (I suggested Latin or Maori)? My penultimate interview with Mr Thompson did not go well: he wasn't going to allow me any room to move and I wasn't going to budge. He had the authority to enforce his decrees; all I had was the power to withdraw from his influence. I told him if he forced me to take bookkeeping, I would leave. This set him back for a minute and he attempted to entice me with the possibility that I might be up for dux of the school at year's end. I said I didn't care. Stalemate. I would take bookkeeping, there was to be no compromise. What if I just went to the class and did study for my other subjects? No to that also. I was never going to back down. Pride insisted I had to leave.

It had come down to a battle of wills. I was extremely stubborn when it came to it and had lost respect for Mr Thompson, completely. He was not going to be outmanoeuvred by a teenager, and I suspect he sensed my contempt. I went home and told my parents the outcome of the clash (they were aware I was having issues). To their eternal credit, they did not say I had to pull my head in and do what I was told. When I said that I wanted to leave school, they stood behind me. I know they would have felt some disappointment, but neither of them had been near a university. It wasn't the kind of rebellion or leaping off the escalator to success and security it would have been for a middle-class family. My Depression-bred and Royal Navy-schooled father was practical and decisive: "If you leave school, you have to get a job" — and so saying, the next weekend, he went to the pub and found me one, in Donaldson's sawmill.

9

Skiddie

Taking my leave from the safety of the familiar entailed feelings that I had neither the time nor the ability to address. I was excited, afraid and ashamed: I said nothing to my classmates, walked into the headmaster's office, told him I wanted a leaving certificate and began returning my textbooks to their various homes. I dodged some of the teachers, but couldn't leave without saying goodbye to Snowy. After my last class, I went to see him in his back office where all the world lay waiting on maps and folders, ready to be revealed — the landforms and the geology, that in my case, I would not now be studying. I told him I was leaving as I'd got a job in a sawmill.

Perhaps the motor neurone disease that would kill him before the year's end was at work even then, as he did not seem to register the import of what I was saying. "The forestry, that's a good career, Jeff," he enthused. "We'll be sorry to lose you." He thought I was talking about the Forest Service. I wasn't up to correcting him, to say I was leaving because of a man he also had resisted in not-so-subtle ways. Snowy would walk past the French doors of the school's Coxon Hall as we gritted our way through another assembly, mock singing his beloved Gilbert & Sullivan, theatrically reading a copy of the *Press*. He had given me so much, this marvellous man; at least I'd managed to farewell him.

I got out of there before one of my classmates asked me what I was doing, before I changed my mind and caved in. There was no backing down now. Next Monday, I was to start as a skiddie at Donaldson's sawmill up the valley near Red Jacks; for now, this period of my education was over.

If I'd thought that school under John Thompson's rule was unbearable, working in the world outside was the cold bath of reality. Dad's search for Situations Vacant over the bar of the Club (a game of darts with Porky Donaldson, I assume) had dropped me into another dimension of the world we'd entered through the Otira Tunnel those years before. There were few easy jobs on the Coast; bodies went on the line. People would complain now and then about how easy some of the railway track gangs had it ("spend half the day lighting the billy and the other half putting it out"), but for the most part the work was demanding and often life-threatening.

My first day at work was only two years before the Strongman Mine explosion that killed nineteen men, including two of my old high school mates. Fishermen would drown when their boats broached on the treacherous Grey River bar; bushmen felled like trees themselves when winch ropes snigging logs out of gullies snapped their moorings, whipped like scythes over the ridge and into the logging crews who weren't quick enough to dive face down into the dust. Maurice's dad once had a dice with death like that: a sprag from a rogue whiplash wire had sliced open the back of his woollen lammy. His mate was not so lucky. It wasn't unusual to see men missing fingers; my new boss's face had received the wire rope treatment years ago, his smile now a scar, his scar a smile.

But youth is oblivious to danger and I got ready to go to work. My mother bought me a thick bush shirt, rubber boots and a shiny black vinyl fur trapper's hat with the furry flaps. Canadian Jim Shields, the local men's outfitter (he ran a cool, black '55 Chevy) must have thought he was back in the Rockies when I walked out of his store that Friday night. My father showed me how to make a sugarbag knapsack for my crib tin (lunch box, for outsiders) and my flask of tea; come Monday morning, when Pete Donaldson pulled up outside in the green VW Kombi work van, I would be ready for my first day at the mill.

My working life began as a green little skiddie at a small family mill that looked like any one of a dozen up the many West Coast valleys, where rimu was still being milled under the supervision of the Forest Service. There still existed at that time a pioneer culture of timber workers and a parallel school of public servants tasked by the government to train workers and supervisors in forest management. Vast natural plantations had been established up north at Kaingaroa which supplied pine logs for the pulp and paper mills at Kawerau — newsprint for New Zealand and the world. Pinus radiata was now being planted on the Coast on cutover second growth, cleared to supply the newer, large factory-type mills owned by companies like Fletchers and Piesse-Blacklock.

My job was in one of the traditional mills that cut most of its timber for scantling: sawn timber for use as framing, studs, dwangs and rafters in house building. Little more than roofs on stilts, these ramshackle structures consisted of skids (where the cut logs from the bush were hauled off trucks and up into the mill); a breaking-down bench, where the logs, cleaned with high-pressure hoses, were cut into manageable lengths, rolled onto

A skiddie (who looks much like me), is axing the rimu bark to get rid of stones, Ngahere sawmill, 1971.

The skiddie hoses the bark with a high-pressure hose, flushing out embedded gravel before the log is sawn, Ngahere sawmill, 1971.

a moving trolley and split into workable slabs by the twin circular saws; a heading-in and tailing-out bench where the slabs were sized, and then dispatched to the docker who cut them off to length. Slabs and offcuts were carted away by winched rail dollies, to the fire to be burned; every West Coast mill from Harihari to Inangahua announced its presence from far away with a watercolour plume of blue-grey smoke. That was the way it was done back then.

On my first day I knew none of this. I was standing in my Skellerup lace-up rubbers ("Get rid of them, boy, get leather boots, or you'll be on your arse in no time") and my beaver trapper's hat, waiting for orders which were not long in coming. My job was to haul the logs off the old GM war-surplus truck when it chugged in from the bush up the road, then wash the logs down with a high-pressure hose. You had to get rid of a mix of mud and stones ground into the bark when the felled tree was dragged along the gravel tracks in the bush. Next, I had to winch the logs up the skids and slice them into lengths with a chainsaw. The breaker-down would do the rest. Imagine: you've never tried any of this before and now, learn it fast or you're down the road.

There were several ways you could be maimed, or die. You could get inside a right-angled force field when the logs were winched off the old GM (that was the first warning, stay outside the pull zone). You might miss a decent-sized stone embedded in the bark, one not dislodged by the hosing and have it fire back at you when the whizzing teeth of the breaking-down saws picked it up and spat it out: David and Goliath (second warning). You could tip a log off the skids as you hauled it in with the English Electric winch, and rip the floor up (I almost did that once). Or, you could get into a fight with the massive Remington chainsaw through being careless and lose some body parts (and while I never did that, I lost skin at the beginning of our relationship).

My teacher now was Dad's darts partner, the foreman, Porky Donaldson: grey jersey, grey strides, leather boots and fag hung on lip, he was charged with breaking me in, like one of those logs — and quickly. You had a day or two to learn the basics. I had problems right away with what soon became my worst nightmare: starting the chainsaw. I'd never done a full day's work in my life, and I was pretty unco-ordinated. Porky showed me how to measure the length of log to be sliced off the giant rimu poised on the skids like harpooned whales, then gave me the ABCs of chainsaw use and safety.

Ear muffs: what? Goggles: huh? This was 1965 and workplace safety was dependent on good advice and intuition, not rules on the wall. My ears

Remington 660 chainsaw, 33" blade.

still ring today from the decibel hell of those mills and factories. The roar of the big Remington 660 was deafening close-up, but it was only one instrument in the symphony of groaning winches and screaming saws. So began Chainsaw 101: check the blade is tight and the chain firm in the runners; make sure the chain oil is full and working (squirt onto chain, and often); check the two stroke petrol-oil mix is topped up — then flick the on switch and get ready for the first pull on the starting cord.

With a cold saw, that meant pulling the choke lever open and sliding it back in once the engine had kicked over and was idling; give her some revs and press the chain oiler. You're ready to go; well, that was the theory. In practice, I was unable to sit the 17lb saw on the log the way Porky did and with one clean strong heave on the cord, start the beast. He showed me how to do this on the floor ("Just keep the bloody chain off the boards!") by shoving my boot in the handgrip and hauling away. "Give her a good tug!" he exhorted with an evil grin. "You know about that eh, boy?" Whatever I knew made no difference: every time I snatched at the cord, the saw would backfire, over and over, until it was flooded. Finally Porky started it for me; then I had to haul it up onto the waiting rimu trunk and try my first cut.

This demanded more muscle than I then had at my disposal. Keeping the Remington going, the oil to the chain, starting the cut straight on the line, all the way through till the job was done and a length of log rolled down on the floor — this was a labour of Hercules. Engine roaring, sawdust spewing, it was easy to veer off target and cut on an angle, or stall the saw by trying to force it. Having that power suddenly was fearful and intoxicating, but it didn't take long before my shortcomings as a starter showed up after Porky left me to it. The next time I tried to ignite the 80cc power plant, I came unstuck. The saw backfired constantly, laughing at my puny attempts to get it going.

This would not have mattered if my hands were not baby-soft from the schoolroom; it was the blisters that killed me. Every backfire, every time the hard rubber handle on the cord whipped back through my fingers, the rawness grew, until presto: I had four big blisters across my palm. My skin was just doing its job. This was a sign to desist from such punishment, but of course I was not in a position to do that. I kept on hauling on the starter and the blisters kept swelling, until they burst. Rimu sap and sawdust are not exactly healing agents, and the exposed skin near made me cry. School quickly began to seem attractive, even with bloody bookkeeping — but there was no way back, the door marked *Pride* was locked.

Blessed relief it was when the chain would get blunt and Porky would be summoned with his file to sharpen it. My job then was to sit on the big red and white beast while he, with all the insouciance of the expert, filed each tooth back sharp. It had to be done just so, else the blade would cut on an angle. Porky puffed away on his Rothmans filtertips and I on my Three Castles Plain. Job done, it was back to the sawing again. My skin would split and bleed through the blisters; I gritted my teeth and pressed on. Smoko and lunchtime in the tiny office brought forth all sorts of fatherly advice on my skin problem: "Ooh, that looks nasty! Piss on them, boy — that'll fix it."

My co-workers were all local axemen, as tough as the timber we were felling and splitting. There was Denny McLoughlin with his big grin and curly quiff; Rusty Lemon, the freckled redhead (heading-in and tailing-out); and Len Fluerty on the docking saw. They all played league and competed in the local chopping competitions: hard-muscled athletes in white slacks and singlets with their razor-sharp axes, precise vision and well-honed reflexes. Why didn't they chop off their toes in those sandshoes, I'd often wondered? Axe head thwacking down inches from your foot?

Les Gilsenan, champion axeman, attacks in the standing chop.
West Coast Photo News

Len or Rusty put me right: "Look at what you want to hit, boy. Look at your toe, you hit your toe." They were right: that's the one thing I was taught there that has stayed with me.

They razzed me without mercy, but as I hung in there and got some kind of purchase on what I was doing, acceptance followed. I kept my head down and tried to fit in, until a letter I wrote to the newspaper about Vietnam got me some stick. I'd argued with a local elder in the pages of the Greymouth *Evening Star* that New Zealand and the Americans should keep out of Vietnam. We weren't in any danger of a Domino Theory communist takeover here, I declared. The next day at work as I sat down for smoko there were mock homages and doffing of caps, "Well, I couldn't understand all them big words you were using there, Professor!" they chuckled, me flushing red. The boss's son, home for the holidays from the St Bede's Catholic school in Christchurch, accused me of being a communist — which I took as a compliment.

The homespun remedy of the smoko room for healing my hands — urination — I didn't try. It was bad enough getting into the bath at night while the skin was still toughening up and I was growing callouses. With the bathwater at a bearable temperature, I would lower myself in, take a deep breath, then slowly immerse my cracked and bloody hands in the water. The sting! I wanted to yell and jump straight out, but I learned to suck my breath and wait. Gradually, the stinging would ease and fumble-fisted, I could get on with bathing my sweaty body. Eventually the blisters healed, my hands hardened and the purple juice of rimu sap outlined every track in my palms in a pattern I was proud of. It was proof I was becoming a man.

I learned more about the workings of the mill; later, relieving for Denny as a tailer-out, I saw just how easy it was to lose concentration. The header-in and the tailer-out take the sawn flitches from the breaking-down bench, slice the remaining bark off and turn them into planks and studs for house building. The header-in — as you might expect — runs the flitch over the rollers into the saw and signals the tailer-out if the plank is done, or needs to come back to him for another slicing into size. That's how you get four by twos, or it was back then. The finished piece of scantling slides down onto a feedline of rollers for the docker to size for length. This day, Rusty Lemon was heading in and I was on the receiving end; a piece of bark got caught in the back of saw between the whizzing teeth and the guide fin behind them.

He reached over with stick about the size of a ruler to flick the blockage free. He must have done it a hundred times, but this one went wrong.

Jack Brothers' mill, Bell Hill, West Coast.
Kotuku Heritage Society Inc, courtesy Marilyn Smithem

It happened too fast to see: his hand came near the saw and bang! He whipped it back, his face gone white in an instant. The stick had caught and dragged his thumb onto the blade, just enough of a nick to take his knuckle. Minutes later he was in the front seat of Porky's '52 Chevrolet, hand swaddled in blood-soaked towels, roaring off up the dusty gravel road to the hospital. I was temporarily promoted to tailer-out, while Len moved from the docking saw to header-in. Now I understood better why some of those old timers around the valley were missing bits of themselves; but not yet why some were missing from the face of the earth. Death was still to come.

I was getting some confidence: surviving the first few weeks and months, saving most of my £12.5s.6d per week thanks to my parents charging me a mere thirty shillings a week board (all in aid of my going on to university the following year). I was daring to let my hair grow longer each month, like my pop idols; but the short-back-and-sides culture of the mill soon put me in my place. Len was having fun with me, teasing me about being a girl; I fired some cheek back and he wrestled me to the ground (tough bastard). He rubbed his axe up and down on my neck, laughing me to scorn as the cold blade moved over my nape, and I froze.

It wasn't till I felt it was the head of the axe and not the edge that I knew for sure he was kidding. Len was reminding me of where I was on the pecking order, and maybe reminding himself of what had been done to him in his day. Compared to some of the tortures that apprentices still endured in the 1960s, I got off pretty lightly. He had the last laugh on rubber-booted me, tailing out one day, when I slipped walking backwards and a huge 20 × 8" piece of timber slid back down the trolley and pinned me to the wet wooden floor. I was cast. I couldn't get up, lying there with this huge wooden erection projecting from my stomach. I was winded too, but not so much that I couldn't shout for help, "Get this bloody thing off me!" Len came round, examined my plight and quietly pissed himself laughing. For a minute there, I thought he was going to walk off and leave me.

The deep winter was the killer; sometimes I still yearned I was back in a warm classroom. The Kombi van was like a deep freeze first thing in the morning: when Pete sped across the Blackball bridge, almost flying blind as the single wiper on the driver's side of the split screen waved across the barely defrosted glass, I would hold my warm hands on my side of the glass so I could melt the ice, just to see my death approaching. At the mill, the plaited steel winch rope was frozen. The hose was frozen. The skids were iced over and treacherous, and when you did get the water flowing, your hands were soaked and you froze again. When the iron on the roof began to thaw in the morning sun, leaks from everywhere dripped cold water down your neck. We grumbled and cursed and kept going. You had no choice — except to walk away.

Salvation came late in the winter with a letter from my brother Eric, up in the Wairarapa on a shearing gang. Did I know that if I wanted a job as a rousie, I could be earning ten bob an hour for the season, from October to Christmas? That was more than the mill was paying me, and you were fed and housed by the contractor and the cockies. I ran it past my parents and got the nod; just give a month's notice and I could go. Nervous, I approached Porky in late August and told him I wanted to go up north shearing (I had a tinge of guilt, as they'd not long given me a raise after six months). He wasn't fazed; they'd have to find another skiddie, but they couldn't be much worse than I was when I started, could they? He winked. I found out later his assessment of my progress, while sharing another beer with my dad: "He wasn't worth much when he started, Bill, but we'll be sorry to lose him."

The night before my last day, I asked my father to fill up a flagon so I could take it to work on Friday and shout the men. I smuggled the half-gallon jar in my crib bag into the smoko room and waited till afternoon teatime before revealing my gift. The assembled gallery of timber gods looked down on my offering, bemused. Porky swooped on the half-G, declaring, “Well, that’s my one, boy, where’s all the rest?” to snorts of good-natured laughter. They were the best of men: ordinary, extraordinary, hardened, brave and self-possessed. We drank the warm draught beer in good spirits and passed a farewell without other ceremony. I didn’t know then I would never forget them, but I never have.

As I got ready to leave and catch the railcar, the inter-island ferry and then the train to Pahiatua, I heard from my school friend Colin Heinz that Snowy Hutton was seriously ill. I stayed with Colin in Cobden that last weekend and we rang our old teacher’s wife to see if we might visit him. Permission was given and together we reverently entered his home in Marsden Road, Greymouth, and were shown to his bedside. To see such a charismatic figure laid low was a shock. I had never realised how old he was during those four years he taught me; old, in the sense of vulnerable. We spent a precious half hour at his bedside and said goodbye, wishing him a speedy return to good health and a happy retirement.

I had to pack whatever I thought I might need for a job I knew nothing about, but this was an adventure. I was moving further from the moorings of home and the familiar objects that had anchored me for years: the miniature rubber wheel ashtray surrounds Dad had got from working at Firestone Tyres in Christchurch, the matchstick art he’d made in prison, the German beer tankards that sat on the nest of tables, all the models I had made that perched on shelves in my bedroom and in the kitchen; leaving my parents, my sisters and my grandmother too, calling out for attention from the sun porch. I got on that railcar on 28 September 1965 and rode to Christchurch, sailing overnight on the *Hinemoa* to Wellington and catching another railcar to Pahiatua the following day. When I got to the farmhouse home of my brother’s friends at Makairo, a few miles out of town, the Hopkins family made me welcome, before handing me a telegram from my mother: “SNOWY HUTTON DIED LAST NIGHT.” That was my childhood’s end.

Tom Roberts, 'Shearing the Rams', 1890.
Wikipedia Commons

10

Wool away

I had a few days before the shearing season kicked off in the first week of October, spent getting to know my brother's adopted Wairarapa family, the Hopkins of Makairo. Small farmers, on a property cut in half in the Depression that was hardly economic to run, Sam and Moira were warm and slightly bohemian, for farmers in a true blue National seat. Sam, lean and brown with a penchant for striding about the farm in brief black swimming togs and sleeveless cardigans, was a do-it-yourself radioman with a taste for Jaguar cars. Moira worked in the Woodville telephone exchange twenty miles away, probably one of the few toll operators in the country who drove to work in a Jag. Each morning there was a huge pot of porridge, tinned Carnation milk and brown sugar, a fog of roll-me-own smoke from Pocket Edition tobacco, and plenty of tea. They became my family and a second home that first hard season away.

Up from working on the Haast Road the year before, my brother Eric had got to know their oldest son John and he too had been adopted by these generous people. John was atypical: a new shearer on his first year out, he drove a 100 mph-plus Daimler Dart V-8 sportscar he'd saved for as his first vehicle. His brother Graeme, who became my first new friend, was more conventional with his green and gold Ford Zephyr Mark I, but to say they were colourful was an understatement. I was in awe of their material abundance and energy. I got used to fast drives on back-country gravel roads, the sound of the stones spraying up under the bodywork as Graeme did controlled slides in the Zephyr, to show me "what she could do".

Those classy Fords had two main purposes: to find alcohol and girls — in no particular order. Cruising and boozing, in between racing each other and dodging the local traffic cop, were the main attractions and I joined the fun. The weekend before we were due to start work, they took me to a party where I met some of my future workmates and proceeded to get hammered. My binge-drinking career began that night; before long I was hanging off a rotary clothesline, spinning in circles and throwing up. My hosts were greatly amused at my puny attempts at swallowing Tui East India Pale Ale and encouraged me to try more. The next day I was crook as a dog. The day after that was my first as a rouseabout in an industry as old as Father Abraham. I didn't know what was about to hit me.

Shearing in the North Island ran nine-hour days, with five o'clock starts. Ponder that: 5 a.m. to 5 p.m., seven days a week. It was a contract industry with the shearers paid by the hundred, a real incentive to maximise their income by shearing clean and fast, as well as beating the man next to you — and if you were good enough, 'ringing the board' (shearing the most sheep). They were akin to Olympic athletes (a suggestion they would have mocked): fit and competitive, they raced the clock all day. Rousies were there to get the fleece off the board after each sheep, onto the table for skirting, classing and then pressing into bales (the presser also had the job of penning up, to keep up the flow of sheep into the catching pen). A rousie was the lowest on the food chain; you were there to work your arse off, running all day for ten bob an hour, good money back then. It was all before me that first black and cold October morning: shaken awake in the shearers' quarters, stumbling through the dark and the dew to my first early start.

The shed was an island of light and action in the pre-dawn murk: voices, dogs barking, the whirr of handpieces, a quick starting check, somebody swearing, sheep bleating and the overpowering smell of lanolin, a greasy air of sheep shit and piss stink. Introduced as Eric's brother — "Jeez, you two sound the same" — I was left in the hands of an older rousie who said, "Watch me, boy, you'll be right." In their navy woollen singlets, heavy stockmen's trousers and sacking moccasins, the three shearers stood at the pen doors as the clock hand moved up to five. "Go!" They flipped the catch and dived into the pen, upending and dragging out a hogget; with one smooth action, they pulled the cord and grabbed the buzzing handpiece. Blow by blow, whipping off the belly wool, working their way around the sheep, the long blow, the shoulder, till the last blow of the last side, heaving the naked animal down the chute. Bent low, they raced back in for the next and the next, for two solid hours.

There was no time to gawp. I was shown how to grab the fleece and throw it on the table; my efforts were a disaster. I'd trip on the fleece, or fire it at the classers in a tangled mess. I got sworn at for not sweeping the floor fast enough before the shearer hauled out the next sheep. My head was spinning, still hung over from the weekend's binge, and the pace was frantic. It was pressure from go to whoa, adapt or die, run, run and run again. I survived those first two hours till seven o'clock and a welcome breakfast. Chops and spuds never tasted so good, a mug of tea and then the chance to catch my breath and have a smoke. If I could just get through this day, I knew I might survive. Too late now to go home.

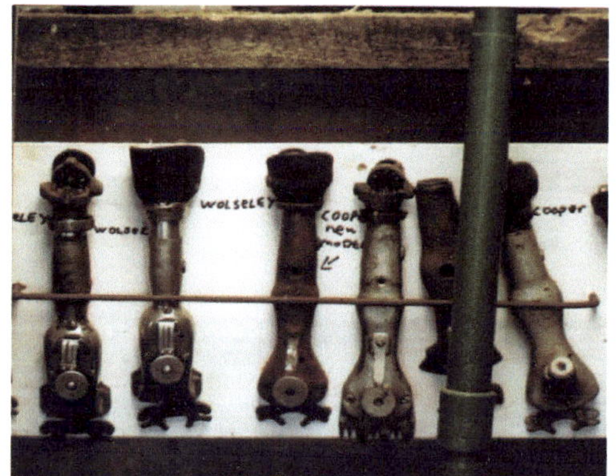

I was working for a contractor, Peter Travis; it was several weeks before I saw him, a former shearer himself who now ran a string of three-stand gangs, 'cocky shearing' on a run of smaller farms, a thousand ewes and a few head of cattle. He'd shorn on the big stations as a young man and worked fencing contracts on some of the near-vertical hill country properties around the Hawke's Bay and the eastern Wairarapa coast. He was tough and surrounded himself with like-minded workers: no-nonsense rural conservatives, the physical match of the men from my mining and milling background but politically Tory and pragmatic. Many of the shearers were farmers' sons, saving to get onto a farm or buy into the parents' land; others were transients like me who worked and drank from season to season with not much to show at the end. I was in another world and it wouldn't be long before my big mouth would get me into trouble.

Expecting to find myself working with my brother, it turned out he was on another gang and I was bunking down every night in the shearers' quarters with a bunch of strangers. You soon got to know each other, working under daily pressure from start-up to cut-out, one shed after another. In October, it was the hoggets — last year's lambs — and then on into the warmer November when the ewes and new lambs came in. The quarters were often old farmhouses, or sometimes purpose-built cabins with bunks, showers and a kitchen where the cook made all the meals from breakfast to dinner, mutton supplied by the farmers as your staple diet (porridge, chops and spuds, cold mutton salads, roast dinners, plum duff and custard — Kiwi fare). The cooks were treated with respect as they were hard to find; woe betide anyone who upset our Mrs Petersen.

It wasn't her I got offside with, but Tinker Smith, an older man my brother used to stay with. Tinker was a genuine country conservative who walked slow and talked slow and wore a big hat. He drove a flat-nosed Morris J2 van, which Daimler Dart man John Hopkins christened "the goldfish bowl". Salt-of-the-earth and amiable enough he was, until I managed to offend him by revealing republican sentiments I didn't even know I had. After work one night, writing a letter home, I offered my thoughts out loud on the subject of the Queen's head on our postage stamps. "Why is she on our stamps?" I declared, "She doesn't even live here." Tinker disagreed strongly; me, the know-all enjoying a joust, arguing back. The silence made the room go cold and he sent me to Coventry for several weeks.

So now I was a smart-arse. Living at close quarters with people for weeks on end could be a trial, but my friendship with Kathy, our lone female rousie, began to make up for it. She was an expert wool handler, one of a legion of Maori working in shearing gangs. I soon discovered there were whanau gangs working around us. This was a way Maori could get into the colonial economy, after their land losses in the 19th-century wars. Kathy was always immaculately dressed and coiffed: to watch her on the board with that broom, whisking the wool with such ease and grace any which way she chose was alluring. There was no nonsense: she kept herself to herself in the evenings and, like the cook, was treated with a degree of respect not accorded to us boys. Respect, that is, until our ganger made a bad error of judgment one day. Jim Davies, you so deserved what happened next.

Jim was a typical alpha male: full of testosterone, competitive and aggressive towards the rousies. He was a good shearer, a hard worker ... and a bully. He had a mean streak that let him think it was fun to trample over us as he vaulted you to get the next sheep. He also enjoyed the 'handpiece on the arse' routine: as the rousie in front of you bent over to pick up the next fleece, you planted the buzzing machine on their backside with a yell, scaring the crap out of them. I'd had it done to me and knew to grin and bear it as part of the initiation into the culture. But Kathy hadn't read that script and the day he tried it on her is one for the ages.

As she bent over to get the fleece, Jim struck: *buzz, whizz, yahoo!* Kathy stood bolt upright and her face changed colour several times, a spectrum running from fright to rage. She didn't hesitate: she lifted her broom high and whacked him hard on his bent back. We sucked our breath and silently cheered: got you, you bastard, got you! He looked like an idiot, of

My shearing handpiece, with New Zealand and Australian forks.
OPPOSITE Woolshed brand, Wairarapa.

course, and just kept on shearing. "Don't — you — ever — do — that — to — me — again!" Kathy snarled. He never did and even started to show more respect for the rest of us. Out there in southern Hawke's Bay, you had no real comeback with people like him, except to risk more torture if you resisted. Kathy showed us how it was done, and being a woman surely helped. He would have whacked me back — or sacked me.

Kathy (who I must have been in love with by now, but no chance there) led an expedition after work one day to gather puha for one of Mrs P's stews. We filled up bags of the sow thistle and carried it back to the quarters, she as dignified as ever and always a hero in my eyes. She never came back to the Travis gang the following year, and who could blame her?

Around the same time my drinking was starting to take charge. It was damned hard to get access to alcohol out in the country back then if you were under 21. Publicans would take one look at you and kick you out. We relied on the older men to get us a dozen of beer for the nightly bottle or two after work. When it came to the shed cut-outs, when the last sheep was counted out and the last bale of wool pressed, the farmers would shout a crate of flagons or a couple of dozen — and then we could truly let rip.

By mid-November I was getting the hang of the rouseabout's job and could throw most fleeces without getting them in a tangle. It was all to do with technique and repetition: the way you picked up the fleece as the last blow separated the sheep from its coat, the raising of the held coil of wool above the classing table, the practised flick of the wrists that propelled it like a cloud to settle flat in front of the wool handlers for skirting. The process — not that we had time to contemplate it — was a thing of beauty. Like the thousands of unseen and unheralded repeated acts that underlie a country's wealth, this ballet move of eye and body co-ordination is virtually ignored in our visual and literary arts.

I was starting to take an interest in shearing itself and asking to have a go. Watching these men was hypnotic: there was something about their fluidity and poise that called for you to emulate their mastery. Shearers are happy to have a keen young rousie take a few bellies off the sheep in their pen before a run starts and later, at the end of the work period, finish off a last side. Working forwards and backwards, you eventually got to shear a whole sheep. I was penning up sheep and pressing the wool; at the end of a shed cut-out, everyone got stuck in to load the press and finish the last few bales. I got to know how the old Donald presses worked, how to avoid pressing the pins, the art of lock stitch and running stitch, and branding the bales.

Shed cut-outs had a psychological bonus: the job was done, you could draw a line there and move on to the next one. My starring role in one such celebration came in December at the end of a tally day on lambs, at Boltons' farm near Pahiatua. In the month before Christmas, with the ewes and the hoggets done, it was time to shear the lambs and set a few personal records. Lamb shearing is another world: lambs are tiny, wriggly, hard to hold and control, needing the perfect grind of comb and cutter to avoid a cut that irritates the animal and picks up the skin, it's an art of its own. Massive men bent low over lambs that look almost like infants is a sight to behold. Everything happens at high speed, with lambs dragged on to the board, shorn and flicked down the chutes in under a minute.

Tally day means there is a record attempt going on. Everybody runs: rousies sweeping the wool, picking it up with a pair of small boards; the penner-up keeping the pens full; the presser filling the bales; the farmer and his dogs directing the stream of lambs flowing into the shed. One particular day, there were three shearers looking to do four hundred lambs each to break a previous shed record — and I was the presser and the penner-up. As well as keeping pace with the wool coming into the press, I had to keep the lambs up to each shearer. There should have been two of us for this, but there I was, running all day, sweating hard and giving it everything. Any sign that the pens were getting too low would bring a rain of curses.

At the end of each run, the count out of each shearer's tally let them know if they were on target to make the four hundred and the shed record; each time, we stayed on track. Breakfast, smokos and midday meal were heaven-sent; the day was warming up and the cold morning dew evaporating. I didn't realise that by not replacing the moisture I was losing, I was getting badly dehydrated. When it came to the last run, the prize was there and the three shearers flew at their work. As the clock wound down to five, we were all close to our limits, but this was it — the tally was nearly ours. When the last lamb skittered down the chute the machines were turned off and the count out began. We waited for the result.

There it was: the magic twelve hundred and a new shed record for the Travis gang. It was time for the shout, and the farmer broke out the beer. I was finishing sewing the last bales as crates of flagons were carried in and celebrations began. Warm draught beer in enamel mugs doesn't sound that attractive, but on the day it was mead from the gods. The Tui flowed, stories and voices were raised and I joined in with a manly thirst. The beer went straight to my head and within the hour I was drunk; nobody noticed me wandering off to have a leak in one of the catching pens, where I collapsed. There were still a few lambs left unshorn and they proceeded to play jump the rousie. I was lying there when one of the shearers came up on the board and spotted me flaked out, with my little friends gambolling over me.

This caused much amusement, apparently, and gave the men a chance to do what they'd been threatening to do since we met, half in jest and half not — give me a haircut. I was hauled out onto the board, a handpiece set up and they shore me, all my Beatle locks ending up on the floor. The joke went sour when I began fitting. I was suffering from alcoholic poisoning and the sudden onset of epileptiform seizures sobered up my barbers in a hurry. There was a degree of panic, they told me later, as I was carried me back to the shearers' quarters and a doctor called. He examined me, a little recovered, told me I was lucky this time and to lay off the beer. It was a warning I went right on to ignore.

I managed to survive the rest of the season, got my cheque and banked it: over £300, a handsome sum at the time and one I needed to put aside to get through the next year at university. It was still the plan to go there. My adventures in the shearing world were, like the sawmill days, stepping stones to that fabled degree my high school teachers were convinced I needed. The problem was that I had no ambition to be a teacher, the usual assumption when you said you wanted to study English. Beyond that negative response there was no Plan B; since my dream of being a fighter pilot had been quietly shelved, mentally I was drifting.

I said my goodbyes to the rest of the gang and the Hopkins family and with my brother, caught the railcar south for Wellington, the ferry and the journey back to my childhood world for Christmas. In the New Year, 1966, two of Eric's shearing mates, John Hopkins and Earl Sowry, arrived on a South Island tour to go tobacco picking in Motueka. Eric had been with them on the tobacco earlier that year, but this time opted not to go. Earl had been on my gang in the run-up to Christmas and shown me a thing or two about shearing. He was cool: he had a two-tone red and white Mark II Zephyr and drove it like the wind it was named for. They disappeared down the road and soon I followed suit, donning my newly acquired student's fawn duffel coat, departing for higher fields and the halls of ivy.

The English student says goodbye to Blackball.

1937 Vauxhall Fourteen Six.

11

Dropping out

My university career had to wait for a few weeks while I got myself settled with old family friends in Christchurch, my dad's former naval pals, the Shepherds. Like my parents, Ted and Mary had emigrated in the early 1950s, ex-Royal Navy joining the New Zealand fleet. I would board with them while I sorted out somewhere to stay, and in the meantime found myself a job at a local timber yard. I partied with their sons Geoff and Cliff, upping my payday drinking along the way with the men from the Wainoni Timber Company. I found a place to board for the coming year with an elderly woman in Bower Avenue. When enrolment day came around I left the timber yard and walked into the university registry on Montreal Street, signing up for three units, as they were called back then: English, History and Philosophy.

Why the latter I'm still not sure: perhaps it sounded intelligent, or maybe I was just curious. It was not long before I was unmasked as a non-philosopher. University itself was intimidating, never mind the bearing and the accents of other students. They all looked smarter than me and sounded better bred (a great many were from the top Christchurch schools). It was a relief to make contact again with some of my former classmates from Greymouth High, but we weren't in many of the same lectures. I began to suffer those curses of the provincial fresher: a sense of inferiority, loneliness and culture shock. In the evenings I would cycle back to Mrs Sanders' place at North Beach, usually against a cruel easterly, eat my tea and listen to her solemn and depressing classical music on the radio. I was allowed a maximum of three baths a week and had to study in my bedroom; it was like being back to the 1930s and I wasn't adjusting at all.

On a radio station one morning I heard a car yard advertising bargains for students: Crowes on Colombo Street in Sydenham had just the vehicle for your transport needs. Madly, I found myself that day in the car yard about to be sharked, my hard-earned £60 going his way and a green 1937 Vauxhall DX coming mine. It looked lovely but I was as green as the car. I failed to notice the blue smoke pouring from the exhaust and took his word that the battery — "crash charged" — just needed a wee run to top her up. Innocent of such details as a driver licence, with almost no time at all behind the wheel, I was soon nosing out of the yard and down Colombo Street towards the university.

The problems began at the first set of traffic lights: I jumped the clutch and stalled her. A few grinds on the starter produced the sick sound of a dying battery; obviously, I hadn't given the car enough of a "wee run". Over my rising panic, the motor fired and I took off, encouraged by the angry horn blasts behind me. This process continued all the way down the considerable length of Colombo Street to the Square. I threw a hard left and dashed down Worcester Street to the first car park I could find near the university. I was a bag of nerves by then, so decided to leave my green beauty to cool off and come back later — perhaps the battery would come back to life?

No such luck. I had to call on Ted Shepherd to tow me back to Bower Avenue and think of what to do next. I resumed my brief university career on two wheels. A consultation with the mechanic who lived next door was sobering: "That motor is stuffed, he wants hanging, selling you that one." That left me with little alternative but to kiss my sixty quid goodbye — or see if the car yard would take it back. I cycled over there the next day and told him of my plight. Tough: I'd had a test drive, the vehicle was inspected by me, I got what I paid for, what did I expect for that price? All of this was rattling my unsettled state of mind; beneath it all, I was already making plans to bail out. The bad experience with the car was just the catalyst: lonely, insecure and almost certainly budding for another binge.

My old Blackball friend Frank Pendlebury had just turned up in Christchurch to study at the polytechnic for his A-grade mechanic's apprenticeship in Greymouth. We connected: he was the right person to make me feel at home, a working-class kid with a good brain and a bunch of issues. My chats with the mechanic next door told me I couldn't afford to repair the car, but I discovered he had a 1947 Austin 10 for sale at £80, which was perfectly serviceable. He was prepared to take the Vauxhall off me in part payment, and he'd repair the engine himself and on-sell it. We had a deal. I told Frank I was leaving varsity, it didn't suit me any more. I was going home and offered him a ride back to Blackball when his time at the polytech finished.

On the broken Blackball bridge, 1966, with Elisabeth, Jill and Mum.
Gordon Howitt West Coast photograph collection (MB1072, 7572), Macmillan Brown Library, Christchurch

OPPOSITE 1960s Mark II Zephyr, Earl Sowry's ride.

It's easy to see now that I was developing a pattern of dropping out when things got tough. Like many smart kids from the provinces, I was intimidated by the urban setting and unsure of myself. Unlike my classmate Maurice, whose parents had moved to Christchurch when he began a law degree, I had no family support network, nobody I could go to and talk things through. Just as I had done at Grey High, I packed up my books. I said goodbye to my landlady, loaded up the grey Austin, picked up Frank from his lodgings and headed towards the Coast. We broke down on the Lewis Pass in the middle of the night; with my friendly mechanic on board, an air lock in the fuel pump was soon fixed. We drove all night at an average speed of around 35 mph. I was free again, but free for what?

At home there was warmth and comfort, but no future: I needed another job. I also needed a licence to drive, so used my time studying the road code and getting more practice.

I decided to take off back up north and look for work around Pahiatua. There was bad news before I could get that far: Earl Sowry, the man with the cool Zephyr, had been killed after a drinking session at the Swan pub in Motueka, a head-on crash with a lime truck on the Takaka Hill. The Hopkins brothers, John and Graeme, were following him in Graeme's

Mark I and saw it all. John had changed his mind at the last minute about riding with Earl, and he lived. Earl was twenty years old; it was my first realisation that it wasn't just old people who could die. My brother should have been with them too, but he'd decided to go back up north and give the tobacco picking a miss that year.

Something of the itinerant existence of seasonal work, the lack of serious commitment to anything long-term, was part of what drew me back; the chance to be young and feckless, to drink and drive and party. Whatever ambitions I'd had were all on hold for now. I booked the ferry from Picton, loaded up the Austin and set off to a life of shearing, fencing, scrubcutting and all the other physical challenges that came with that world. A part of me was sick of being seen as a 'brain'; weighed down by my primary school fat boy image, I wanted to prove myself on a primal level. It was a straight swap between this, or the glorified schoolwork on offer at the university. I'd had a conversation in a philosophy tutorial before I left: playing the cynic, I remarked that philosophical problems seemed to go on "ad nauseam". "I prefer *ad infinitum*," the tutor parried. That about summed me up back then.

The faithful little Austin got me all the way back up north, the only hiccup a dodgy bearing that meant no first gear. To get her up onto the car ferry I had to race up the ramp in second. The Hopkins family took me in again and I soon took up partying with Graeme, right where we'd left off the previous season. I was impressed with his ability to do controlled slides on gravel and decided one day to try the same trick in the Austin. I charged at the corner, got the car into a rear-wheel slide and over-corrected; next thing we were airborne, leaping into the grass, over a ditch and thumping to a stop. I'd bounced from one side of the cab to the other, wrestling the steering wheel, suffering a pounding as I landed on the handbrake between the seats.

In a vain attempt to drive off, I wound away at the starter, but the engine was not going to fire for me — not now, not ever. Graeme was called in to tow me out and a plan was soon hatched to haul the defunct Austin to the wreckers in Woodville (I had no money to fix the engine, and couldn't leave a wreck to rust on the Hopkins' farm). Graeme and his mate kindly offered to borrow the parents' Jag and tow me the twenty miles to the wrecker. Away we went: once they'd got me off the gravel and onto the tarseal, they wound the Jaguar up, waving out of the windows as we hit first 50, then 60 mph on my speedo. I'd never had the car much over 45 miles an hour. On the main road from Mangatainoka, past the Tui brewery, there are long sweeping corners; these maniacs pushed the Jag with me in tow up to a nerve-wracking 70. Madness.

I was terrified. I hung on grimly to the shuddering steering wheel, swearing at them to slow down. I doubt the car had ever gone that fast; its last act on the planet was probably to set a land speed record for Austin 10s. When we finally got there, abusing my two 'tow truck' drivers was a waste of time — they just couldn't stop laughing at me. That was the sort of fun I'd bought into now, hanging out with guys who ran on adrenaline. Wild colonial boys, like poor Earl Sowry. Now I needed to get work, but at that time of year there wasn't much to be had. Graeme had another bright idea: scrubcutting. The hills around the Wairarapa were overrun by manuka and gangs of professional scrubcutters took contracts to clear them. Graeme knew somebody who knew somebody and lined up a contact for the two of us (his mate, being better informed, pulled out).

The old method was to attack the scrubby low trees with slashers: backbreaking work on slippery hillsides. A more recent innovation was the use of chainsaws with long booms attached to the clutch housing and a circular saw at the end of the boom. Handles like bike handlebars crossed the boom; the operator strapped the device over his shoulders. Starting the saw, you advanced, lined up a manuka on the slope and with a burst of revs, felled each tree. This required a good bit of effort to stay balanced on the slopes, but it was nowhere near as tough as hacking away all day with a slasher. We had a small problem: money to buy saws. A local McCullough dealer had just the thing: two second-hand saws complete with everything we'd need to get started. No doubt the capital came from Graeme's long-suffering parents. There I was, an independent contractor in the scrubcutting business, with a saw, a partner and a vehicle to get us out to the job on the road to Pongaroa.

What the farmer thought when two long-haired boys turned up in a green-and-gold Zephyr with whip aerials and a couple of saw booms sticking out of the boot, heaven alone knows. We set to work: at first it was exhilarating to see bush after bush, tree after tree topple over before our attack. Not quite so thrilling was the slipping and sliding when it rained, gouging your knee on a stump. It was dangerous, like all jobs involving machinery with moving parts. Neither of us were saw doctors and we only had a couple of spare blades; once they blunted, there was a trip back into Pahiatua to get them sharpened at the chainsaw shop (we later recruited Sam, Graeme's dad, to help out).

Then there were the breakdowns needing more trips to town, the cruising around talking to girls we knew, hanging about in milkbars while the saws were fixed, going home early as it wasn't worth driving back out to the farm. Not yet twenty, we were green as grass and poor prospects to run a business. The scrubcutting empire folded before it even got started, leaving us with little to show but a couple of burned-out saws and a reputation for being useless. Salvation arrived in the spring with the prospect of another season on the Travis gang. With the promise of a presser's job, I signed up again. Once we got to Waipukurau in Hawke's Bay, I was quickly disabused of this notion when I met Brian, introduced as the new presser.

I protested to Colin, the ganger: I'd been promised a job pressing at the end of last season, Peter Travis himself had said so. Colin was unimpressed: it was like it, or leave; reverting to my usual strategy, I said I was leaving. He drove me down to Dannevirke to talk to the boss. Travis too was unmoved — "Just quietly, boy, your pressing wasn't worth a tin of shit" — and he seemed to have a memory lapse about his promise. With some persuasion, reality sank in; if I stood on my pride, I was about to be jobless and penniless. I pulled my head in, and with promises of maybe getting some pressing later in the run, we trekked back to Waipukurau.

We were working on a property named Tangmere, a returned serviceman's ballot farm drawn in 1959 by Wilf Clouston. He was a wartime Spitfire pilot who strode around the shearing shed in a military manner like an English country squire. When we'd shorn there the previous year, our presser Clem had amused himself by hauling out the long steel pins from the top box of the press and dropping them deliberately behind the wing commander. The crash startled Clouston and he stopped dead; readjusting his military bearing, the old airman strode on. None of us knew that while surviving the Battle of Britain, he spent the years after the fall of Singapore in 1941 as a prisoner of the Japanese. With my romantic notions of air combat, I longed to ask him what it was like to fly planes like the Spitfire, but could never summon the nerve.

Flight Lieutenant Wilfrid Clouston (right) and Squadron Leader BJE 'Sandy' Lane of No. 19 Squadron at Fowlmere, Cambridge, 1940.[10]

Old flyers

for John Ritchie

From *Fly Boy*,
Steele Roberts, 2010.
John Anthony Ritchie (1921-2014), emeritus professor of music, Sub Lt RNZVR, FAA, WW2 Spitfire pilot.

Each day they glide to never's never, each
night a raid above wherever flak falls

silent back to earth and medals glitter
behind the broken glass of winter. We

need to ask them but never do, what
it was like to hover above the earth — and die?

Hover over death and kill, kill then laugh
till you were killed? Night and day they

leave the earth and we're none the wiser: old
flyers, rising up through the clouds of unknowing.

The season progressed as the last, from shed to shed, pub to pub, working every day God sent until bad weather stopped the gang. You can't shear sheep wet without associated health risks to the shearers, and you can't press the wool wet either; it discolours and hot, damp wool bales can spontaneously combust. Longing for a break, we rousies loved the wet, but the contractor and the gangers sweated on a spell of fine weather to finish the run before Christmas. Getting into town for a decent feed of steak, eggs and chips, then a session in the pub, was a highlight. It was when we were stuck in a wet spell near Makuri later that the downside of wet sheep and long sessions in the boozer came home to me after a bad judgment call from our Australian rousie, Fred.

Fred was a tough nut from Melbourne, a street kid who loved the Rolling Stones, and we were getting on well. He did have a major problem: the streets of Footscray had taught him that you got in first, you got in hard and then you got out. We weren't in Footscray when the trouble arrived; there were no back alleys around the isolated Makuri pub where we'd been drinking for most of the day that our Fred decided to pick a fight with a gang of shearers from Eketahuna. This included some well-known scrappers by the name of Cadwallader, men who were best avoided. It was the same old story: Cadwallader man to Fred, "Who you lookin' at?"

Fred, "Lookin' at you, so what?"

Cadwallader man, "Wanna make something of it, prick?"

Fred, "Okay, outside!"

Fred's opponent walked out the door of the bar with Fred right behind him. The other young rousie was looking at me, we both knew this meant trouble. There was a scuffle and swearing outside as the rest of the

Cadwalladers followed their man out to watch him finish off the Aussie. "Stay out of it, or you'll fuckin' get it too!" they glared at us. We obliged. Neither of us was a fighter or wanted to get killed, but we did poke our heads out of the door, only to see Fred on the ground getting a good old-fashioned kicking.

"He king-hit him, the bastard!" they shouted. "You two, stay out of it!"

In true Footscray style, Fred had smacked the other man in the back of the head, so the rest of gang got stuck into him. He managed to get on his feet and ran off as the victorious Cadwalladers threw curses after the fleeing figure.

He was lucky they hadn't killed him. We walked back to the shearers' quarters, going over and over the night's events, wondering what had happened to Fred. We weren't left in the dark for long. He'd made his way back too, hidden until he was sure his tormentors were not coming after him, then listened to us outside the door before bursting in spewing hate and brimstone. "You fuckin' bastards!" he yelled, swinging at me and knocking me down. "Why didn't you give me a hand?" I hit the floor and rolled underneath the bed, while Fred kept up a rain of kicks in my ribcage and tried to rip the bed from over me. My mate tried to calm him down, pleading that we couldn't do much, we weren't fighters and anyway, we were outnumbered by the other gang. They were going to kill us if we poked our noses in.

This didn't impress our street fighter, who kept on raving, but he did stop kicking me. The other guy saved my skin by talking Fred down. The Aussie was a mess, beaten black and blue; he finally collapsed onto his bed and fell asleep. We followed suit. I woke up sore and sorry in the morning, but Fred's bed was empty. Colin the ganger walked into the bunkroom and looked down at me with not a hint of compassion. My ribs were hurting me now, and I wanted to crawl away. "I'm fucked!" I moaned. "You're not fucked till you're dead," he replied helpfully. I only found out on a trip to the doctor weeks later, to get to the bottom of the ongoing pains in my chest, that my ribs were cracked. I worked the rest of the season like that.

Ignoring his hard-man bedside manner, I asked the ganger where was Fred? "On the train to Wellington. We sacked the bastard," said Colin, walking out. The cook had called them in the night: they'd driven out from town, dug Fred out of bed and removed him. I guess he didn't have much fight left in him, but he still had my Rolling Stones *Aftermath* LP, which was a kind of poetic justice. I wondered afterwards — ashamed of my lack of courage, still convinced he'd brought it all on himself and we didn't owe him getting ourselves a hiding — if he made it back to Melbourne and out of street fighter mode before somebody killed him.

That pub binge should have been enough warning to me about out-of-control drinking sessions, but after a while it wore off. Another shed, another run of wet weather and we found ourselves in one of the few Pahiatua pubs that would wink at under-age drinkers. I'd discovered by now the charms of Bacardi and Coke: after a few beers and some games of darts we hit the top shelf hard. By the time we got home for tea several hours later I was well plastered, and made the point by opening the car door and falling out onto the grass. I couldn't stand up, so they carried me to bed and left me to sleep it off. I promptly rolled over and fell out, ending up underneath the wire-frame bed, which I tried to kick off me. Somebody came back to investigate the ruckus and there I was, fitting again. Some bright spark tried to revive me with a vinegar-soaked rag — shades of Jesus!

I managed to come through that episode without the arrival of a doctor and dozed for a while into the twilight; still drunk, I got up and wandered outside. There was a swing bridge over a creek near the quarters, which we had to cross to get to the shed. I sallied forth and was soon spotted hanging onto the supporting wires, my feet just on the slats of the bridge, raving. It was about fifty feet or so to the dry rocky creek bed below; if I'd fallen, I'd be dead. This was the second year running I'd inflicted an injury on my developing brain, but in 1966 nobody talked or thought like that. If you wanted to be a man, that kind of man, man alone emotionally, you got pissed.

I was still keen to learn to shear, and I'd found a willing teacher: Leckie George. Leckie was a short, stocky Maori shearer, the only one in the three gangs who wasn't Pakeha. I warmed to his sense of humour and constant singing. He pissed the other shearers off at times: he was friendly to us rousies and seemed to take it all in his stride, not an uptight tallyman like a few of the others. Leckie would sing along to the latest hits, 'Black is Black' by Los Bravos a special favourite, added to with a few lyrical changes of his own. "Black is black, I want my Maori back ..." he would warble, working his way around the sheep, chatting to me as I picked up the fleece. I asked him if I could take some bellies off for him and would he give me some tips? Leckie was up for this, on condition that I first learned to make shearer's moccasins, "You have to do that boy, if you're going to be a shearer." So Leckie got his moccasins made for him and I got the benefit of instruction. This also seemed to annoy the other shearers, who let me know he was having me on. They were just jealous. Ten minutes before the start of each run, I'd haul a sheep from Leckie's pen and shear the belly wool, which I could do pretty well by now. As the clock neared the hour, I would have belly-shorn half a dozen. I got to go over the first hind leg on the last one, before he took over. This meant that for the first thirty minutes, Leckie — who was not the fastest of the three — would ring the board, dragging out bare belly after bare belly, laughing and singing.

Anyone who has ever listened to the words of 'Click go the Shears' knows that the old shearer, who had his gaze fixed on a bare-belly Joe, was going to put pressure on the top man. "Glory, if he gets her, won't he make the ringer go!" Leckie did just that. The other shearers didn't thank me for it, but I learned fast. By the end of the season, with finishing off the last side and later the long blow, I could shear a whole sheep. We kept on shearing and we kept on partying till Christmas, then went our separate ways. I never saw Leckie after that year, but before we left to go home I'd made a friend with one of the farmers we shore for near Makuri — Doug Falconer, who ran Skye Farm on the Pori Road over to Tiraumea.

It was reputedly the highest homestead in the Wairarapa; after a few misty mornings that proved to be low clouds setting in, I found this to be true. Doug was a bachelor, a former schoolteacher who hosted us in his house right next to the shed, on a steep hill country farm that ran Perendales. These were crossbred sheep more like mountain goats in their nervy, highly-strung nature, but tough and ideally suited to that hard country. As was Doug: we got on well, drinking after work in the kitchen and heading down to the Makuri pub in his old ragtop Land Rover. When the shed was cut out, I said I was coming back up next year and he offered me a job as farmhand after Christmas. We shook on it: having something steady to come back to was way better than my efforts earlier in the year. I packed my bags, picked up my cheque and said goodbye to the Travis gang until 1967.

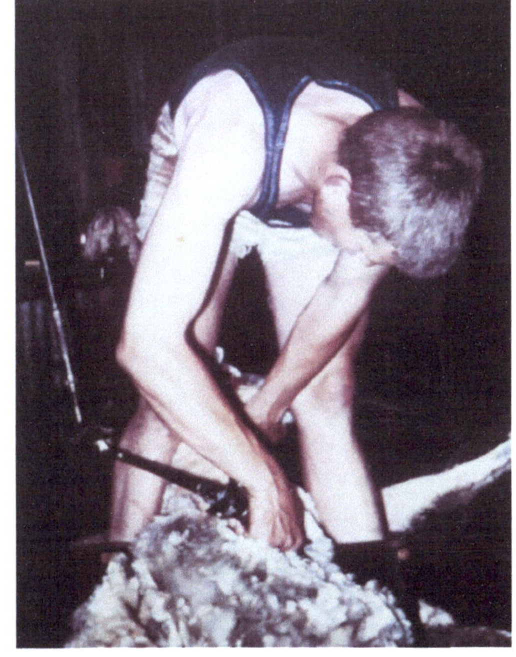

The learner, over the last shoulder.

12

Skye Farm

The trip home that Christmas ended in anything but a season of cheer and goodwill. Our parents' wartime marriage, contracted in haste in 1943 at a time when death for civilians and the military was an ever-present reality, was at breaking point. While my brother and I were drinking with Dad in the Dominion Hotel, Mum took an overdose in the middle of the day, leaving a note. She was quickly discovered by my distraught sisters and rushed to the hospital in Greymouth. It was a cry for help, we could see that even then. Once she had recovered enough to talk to us, to say how sorry she was, she asked if we would help her get out of a marriage she should have left in 1962, but stayed for any number of reasons: unable to break free psychologically from her abuser; for the sake of her children; and the frightening question of how she would survive with no income. It was five more years before the Domestic Purposes Benefit gave battered women a window of hope, a way of escape.

Desperate by now, she needed our help to escape the ashes of a wartime romance that had soured into bitterness and recrimination. Warning Dad we were leaving, we hired a van and moved my mother, grandmother and my two sisters out of the family home and into a run-down property in Greymouth. Eric and I stayed around long enough to help them settle in and then left for work again up in the Wairarapa. I had promised Doug Falconer I would be back in the New Year, so had little choice. It was the worst Christmas I'd ever had, and we left with all sense of a home leaving with us. Nineteen and twenty-year-old males of our generation were not encouraged to deal with their emotions; there was no grammar of feelings, no dictionary of damage limitation.

We swallowed the family pain and moved on, wounded. Eric had a job with a shearing and farm contractor in Tiraumea, over the hill from Skye Farm, and I went to work for Doug. A former teacher, he had resigned from the profession and gone on a world tour. He'd returned to run a shearing gang with his brother, finally buying a neglected hill country property the doomsayers reckoned would break his heart — Skye Farm. Wiry, feisty, intelligent, with a short fuse, Doug was a pocket dynamo.

The farm was certainly high: on cold autumn mornings the clouds would swirl in and we were fogbound for hours. The old farmhouse was clammy and damp, tall pines and macrocarpas conspiring to block the sun whenever that pale orb finally emerged from the gloom. With the shearing shed right opposite across the gravel drive, a bulldozer almost at the back door and dog kennels populated as always with lean and hungry chain-rattling animals, the scene then was what would now be understood as Kiwi Gothic. A venerable International KB6 truck, born in the same year as me, completed the farmyard scene. Doug was used to a pioneering lifestyle and I was soon inducted into this rough male world.

Skye Farm was as rugged as they come: ridges mostly, with barely any flat, running a mix of sheep and cattle amid the totara stumps from the days when pioneers had cleared the land, way back. Doug had chosen his Perendale sheep as the breed best suited to the steep and rugged nature of the place, a Romney-Cheviot cross developed at Massey University. They were semi-wild, relentless foragers, good mothers, able to lamb with little assistance, ideally suited to the geography. They were also mad, flighty and fast, not unlike Doug; it needed a good heading dog to round them up and keep them coming in a single mob. That was where his cunning eye dog, Jean, came in (more of her exploits later).

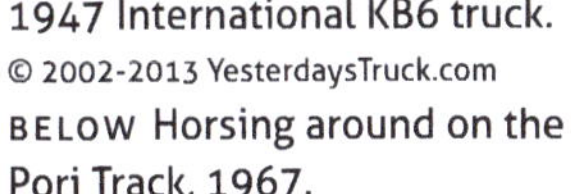

1947 International KB6 truck.
© 2002-2013 YesterdaysTruck.com
BELOW Horsing around on the Pori Track, 1967.

The beef herd — run cattle — were wilder still. These were not your tame old dairy cows meandering to the shed in time for milking. These beasts were left to their own devices for long periods, then rounded up for drafting after the calves had grown, or when it came time to send the steers to the works. On those days when the dogs were sent out to herd them into the yards, it paid to keep an eye on their potential to have a go at you. I was completely green to farm work and stock handling, needing a crash course to learn survival skills. Once I'd settled in, Doug gave me a tour of the place and we were ready to begin my new life as a hill country shepherd and cowhand.

To say I was pretty useless for the first few days and weeks would be fair. I hadn't been brought up in a farm culture where kids learn stock handling and DIY maintenance, running around with their parents. I was soon confronted with Johnny the surly packhorse, whose services were needed in the hilly, slippery conditions. Doug showed me how to put a pack saddle on the recalcitrant nag as we packed in some split totara battens from beside a swampy creek, up to the fenceline where they'd be used. Needing to visit town on business, my boss left me to it; this suited Johnny completely. From long experience, he could recognise a greenhorn when he smelt one. As I tightened the cinches, the cunning white gelding breathed in, so that when he breathed out, the saddle would be loose and more comfortable.

Reaching the stack of battens, neatly bundled with wire for packing out, I loaded them onto hooks on either side of the saddle and led the horse along the gully to the first creek. Johnny balked. He was not going to cross. I hauled on the reins: he resisted at first then gave way, leaping over the boggy stream, dislodging the saddle and the battens as he did so, kicking the lot into the swampy creek. He stood there snorting, looking satisfied: "Your move, son," was the message as he twitched his ears. I was snookered. There was no way I could get the saddle back onto him on my own. I had to lead the smirking nag back down the hill, along the road to the house and the horse paddock. I waited for Doug to return while the sly old gelding returned to its grazing.

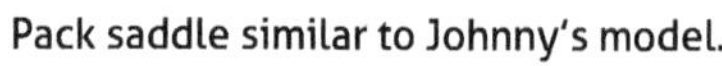

Pack saddle similar to Johnny's model.

Doug had a good laugh when he heard how Johnny had outsmarted me — but was not so amused when he heard the leather saddle was still up there by the swampy creek. Didn't I know how much those things cost; that water would ruin the leather? Sadly, no; my first attempts at being a farmhand were much like my early days in the sawmill. Johnny was re-enlisted to go with us and retrieve the saddle. I swear his lip had the healthy curl of a sneer when he looked me up and down. He soon got the better of me again in my time on Skye Farm: I was deputed to retrieve the carcass of a cow that had died after falling down a hole on a steep hill, breaking its spine. Doug had butchered it on the spot; my job was to bring the meat uphill to the shed, on Johnny, on the pack saddle. His last win over me fresh in his equine memory, the horse waited as I came into the yard with the saddle and promptly turned his bum to me. Every time I tried to get close and hoist the saddle up, he either moved away or presented me with his rear end and the prospect of a good kicking. This went on for quite some time as I swore at him and got nowhere; in the end, of course, Johnny won. I traipsed down the hill and carried the butchered beast up to the shed myself, entailing several difficult trips, all the while watched by a smug, relaxed Johnny who was quite content to avoid such a troublesome task. Doug's later advice — "You have to show him who's boss, give him a smack on the nose" — was something I never got around to trying.

Not all of my early adventures in farming turned out so badly, nor resembled the hard-luck stories in the *Me and Gus* books I had devoured at high school. I was never going to make Young Farmhand of the Year, but I did manage to become of some use to my fiery employer. Doug was renowned in the district for his tendency to fly off the handle when machinery or the universe in general was not co-operating with his plans. Variously, in the few winter months I was there, I saw him fling to the ground a stubbornly unco-operative chainsaw from the upper branches of a pine tree he was trying to top near the house; hurl a wrench that was not budging a stubborn nut on a machine in the woolshed, at which point the spanner dropped through the slats of the shed to the sheep shit strata below, from whence he, cursing, had to retrieve it; and midwinter, cutting with a butcher's knife the frozen ropes that held the tarpaulin to the bulldozer, when his numb fingers had failed several times to untie them.

I learned plenty about self-control, about not messing with run cattle and never getting between a cow and her calf; I came to admire the sheer poetry of Jean the eye dog holding up the mob of sheep with no more than a look as we shifted them on the winding public road from block to block; I winced as Doug thrashed the same dog with a fence strainer chain after she'd killed a ram; I learned to drive the beat-up old short wheelbase '52 ragtop Land Rover in four-wheel drive on slippery clay hill tracks; and I discovered the combustible power of Captain Morgan Navy Rum, passed around after a freezing morning's deer-stalking on the back of the property. I learned some limits and began to feel the small stirrings of physical self-mastery, easing the way I felt about myself.

In spring, the plan was to leave Doug's employ and go down the valley, east to Tiraumea and work with his relative, Laurie Kidd, my brother's boss. I was saving money — having nowhere much to spend it — and would soon step out and buy another car, a green and white 1952 Chevrolet De Luxe. My last act before doing this and leaving Skye Farm was to give Doug a story he probably dined out on until he died in Waipukurau years later, in the 1980s.

While a shearing contractor, he'd bought a canning plant to preserve the season's tomatoes while they were cheap and plentiful, to serve them up to his shearers with the usual meat and veges. With some venison he'd preserved and other meats, Doug concocted a variety of stews to use for quick meals after a hard day on the farm. Once they were cooked, we ladled the stew into large cans and sealed the lids with the canning plant.

There was one more step: the cans had to be heated for half an hour each in the oven to help expel any air and complete the seal. Once more, Doug had business to do in town; as it was a wet day I was left to load the tins of stew into the Shacklock 501 wood stove, supervising their heating and removal. He drove off and I pulled up a chair to the stove, reading a book while waiting with my feet up on the fire surround in the kitchen. Engrossed in whatever story it was, I neglected to keep an eye on the time. There was a sudden explosion and I was knocked from my chair by the oven door, blown off its hinges. Book in hand, shocked in a pool of hot stew with three large cans of the stuff burst open in the oven — disaster! I jumped to my feet and surveyed the wreckage — what would Doug say? He'd kill me, he'd blow up big time, like the stew.

Something about my time in Cubs and St John's must have stuck, so I set about cleaning up. The cast iron hinges on the door had been snapped clean through by the force of the blast, but other than that there was no damage and I was unhurt, save for pride. I looked at the stew-flooded lino and saw one of the cats had taken to lapping away at the unscheduled feast. A light went on in my fevered brain. I went to the door, walked outside and let Luck and Jean off their chains. I called them over to the house, right

The '52 Chevrolet at Timmins' woolshed, Tiraumea, 1967.

to the kitchen door, and invited them in to clean up the stew. Trying to get farm dogs into a house is no easy assignment; they're habituated to living in kennels far from humans and they know that such places are forbidden. They stood at the doorway, half-frozen by taboo, but drawn within by the prospect of a free meal.

Eventually, one of them moved in far enough to start licking the meat-spattered floor and instinct took over. Cats and dogs together, they cleaned up most of the mess; the dogs were then returned with full stomachs to their kennels under the macrocarpas. I got out a bucket and mop and cleaned the floor, leaning the stove door forlornly against the oven and waited for Doug's return. On hearing my tale, he actually saw the funny side and marvelled that I'd managed to get the dogs into the house. The next day, he bronzed the hinges back and restored the door to its oven. Doug Falconer was a generous and forgiving boss. While I gave him a few grey hairs in the three months I was up on Skye Farm, the main reason I was there — as company, as a balm to his loneliness — was at the heart of my employment. I know he got something of value from our relationship; we both did.

Laurie Kidd and his wife Coral with their two young children gave me a completely different domestic and work environment to the bachelor existence Doug lived, high on the hill. You descended to Tiraumea from the Pori by way of a track hardly deserving of the name 'road', tiny houses and sheds visible in the valley far below. Their home was near the junction of the gravel roads that ran north-east to Pongaroa and Hawke's Bay, then south-west to Eketahuna and Wellington: isolated, unvisited by most New Zealanders. After the descent, at the crossroads, a white stadium-sized ten-stand woolshed announced the presence of George Timmins, the largest landowner in the area, a polar opposite to Laurie and his start-up contractor business.

I trundled past all this in my big Chevrolet, wondering what lay ahead. It was close to spring lambing: when the season came around in October, I would be working with my shearer brother and his new boss. Laurie's wife Coral leant a definite feminine presence to the old but tidy farmhouse the Kidds owned. She brought home to me again that I missed my mother's comforts and liked having a family around me. Young David and his impish sister Tracy were a tonic; sitting down to a meal with them all was a pleasant relief from the roll-your-own smokes male culture of Skye Farm's kitchen. Not that Coral was your typical farmer's wife; she was bolshie and hard-nosed about males in the house expecting her to be the kind of maternal figure I was missing. I suspect she never intended living at the end of a remote gravel road; we were getting the rough edge of some disappointment, and at times, her tongue.

We settled in and got to work. As well as shearing, Laurie had other contracts for fencing and gorse spraying, all of which I had a go at (I'd done fencing repairs with Doug). We ended up in a caravan somewhere in the back of beyond, climbing steep inclines, digging postholes while trying to keep our footing, and hauling wires, hammering staples and ramming the dirt. Fencing is an art little-known within the city limits, strange for a country that is spider-webbed with thousands of miles of the stuff in various states of repair. Fencing is the ultimate statement of private property, cutting us all off from the shared commons enjoyed by our medieval forebears before the enclosures that made us what we are today: individualists. There's nothing like nice straight fenceline to delight a cocky's heart.

I hadn't been at Laurie and Coral's place for long when my brother and I got a phone call from my mother: Nanny was dead. My dear old grandmother, pushing ninety, had come to the last heartbeat. "Don't come home, dear," my mother told me. "There's nothing you can do." There was a loneliness in her voice that was new; they had seldom been separated since my mother had come out of a five-year stint in an orphanage, abandoned and imprisoned there after her father had died in Liverpool in 1930. I was torn. I had no money to speak of, having blown my meagre savings on the car, which I was paying off over the next twelve months.

Laurie would have advanced me the train and ferry fares and taken it out of my wages later, but I did not go and later regretted it bitterly. Nanny was my history maker, my Tusitala, teller of tales, my war correspondent, a link to the distant past. I went to bed that night and cried into my blankets as the mad Tiraumea winds blew outside. The district was known for the endless gusts that drove you crazy after a day's fencing, or worse,

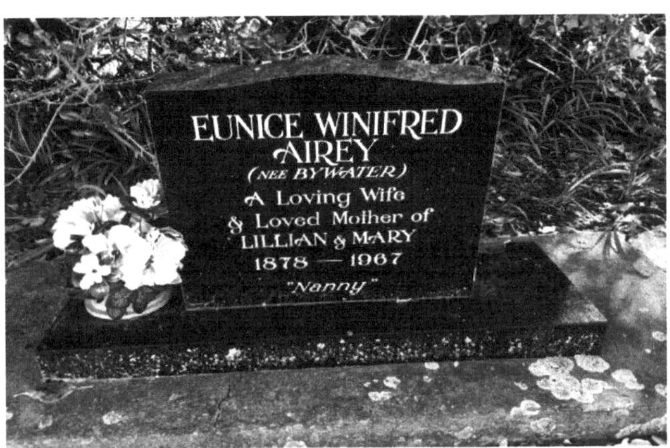

My grandmother's grave, Karoro Cemetery, Greymouth.

gorse spraying with 2,4,5-T and arriving home with a suspicious headache from exposure to the chemical mist. We were not supposed to spray on windy days but the wind hardly ever stopped in the winter months. I kept my head down and pushed the grief inside. I would go to the grave at Christmas time and say my goodbyes.

For now, there was work to be done: lambing was here, and down on George Timmins' place a fresh crop of land girls hired for the lambing beat. The arrival of a bevy of single women in the backblocks was a magnet to the young males of the district. Parties were soon organised on the weekends and we were introduced: there were two Aussie girls, Lyn and Fran, and Jane from Yorkshire (who had the dubious honour of owning an underpowered Ford Prefect that almost stalled changing from first to second on a slight rise). My brother Eric would go on to form a relationship with Fran, an outgoing and strong-minded West Australian woman; early in the following year, newly engaged, they would leave for Australia. Eric had acquired a new Fiat 1500 car, a payout for an injury suffered earlier when a hammered staple had bounced back at him from a fencepost and pierced his eye. New cars were hard to come by then, with the need for overseas funds as part deposit — Fiats were somehow exempt.

Each with a set of wheels, we were in party mode and could travel to football games and films. I once drove my boss Laurie to a segregated showing of the film version of James Joyce's *Ulysses* in distant Palmerston North. In the dark with him, listening to Molly Bloom's sexual soliloquies, I didn't know where to put myself, or what we had struck. The homebound conversation in the Chev would be worth hearing now.

The shearing season came around again and we headed into my third season. I was picking up and pressing, taking every chance of shearing practice and getting good enough to shear a whole sheep. I was hoping I

Black sheep of the family: one I shore earlier, Tiraumea.

could come back next season and get on a stand myself. Watching the pain my brother Eric was going through with his back problems, I should have been warned. It would come to me down the track.

I was drinking again in heavy binges but there was no repeat of the severe insult to my brain of the past two shearing seasons. It still wasn't pretty: after a day docking lambs, I got so drunk at the Pongaroa pub one night with a mate Roy Bennett that I collapsed on his couch and overnight, pissed myself. The shame of it: a recidivist bedwetter caught out in public this time with no mother to cover for me, stripping the bed and airing the mattress. It is only years later after sharing such embarrassments with other recovering alcoholics that I have been able to own up to the degrading outcomes of addiction. Roy's wife was a saint and no mention was ever made of my lapse. She was a former rural schoolteacher so I suppose this childish behaviour would have come as no surprise — in children. Slowly, I was driving my emotional life into a dead end, filling stalled ambition with booze, cars and fumbles at desultory sexual experiences. I was searching for myself in all the wrong places.

My Chevy became a kind of shrine to mobility: I loved the size of the beast, and its grunt on gravel roads, the crackly Air Chief valve radio that took ages to warm up. I was dead impressed when Coral's brother Bee Herbert arrived to do some shearing with us, roaring up in his 1955 Studebaker Commander V8 automatic, then taking me for a spin. Those gravel roads were narrow enough for a conservative driver; the skill needed to mount the heaped crown of gravel with the driver's side wheel while keeping the other wheel on the verge was an art form at the best of times. Bee had flawless technique, but 70 mph on the straights and 50 mph into some tight corners was scaring me shitless. I said nothing, of course, white-knuckling: gravel sprayed out from the Studebaker's fat tyres as Bee extolled the might of the machine at his fingertips. You couldn't show fear and be a man at the same time. No way.

That shearing season was a tough one for Eric to get through with his severe back problems; some people are just not built to be shearers. He persisted and was soon averaging his 200 sheep a day and looking ahead to the lambs later to crack 300. It never happened. I picked up and pressed, shore a few here and there, followed my brother around when he visited Fran at the land girls' quarters on Timmins' farm, racing around the countryside hunting for parties which weren't that easy to find in the wop wops. We drove to the beach at Akitio, went diving, lit fires on the sand and drank straight from the bottle in the cold winds. The gypsy lifestyle and smell of lanolin had got to me, but I still kept a diary now and then and wrote an occasional poem. I wasn't ready to admit I should have stayed at university, or even at school, nor to look sideways and see the chips I was carrying on either shoulder.

We survived another season and made plans to go home for Christmas, Eric arranging to meet Fran down on the Coast when her work in the valley was over. We shore the last of the 1967 season's sheep, pressed the last bale with the Kidd gang, picked up our cheques, said our farewells to Laurie, Coral and the children. We booked a flight for our cars on a SAFE Air Bristol Freighter, then drove to Wellington for the flight over Cook Strait (we'd left it too late to get on the car ferry). We watched our cars being driven into the clamshell nose of the bulbous freighter; somebody handed us a manila envelope each and told us to climb in the back. Inside the envelope were balls of cotton wool. When asked what they were for, the grinning operator replied, "Ear plugs, you'll see!"

He was right. In the canvas seats as the Bristol revved up and lumbered down the runway, the noise of the twin Hercules radial engines spattering glycol over the smeared Perspex windows grew to be deafening.

Years later, in 2010 I would write of this in a poem: "it felt like a factory, thundering onwards/with rivets alive in the trembling wings".[11] We stuffed our ears with the cotton wool and watched as the land left behind became

RNZAF Bristol Freighter.
Peter Tremayne

first sea and then, over Blenheim, land again. We would be back for Christmas in our mother's new home at 30 Murray Street, Greymouth, in the heart of the Catholic zone — no longer the Holmans of Main Road, Blackball. Driving our cars off the airfield and heading south, it felt pretty damn good to have a summer on four wheels just ahead, with a wad of cash to play with. We passed and re-passed each other as the sun went down, into the summer evening and the oncoming year.

OPPOSITE The *Wahine* sinking in Wellington Harbour, 1968.
35mm-01149-28-F, ATL

13

Frankland River, Western Australia

The Wahine storm of April 1968 was the worst ever recorded in the country. Greymouth had felt the force of it overnight on the Coast as the Antarctic storm that met Cyclone Giselle in Wellington Harbour at one hundred miles per hour battered our houses and flooded our streets. We were used to rain and gales on the edge of the Tasman but this was a weather bomb of almost nuclear proportions: roofs ripped off, buildings pummelled, streets flooded as the storm rampaged in the night. What we didn't know as we woke up to the morning chaos was that the Union Steam Ship Co road-rail ferry, TEV *Wahine* was on the rocks and aground in Wellington Harbour with over seven hundred souls in peril.

By mid-afternoon as we all listened to the radio in between cleaning up and battening down, the ship had rolled completely on her starboard side and despite heroic rescue efforts in atrocious conditions, fifty-three passengers and crew were drowned in the country's first ever television disaster, viewed unforgettably in black-and-white on the evening news by almost the entire population. We had our first TV: Mum had bought it after leaving Dad and I wrote later this about that moment:

> Coronation
> Street in black and white with
> static. Mum was back in a kind
> of Liverpool but really it was
> 1968 and the Wahine Storm
> outside.
>
> Yes, that storm. I was there and remember
> it from the television: black hulk, black night.

That weather bomb, whatever it might have been called before the sinking, was ever after in the country's memory the Wahine storm and it signalled to me a time to leave. Our return home for Christmas ended with my brother and his fiancée Fran leaving for Western Australia, as my '52 Chevrolet began showing its age and costing me money. We had shorn on a few smallholdings around the Grey Valley but there wasn't enough work to keep us going and Fran was ready to go home. Eric sold his near-new Fiat for a rip-off deal to get cash for the trip, so our brief shearing partnership ended. I took up with old-time Reefton shearer, Bob Win, and cruised through the remains of summer learning my trade, drinking hard with Bob at the Grey Valley pubs after shed cut-outs. But the work ran out and the Chev developed expensive engine troubles.

The Chev on the Coast near Rapahoe, David Penhall posing.

I decided to sell up and follow my brother to Oz, but first had to get the valves ground to make her saleable. The work done by a local dealer, compression was restored; the motor then blew a rear main seal and oiled the clutch (a frequent occurrence, the garage informed me after the event). Now the car had a slipping clutch: whenever I floored the accelerator to climb a hill or pass another car, it lost traction. My mechanic now advised me that as it was necessary to remove the engine to fix the rear main seal, I should get it reconditioned while they had it out. I was green as grass, discovering the elements of vehicle repairs back to front by opening my wallet. I had learned little from my bad luck with the clapped-out Vauxhall three years earlier. The engine was now renewed from tappet cover to sump and ran sweetly once more. I could promenade up and down Tainui Street to my heart's content.

There was one small problem: the bill amounting to around £250 was exactly the sum I did not have in my bank. There was one depressing strategy left: sell it. I advertised and sure enough a lucky buyer came along and paid what I asked, the amount owing on the repair. He purred away with a brand-new engine; I watched the big bright green pleasure machine turn the corner and disappear — and kicked myself. Broke, no job, no wheels — the only upside was being out of debt. The problem of how to get to Australia was solved when my dear mother offered to loan me the fare, saved goodness knows how from a low-paid cleaning job that only just kept her and my sisters afloat. Promising to pay her back once I'd got myself a job over in Oz, I picked up my tickets from the travel agent and packed my bag.

My next big plan was to surprise my brother when I got to Frankland River. Maybe I feared if I told him I was coming, following him around again, he might tell me to bugger off. I packed a suitcase, loaded up my green duffel bag covered in beer labels — Tui East India Pale Ale, Waikato XXXX — kissed Mum and my sisters goodbye, then drove over the Lewis Pass with an old school mate Murray Webster. A DC-8 was waiting at Harewood Airport in Christchurch as I joined the jet age in my escape from reality. Keep on running, stay ahead of yourself — at twenty, that was me.

Coming in over darkened Sydney, I goggled at the endless carpet of lights on the ground and tracked the car headlights — shoals of Holdens and Falcons — as we roared in to land. It's a big country, they say, and here I was, touching down with only a few measly dollars and my blissful ignorance to get me all the way across to Perth. A shared taxi to the railway station took me through Kings Cross, a ride with two bejewelled demi-mondaines who seemed to know the driver well. The warmth of the night and the sparkle of everything came over me, excited and nervous both. I took the train to Melbourne and rattled through a night full of strange off-centre Australian accents, sounds of a self-possession alien to my Kiwi innards. From the guard to the woman serving tea and toast in the dining car, everyone seemed so confident, so much more real than real.

After not much sleep I arrived early at Flinders Street station for a day's wait to catch the train to Adelaide. From there it was on to Port Pirie, changing trains each time for the final leg across the interminable Nullarbor Plain. The rail gauges in the Australian states were all different then; a couple of years later, I was able to recross the continent in the air-conditioned comfort of the brand new Indian Pacific from Sydney to Perth via Broken Hill on a single gauge.

On the trip from Melbourne I met my companion for the rest of the train journey: a former Latvian refugee from post-war Europe. He was in the carriage compartment when I entered and we exchanged nods and greetings. Tired after a long day at the station with no money to enjoy Melbourne, I didn't take a much notice. Waiting for the evening meal to be called in the dining car, I pulled a book from my beer-labelled duffel bag and poked my nose into *The Rise and Fall of the Third Reich* by William H. Shirer. It wasn't long before the man who had been observing me could contain his curiosity no longer. "Excuse me," he said, pointing at the massive paperback. "Why is it you are reading a book about the Nazis?" I thought I must have offended him, but said that I was interested in history and thought it was a good book for such a long journey. He had

A 1450-page brick: the 1964 Pan edition.
ABOVE Latvian Legion SS troopers, Independence Day 1943.

been in the war, he told me, he was from Latvia. "My name is Jan," he said, offering his hand.

Over the next 48 hours, as we rumbled on towards whatever awaited me in Perth and further south, he slowly revealed his story. Sandwiched between the other two Baltic states, Lithuania and Estonia, the Latvian republic had been founded in 1918 only to be grabbed by the Russians in 1940 and then invaded by the Germans in 1941, finally reoccupied by the victorious Soviet armies in 1944. I might be reading about all this in a mere book, but Jan was an embodiment of those times and he proceeded to tell me what it was like for him. The incoming Russians had murdered and deported any opposition — over 34,000 Latvians in one year — and the Germans in 1941 were welcomed at first as liberators. By 1943, under orders from Hitler, they were conscripting men into the Latvian Legions (the Waffen-SS and the Wehrmacht); any who demurred were sent to concentration camps. Jan, like most of his generation, was faced with the kind of choice that was no choice: fight and perhaps survive, refuse and almost certainly die without dignity.

The German SS Oberführer Adolf Ax put it this way, "They are first and foremost Latvians. They want a sustainable Latvian nation state. Forced to choose between Germany and Russia, they have chosen Germany, because they seek co-operation with western civilisation. The rule of the Germans seems to them to be the lesser of two evils."[12] Jan found himself between the very devil and a bottomless deep blue sea: they had to beat the Russians and the Germans could help them do that; if the Germans could rid the country of the Russians, the Latvians would then have to turn on their German masters as they had done before. If the Russians won, it would mean retreating with the Germans back into Germany territory and taking your chances with the Allied forces advancing from the West.

This was Jan's story: he had fought with honour, he said, and he was decorated in German colours. Now in his forties, he was small and wiry; back in those desperate days he was fast and nimble, used as a runner by his German officers to carry messages from one frontline position to another. It was dangerous work, attracting sniper fire, and he had the scars to show for it. Removing his jacket and rolling up his shirtsleeve, he pointed to a long, livid scar in the fleshy part of his upper left arm: a bullet had gone through and just missed killing him. He had no compunction in revealing himself to me, a stranger from another world, young and green. Trains can be like that: intimacies shared when we think we will never see each other again. He didn't know he was talking to someone who might one day write his story, but he wanted to tell it, wanted at least one other human being to know.

I was fascinated: war was my obsession and here was a man not only willing to talk about his experiences, but one who treated me as an equal, answering all my questions. In the dining car over the journey, the strange quality of that rail trip changed again as we were joined at our table by two nuns en route to Perth. The sisters were lively, intelligent women and the younger one especially pretty; after our first evening together and a few glasses of wine (the nuns joined in, with moderation), Jan teased me on our return to our compartment. "You like the pretty one, yes?" I blushed. "Hmmm, what a waste," he mused. For the rest of the journey, sharing the same table for meals, I couldn't help having impure thoughts as I wondered what her hair looked like under the wimple, her body beneath the black robes.

Jan remained the object of my attentions as we crossed the Nullarbor after the final change of trains at Port Pirie. All that second day I talked with him as he filled out the rest of his story, my asking how he came to be in Australia sparking the rest of the tale. As the Russians pushed forward and his fate became clear if they caught him, he ran deeper into Germany with retreating members of the Latvian forces. If they could not get into Allied hands, they were doomed men (many who did were handed back to the Russians and certain death). Others hoped that the Allies would restore the pre-war Baltic republics to their brief independence, unaware that Churchill had already ceded those countries to Stalin. The bloodbath was already under way as the NKVD commenced fresh Russification purges that would repeat the slaughter of four years earlier.

Jan made it to Berlin and managed to survive in one of the Allied sectors after the surrender. He gave no more details about just what it took to get there, but imagination served me well after reading Shirer on the last days of Hitler's Reich. He told a tale of his involvement in black market activities in the immediate post-war months and his arrest by the German police. He thought his number was up: at the very least, a handover to the Russians if it was discovered who he was and his time in the Latvian SS. The police officer interviewing him held up Jan's identity card and a small portrait of Hitler he still had in his papers. "What is this?" the interrogator demanded. "I thought my time was up," Jan said, so he told the truth: "I fought for Germany and Hitler was my Führer."

SS Latvian insignia.

The man leaned forward, "There are many of us who still feel the same," he confided and let Jan go. He eventually made his way into Austria and a resettlement camp, thrown together with hundreds and thousands of uprooted souls tossed into limbo by Hitler's madness and Stalin's vengeance. There he met his future wife and together they applied for permission to immigrate to Australia. In time he had prospered and now owned a trucking business in Western Australia, another member of the post-war European diaspora that changed the nature of Australian society, shielding a number of war criminals who slipped through the net. Charges of war crimes have been levelled against the SS Latvian soldiers but in general, because of their conscription, few if any were pursued.[13]

I could not have found a more compelling and forthcoming travelling companion. After we parted at Perth I never heard from Jan again, but I had met another traveller who would be in my life when that journey ended: a redhead named Eunice. I was out on the viewing platform at the end of train, watching the flat, dry, scrubby expanse of the treeless Nullarbor unreel behind us. She was there too in the cooling rush of air and we talked — talked and talked some more. I might have neglected Jan after that. I told her I was heading for Frankland River way down south near Albany; she was getting off at her hometown Perth at journey's end. We exchanged addresses and I promised to write when I got settled in. It would be some time before I saw her again, months later in November when she came down to Frankland River for my 21st birthday party.

Suddenly it was morning and I was at the Perth station waiting for a unit to the suburban stop at Armadale. The plan was to hitch a ride on the main highway south towards the Cranbrook turnoff to Frankland

River. I had just enough for the fare, with twenty cents to spare, looking at a 200-mile journey to get me there before nightfall. I was still swaying from the train's motion as I said goodbye to Jan and Eunice. It was good to be twenty years old and crazy. There was no choice but to press on, whistling, with my suitcase and my duffel bag, hopeful my thumb would get me the ride I needed once I made it to the start of Highway 30 south.

I wasn't on the roadside for long when an older man pulled up in a white Holden ute (I was about to see a lot of white Holdens, a popular colour, cooler than anything dark). My kindly driver shook his head when he heard where I'd come from and where I was going and took me all of the 150 miles to the Frankland River turnoff. Wishing me luck, he sped off for Albany; as the afternoon drew on I was alone on a long road with its edges of red gravel and sentinel gum groves stretching to the western horizon and seeming to disappear over the earth's curve. I was hot, tired and thirsty — and the traffic almost non-existent. With no real alternative, I picked up my suitcase and trudged off towards Frankland River — wherever, whatever it was.

14

Waiting for the Albany Doctor

I didn't have to wait long for the roar of an approaching vehicle behind me to raise and then dash my hopes. I stood back and poked out my thumb as a red Holden flashed past and kept right on going. A good way down the road his brake lights stabbed on, the car hauled up and reversed back towards me flat out. That's how I met Arthur Challenor — I would later go shearing with his brother Jimmy — who had a couple of mates with him and few bottles of Swan Lager.

"Where you heading, mate?" he asked me.

"Frankland River."

"Hop in then, shove your gear in the boot!"

We were off at a good clip, the bottle ended up in my hand as introductions and questions buzzed in the speeding car. They discovered I was heading for the Towton family home to meet my brother. "Eric, the Kiwi, we know him," said Arthur, planting his foot even harder as we flew into the western sunset. I would get used to these young Aussies with their flash new cars and need for speed: the Holden and the Ford tribes, with a few outriders in their Chrysler Valiants. They knew their cars and they knew the roads, driving everywhere Bathurst 500 style. Arthur's velocity made me nervous but I needed that ride. There would be more reason for fear in the months ahead when I got into his brother Jimmy's 120 mph Holden Monaro V8.

We rolled into Frankland River and pulled in behind what was to be my new home: the general store run by Fran's dad Jack and his wife Roma. Arthur took me in via the fly screen door and announced my arrival with, "Hey Jack, you've got a visitor!" Introductions made, my unheralded arrival digested, the Towtons took me in with hardly a blink — I was welcome to stay. There was no sign of my brother: Eric had got a job as a welder in Wagin, a hundred miles north and only came home on the weekends. They laughed at my cheek and what a surprise it would be for him. Fran gave me a warm welcome as she hugged me — "Bloody hell, Jeffrey, you're a hard case!" My gamble had paid off, but could have all gone badly wrong if the Towtons had turned me away, thousands of miles from home. They fed me, asked me all sorts of questions and after a few beers by the fire, showed me a bed in the sleepout at the back door. For the next two years, they would be my family.

I'd landed in a small crossroads township with little more than a general store and a garage, a dozen houses, red dust, and gum trees where every morning the kookaburras mocked from the upper branches as cockatoos swooped through hot cloudless skies. Frankland served an older farming community in a radius of thirty miles or so and the newer, further-flung soldier settlement farms on land cleared after the last war and allotted to returned servicemen. The town had a small school and not much more; the nearest pub was at Rocky Gully fifteen miles south, but the store had a major drawcard — a gallon licence. You had to buy half a dozen bottles of beer minimum or its equivalent in wine and spirits; stocking up presented no problem to the thirsty Aussies living within driving range. It was through this portal that I got to know the parade of characters visiting Jack, a retired carpenter and former horse trainer who still had shares in a hopeful nag, Boyleton. These men would sit down with him and Roma from lunchtime on, to share the cup that cheers and tell yarns of life in the bush.

By the time my brother arrived on the first Friday night of my stay I was well ensconced and he didn't seem too surprised or fazed. Things were not going as planned between him and Fran, but the Towtons still treated us both like sons along with their own boy, a blond rascal called Jackie. The word went around that Eric's brother was looking for work and one of Jack's visitors, a farmer by the name of John, said he could use a hand. He was a hard-working newbie breaking in an unsympathetic piece of dirt that Jack reckoned would defeat a lesser man. John was married to a former air hostess with the looks of a beauty queen, who always seemed like she'd got off at the wrong destination and was doing the outback life hard.

I was desperate for money and jumped at the chance to work for John, a slow-talking salt-of-the-earth man who had come into farming from somewhere else and was surviving by sheer grit. He'd had some land cleared of bush and set me to work on a vintage tractor straight out of the ark, an old International Harvester with narrow gauge front wheels that looked dodgy even on the flat. I was set to harrowing roots around mounded windrows of fallen trees, driving on steep slopes. The tractor had a homemade sunroof consisting of four waratah stakes and a scrim covering. After a few passes getting the hang of things, I tried to steer left past a windrow on a slope that kept increasing its angle. I could feel the tractor bouncing almost to the point of tipping over. Then it happened: the right rear wheel hit a large boulder and up we went. The old beast sat on the point of tipping as I leaned hard right in panic — then bouncing slowly, settled back on the ground, still leaning left at scary angle as I cut the motor. The deadly old International Harvester of doom.

My brush with likely death or certain serious injury didn't much impress John. I'd punctured a tyre on the sharp rock; it was a terminal gash and now he had to pay for a new one. I did some more work for him, including dagging sheep (nobody else in the district was keen), but in the end I had to move on and leave him to it. My efforts in the dagging trade got me more work on local farms and I was able to give John back my borrowed handpiece and buy one of my own — still in my possession fifty years later. By this time, Arthur, my ride into Frankland, had introduced me to his younger brother Jimmy and we started doing a few sheds. He had a local shearing run and was happy to have me along when the season started.

In the meantime I picked up more work from Jack's drinking mates, characters like Mac McQuillan, a former soldier with a wooden leg who famously flaked out one night at Towtons after a long session, whereupon his hosts bedded him down on the settee and after removing his shoes, burned his terrible holey socks. On waking, Mac complained loudly that he couldn't wear his shoes without socks as he could feel the difference even on his wooden foot. The district was populated with figures like this: Chum, the alkie farmer who so loved stout that he hid bottles all over the farm (drinking heated stout in the cab of a Land Rover has to be one of the beverage choices on offer in the bars surrounding the entrance to Hades). My drinking too was heading for the hills and once the locals had built their own licensed club (you had to sign up to get a drink), long nights of Swan Lager became the norm. I was saving money for another car; in such an isolated area, without wheels you were completely dependent on others. November rolled around and I'd been there seven months; my 21st birthday was approaching and I'd invited Eunice to come down from Perth for the party (we'd been regularly writing letters). Eric and I decided to put down a hangi and show the Aussies how it was done back home.

I'd never tried our distinctive national cookery method, but Eric had, so we set to work digging the pit and bringing in stones and wood (you had to beware of redback spiders and snakes on such expeditions). A pig was sourced, the fire was lit on the stones and fed till they were red hot, then on went the netting, the wet sacks, the cabbage leaves and in went the porker in its wire cage stuffed with vegetables and surrounded with chickens. Bruce, Fran's new man, looked on bemused but got stuck in and helped; Eunice shook her head. Eight hours later as the party was humming in the dark night, under a string of lights, we dug up the hangi, our Kiwi fingers crossed (if it didn't work, we were sunk). As the meat fell off the bone and the locals tucked in, the murmurs of pleasure and flow of compliments mingled — music to us both, much relieved. "Best bloody pork I've ever tasted!" said Jack and the rest said "Amen."

Eunice had to go back to Perth, but invited me up to meet her family; it looked like we might be going somewhere. With Eric and a Kiwi guy Greg who'd turned up from somewhere, we drove to Perth to get my car. After research in lots of *Wheels* magazines, I'd decided on a rally-proven Peugeot 403, a choice none of my Holden-Ford friends could possibly understand. In the event, when I got into the only car yard I could find that had one — a mint grey sedan — I chickened out and bought a two-tone 1960 Vauxhall Velox, proving once more that engine size seduces men when economy should talk. It was a capacious six that would serve me well. We drove back to Eunice's place to meet her father and her brother; they'd both been up north in the mines making big money and were home now for R&R. I was getting along well with her mother and grandmother and things were looking up: I had a car, a girlfriend, some mates and a bit of work, hardly a year into my time away from the mess I'd left behind on the Coast.

In Eunice's hand on the back of the photo: "Jeffrey's pride and joy."

We sat around waiting for father and son to arrive; once they were welcomed home and having a few beers, the talk flowed to life in the mines up north and eventually, the problem of "the bloody boongas". I'd already come across some local attitudes to Aboriginal people down at Frankland River when "the Abos" would arrive in an old FJ Holden ute or similar and buy alcohol from Roma or her shop assistant, Maureen. Complaints of the smell they brought into the shop and their itinerant lifestyle were common parlance in evenings around the fire with these usually kind-hearted people. The tone in Perth was different, almost a suggestion that it might be better for everybody if "the blacks" just got on with it and died off. As the conversation got nastier, I looked at my brother Eric and could see he wasn't comfortable either. In a state of almost complete naivety, I ventured what seemed a pretty harmless truism, "Well, they're human beings like you and me, aren't they?" The atmosphere in the room changed in a flash.

The son stood up, fists balled, face red and snarled at me, "Are you saying my old man's the same as one of those animals?" I was dumbfounded. What had I said that turned him from friendly to someone who looked like he wanted to punch my lights out? I burbled on some more and he got even more worked up; Eric, playing a pretty good hand of peacemaker, managed to placate Trevor and stare down the faceoff. Greg said nothing and Eunice was looking pretty distressed. It was one of those social disaster scenes that you can't climb out of and you're still not sure how you dug a hole so deep and so wide.

I was yet to understand the depth of feeling lurking below the surface of the racial situation in Australia in the 1960s (ignorant as I also was of realities for Maori back home in New Zealand). I didn't realise — but found out soon afterwards — that my relationship with Eunice had been damaged in that exchange; it wasn't long before Greg had moved in and I was a goner. Back down South, I also didn't understand that my new shearing partner Jimmy was a victim of racist attitudes in the dark underbelly of the Australia I was discovering.

I'd heard him speak negatively about the "Abos" too, only to discover later that he came from an Anglo-Indian family who had immigrated to the country long before. His father had made a successful life as a farmer, and they had prospered. Yet the sons hid their difference, their Indian roots; secretly ashamed of their non-white status, they adapted by living a fast lane life with the latest hot car and a bootload of Swan Lager. This suited me too: running scared of who I might be and trying on any and every hat that would fit, my alcohol problem slowly but steadily took over

Trevor, Jeffrey and Greg, before the racial storm broke.
OPPOSITE New Zealand-width Sunbeam comb and cutter.

my inner life. I was tied up with work, booze, cars and sexual frustration, at anorexic odds with the boy I saw in the mirror, although by now I'd become physically lean and robust.

I'd bought a new Lister handpiece and proceeded to break it in on huge wheat belt wethers out east at Gnowangerup. It ran so hot it blistered my hand; I could barely manage a hundred per day on these monsters. Like a dozen blokes before me, I soon left and went to work with Jimmy back at Frankland River. He had a good run around local farms and we began to work the sheds. I was coming to grips with the challenge of shearing Merinos using the narrower ten-tooth Australian comb and three-tooth cutter (versus thirteen and four on New Zealand gear). The Merino is skinny and all sharp angles with dense fine wool; the Romney Marsh, our typical breed at that time, was rounded and covered in a coarser fibre. A good Kiwi shearer might get through 250–300 on Romneys; in Australia, anything over 150 was pretty good going but the rate per hundred was higher too.

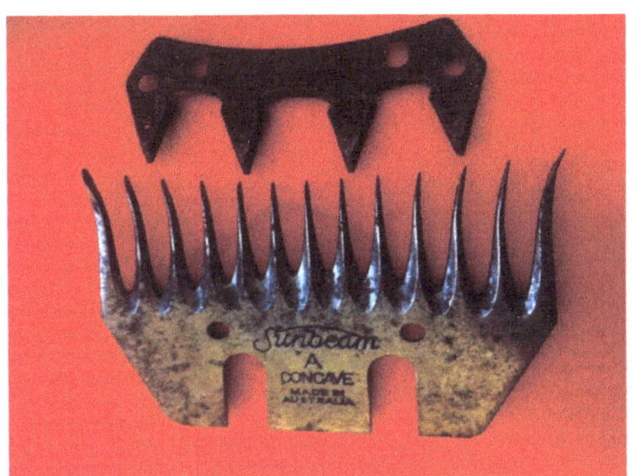

Facts and figures says nothing about the reality of shearing day in day out in heat approaching 100°F under low corrugated iron roofs with a plague of happy flies that sat on your shoulders just out of reach, keeping themselves cool on your sweat. In the end you gave up swatting them off and let them ride it out; I saw it get so hot one day that they fell out of the air and died, little legs-up corpses sprinkling the board. Unlike us, flies are completely reliant on the ambient air temperature. Hot enough to kill flies on the wing? Hot enough to keep a Kiwi shearer like me on a steady diet of salt tablets and water to avoid dehydration; in one shed, way up north near Perenjori, hot enough to make me quit that run and head back to the cooler south-west.

I had a towel on the rail as I went in after each sheep was shorn and pushed down the chute to the yards; my eyes stung with sweat and I had to wipe my face after every animal. Between severe backache — which laid me low a few times — the flies, the sweat and sauna-level heat, I still wonder how I hung on in there until I'd learned to handle the sheep and the conditions. Hangovers were worse: head down the morning after a night on Swan Lager and Bacardi, temples throbbing, sheep kicking, the machine buzzing in your ear — promises of "Never again" were easy to make. Come five o'clock and senses semi-returned, out we went and did it all again. The one sure relief was the daily arrival of the Albany Doctor.

I first heard of this character when early on in the season with Jimmy, about three o'clock in the afternoon, one of the shearers called out, "Here she comes, the doctor!"

"What doctor?" I yelled at him.

"The Albany Doctor, Kiwi, the bloody breeze, mate!"

I got it then, as I felt it brush my shoulders and kiss my cheek. The phenomenon of heat exchange between land and sea, morning and evening, gave us the offshore and onshore winds. The wind from the Indian Ocean was flowing over the baking land; once it hit the shed, the temperature fell quickly and you could feel a cool breath on your sweaty brow. The Doctor indeed: those Aussie shearers earned every cent the hard way. What I learned among them was a kind of stamina that enabled me later to put up with conditions that pushed you to your limits. I certainly found mine in their ranks.

Shearing — the height of my physical phase of 'working with real men' — was a proving ground; after a while, it became obvious I might have to look elsewhere, but for what? Roma, in nights by the fire drinking sweet sherry after Jack had gone to bed, drew me out on my fractured relationship with my father and said to me, "Go home, Jeffrey, go and fix it up with him." Still angry and still stuck, I took her advice, and early in the New Year of 1969 bought a plane ticket back to New Zealand and to my mother's house.

It wasn't hard to track my father down; still in our old house in Blackball with a new partner, Coral, and her children. I hired a car and drove to see him, walking into the childhood home where my father now lived with a new family of strangers. We did our best to make the contact work, but there was little privacy. It was a start and I found Roma was right: healing was needed, forgiveness begun. She had told me we don't know how long we've got on this earth; proven right three years later when my father was diagnosed with a cancer that was rapidly terminal.

In my brief return, I picked up some work shearing in Southland, romanced a local girl, made enough money to travel back to Perth this time on the single-gauge Indian Pacific via Broken Hill — but for what? I probably should have stayed put at home, but I wasn't quite done with the macho world of booze, fast cars and hard work. When I got back to the Towton family, my romantic interest at home was still calling; I was pretty unsettled, but broke again. I found a job working for a contractor

Root rake,
Western Australia.

driving tractors towing massive root rakes, offset discs with metal teeth that ploughed up any remaining tree roots in the acres of land cleared of bush for the sowing of cereal crops. My brother in Wagin was welding these implements of agriculture. I was driving them at night on a 24-hour shift rota in a time that would figure later in the same poetry sequence where I'd tried to capture the Wahine storm:

> Later, in Australia, ploughing way out in the sticks
> on nightshift, men were walking on the moon. They
> had computers. We did not know
> about computers, kangaroos ghosting
> through the tractor headlights.

As I drove around Western Australia in the darkness and mystery of night fogs, broken by ghostly kangaroos bouncing across the path of the chugging tractor, fighting to stay awake for six hours, high above and far away the first moon landing was taking place in circumstances equally surreal. Elsewhere on planet earth, Martin Luther King was murdered. The world was changing under my feet and over my head: on the bookstand in the store Roma was running, I came across something unusual amid the cowboy yarns and car magazines — a poetry anthology. *Poems from Poetry and Jazz in Concert* was a selection of verse from a series of concerts held in London where poets like Danny Abse, Laurie Lee and Adrian Mitchell performed. I bought it and started reading, with no awareness of who these writers were. I'd starved myself of such things since high school, but whatever was in me when I wrote those poems back in class with Peter Hooper had not gone away.

After reading poems by Michael Hamburger, Ted Hughes, Laurie Lee and Stevie Smith, something was switched back on inside. I'd been corresponding with Peter while I was in Australia, keeping up that lifeline of friendship with a writer. I wrote a poem about the journey over on the train the second time: 'Indian Pacific', I called it and sent it to him. He liked the poem enough in 1970 to include it in a small privately published booklet titled *A Pleasure of Friends*, in company with people like John Caselberg, Peter Ireland and Brian Turner. It was very much apprentice work but I was back on the horse.

> Trains rail the stunted-tree interior,
> into which haunted coastal eyes
> fear to gaze.

I stayed around for another shearing season with Jimmy and still got drunk, still sat alongside him in his proud new possession, the grunty blue Monaro V8 he'd bought as soon as it was released, once even hitting 120 mph as he whooped, "Look at that needle, Jethro, look at that, 120 and she still wants to go!" — a suicidal road twisting before us like an animal in the night lights as we covered the thirty miles from Albany to Mount Barker in fifteen minutes. It was not my day to die, in spite of the times we asked for it: inviting death, cheating it when others no better or worse, like Earl Sowry back in Riwaka, spun out and died. Young men from the area were fighting the Viet Cong in the jungles of Vietnam; a kid from Rocky Gully died there and the news spread round the district like the flames in the tops of the gums a mile ahead of the blaze on the ground; old hands from the last war were spitting on Japanese car imports; the Bob Dylan I'd lost touch with in my retreat to the country was suddenly on the airwaves with 'Lay, Lady, Lay'. It was time to go home and find out what I'd left behind.

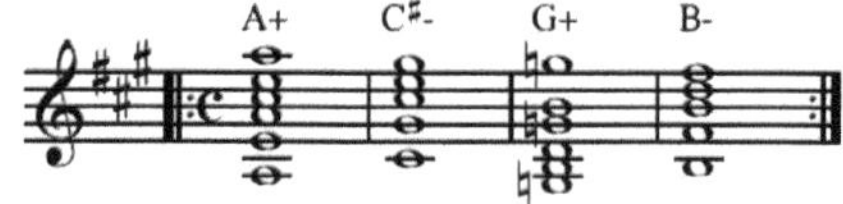

Bob Dylan's 'Lay, Lady, Lay' chord progression.

15

Poetry man

Arriving on the West Coast in 1970, I moved back in with my mother in Greymouth, without any real plan. My father had moved up to Nelson with his new family and Mum had a new man, Dick Buckman, who nervously introduced himself to me (sons of divorced mothers can be pretty hard on the new suitors — ask Shakespeare). He was a lovely man, a porter at the hospital where she worked in the kitchen. Dick was a humble soul who liked nothing better than to take her away up the coast to his bach, fishing and rambling on the beach near Punakaiki. I warmed to him straight away, happy that my mother had found some love and companionship after the wreckage of her marriage to Dad.

I was reconnecting with my sisters and drinking with their boyfriends; a lost soul, I said goodbye to the girl next door I'd met on the previous trip home from Australia and marked time. I needed a job. I decided I'd better sign up with the Labour Department, as there wasn't much around on the Coast at that time for somebody with no real qualifications. There were a few unemployed back then, but the 1960s were over and worse was to come. The days of leaving one job and waltzing into another were numbered. I signed on and found myself on an employment scheme with the Forestry Service, planting pinus radiata seedlings and release cutting older trees in the gorse that grew up on the clear-felled second growth bush, milled earlier by men like the Donaldsons at my first sawmill job. The other move I made was to walk into Walden Books on Albert Street where my old friend and teacher Peter Hooper was running a bookshop.

At a distance, these two moves seem integrated: I was neither ready nor able to take the way of my peers, the baby boom writers who were already hard at work preparing to publish and shake the establishment: people like Ian Wedde, Bill Manhire, Keri Hulme and Patricia Grace. At 23 I was a dropout and damaged goods, unable to separate myself from the wounds of my parents and my own confusion. I had a head full of Bob Dylan songs and close to zero self-worth, but I knew Peter cared about me and that poetry had something I needed. In the words of that man from Hibbing, Minnesota, written when he was my age, "I got mixed up confusion/Man, it's a-killin' me … I'm lookin' for a woman/Whose head's mixed up like mine." [14] I walked into Walden Books and there was Peter with a warmer welcome than the one I'd had from the po-faced officer at the Labour Department. I was in heaven, a shop full of books. I walked out of there with a copy of Pasternak's *Selected Poems* and a slim purple volume my old teacher pressed upon me with a recommendation: Hone Tuwhare's *Come Rain Hail.*

By permission of the Hotere Foundation Trust

I'd chosen the Russian poet because I'd been reading *Dr Zhivago*, so his was a name I knew; the Tuwhare I took on trust from Peter. I bore them home and read them. One of Pasternak's poems, translated by his sister, has stayed with me: 'The Swifts', a celebration of this aerial master, a bird I would have to wait twenty years more to see and love. Hone Tuwhare was different. I wasn't far into the slim purple volume with its red-circled Hotere cover (celebrated within by a poem to the artist) when I recognised he was writing my world. Not "about my world", but actually recreating the floods and the drunks and the work I knew, releasing feelings of recognition I could not have articulated at the time. Demotic, accessible and always from here, the place where I was standing, New Zealand. Whatever was waiting in me stopped waiting and sent me to a stationery shop where I bought a thick red exercise book, just like those I had so lovingly filled with maps and diagrams for Snowy Hutton. I got out my Parker 45 pen and began writing poetry.

The first few days on the forestry gang stood in stark unpoetic relief to my literary stirrings. Picked up by a standard yellow Bedford truck in the frosty morning, crammed in the rear cab with Lenny, Chris, Alan (a scholarly-looking youth who owned a pristine VW) and other sleepy strangers, we roared down the road south to Waimea and Goldsborough for my first day's planting. Alan we picked up at the Kumara turnoff, then dropped there again at the end of the day, V-dub V-dub V-dubbing away in that paua shell-shaped green and white People's Car with its unmistakable exhaust note. Len, a freckle-faced five-foot-two, rode a big Norton 650cc. He would later give me a terrifying pillion experience from the same turnoff, racing the Bedford down the straight and passing it at 100 mph. I know that we hit the ton, as Lenny pointed at the speedo while I hung on for all I was worth. When he dropped me off at home, my calf muscles were burned from pressing on the exhaust pipe; I'd been too frightened to feel the heat through my jeans. It seemed I'd learned nothing from my adrenaline-fuelled blasts in Jimmy Challenor's V-8 Monaro back in Western Australia.

Our gang boss ('Woodchuck') was a serious chap, faced with a group of mixed vocational abilities (we were there because there was nothing else going and no work meant no dole). He did his best to instruct and supervise us in the art of planting pinus to the chant of "1-2-3-tree!" We had to pull a sapling from our heavy shoulder bag, whack the spade into the soil, push it forward to make a home for the planting, then stomp the earth tight around the tender shoot — all in one smooth movement, stepping seamlessly forward to repeat, repeat, repeat the action. This system had been developed in the vast and flat volcanic lands that became the Kaingaroa Forest.

Our problem was that the hills and gullies of Waimea and Goldsborough — steep, muddy, slippery and covered in blackened tree limbs from the summer's burn off — were anything but flat. It was hard enough at times to walk uphill and down, staying upright, let alone attempting to plant a tree at the same time and almost impossible to perform any kind of "1-2-3-tree!" choreography. We stumbled and bumbled on, frustrating Captain Woodchuck with our slow progress, earning threats that we would miss our target and thus, the bonus. This cunning carrot was a system that laid out a target number of trees per planter, per area; reaching it, we had a bonus added to our $70 a week basic pay. The stick was also employed: as soon as you began to reach the target, the next week it would be raised, on the grounds that if it was easily reached, it must be too low.

On the Coast it rained with frequency and persistence; there were times when we all sat in the van, smoking, playing cards, waiting it out. Some days you just had to give up and go home. Trying to plant in heavy rain on greasy papa slopes meant slipping over and injuries. At lunch breaks I would find a moment to jot a few lines on the back of my Park Drive tobacco packet; this was before plastic pouches for roll-your-own tobacco products took over. Many a builder was seen doing calculations on the back of a packet of Greys or Pocket Edition. I always had a pencil in my pocket: when an idea came, I could stop mid-row release cutting young trees in the gorse and write something down. My hands and fingers were pincushions for gorse needles: at night at my mother's place I dug the prickles out. The next day it was out to Waimea again to pick up more.

Surviving the first few weeks, I had a few dollars to play with and I was getting my fitness back. I visited Peter at his home, borrowing books to complete my education (Coleridge's poems, including 'The Rime of the Ancient Mariner' was one). I kept at it, writing in my exercise book. Coming home from a visit to the Recreation Hotel one night, a blustery wind tearing at the palms and the pohutukawa trees bathed in the yellow-gold of the town's new sodium street lights on Tainui Street, back inside the house I wrote, "Wind whip raw bone breaking chill/booming down the dark gut of night." Not earth-shattering stuff, but it was a start, with an instinctive sense of the power of Anglo-Saxon alliterative verse in recreating elemental tensions. I was away. A party at Yogi's place (Bruce was his first name, a local bohemian with Hendrix posters and heavy rock on the turntable) produced this: "In the beer reek flat I see/images of Che Guevara/and a thousand culture heroes/reverberate to numbing music." I must have been reading Longfellow's 'Hiawatha' that week.

I bought a Nina Simone album where she sang some Dylan songs ('Just Like Tom Thumbs Blues', 'The Times They Are a-Changing') and Brecht and Weill ('Pirate Jenny'). Her voice pinned me down, calling from another world. I was so naïve: ignorant of the race war and the drug culture fuelling the pain and the rage of these songs. Wherever I was, without knowing it, I was on my way to somewhere else — music and poetry were taking me there. The forestry job had reached a certain limit for me in the wrestling match for my identity. Was I going to spend a life as 'one of the boys', or be myself? Which one? I found another alternative in the Greymouth

J-1 Forest Service Bedford: Ahaura-Kopara Road, 1978.
Photo: courtesy Glenn Johnston

Peter Hooper, c.1960.
Hooper family[15]

Branch of the Child Welfare Department: there I was, asking how I could apply to be a Maori Welfare Officer. Why Maori Welfare I don't know; they told me I was more likely to get a job with Child Welfare as a trainee, if I sat through an interview and then applied. I went through with that and waited to hear if I had made the grade. What did I know about child welfare? Nothing at all. Was I qualified? Only as someone who knew what children went through in a family like mine. Whether that was a plus or a minus for a trainee social worker, time would reveal.

16

Narziss and Goldmund

Love for me, when it came, favoured the surprise attack: it ambushed me in the spring of 1970 through the agency of Stephen, an old school friend, who called in to see me at my mother's place. A red-haired drummer, Stephen was the little brother of a classmate first met in 1964 when he was a mere third and I a lofty sixth former. I always liked his cheek and wacky humour. He told me that his friend and classmate Theresa, another third former from high school, was going into hospital and he wanted to ring her in Christchurch. My mum obliged with the phone and soon he was chatting away, before offering me the receiver, asking if I wanted to say hello.

I hadn't seen Theresa for a couple of years, when she was in the fifth form at high school and I was back from shearing up north; half-cut on the streets of Greymouth on New Year's Eve, I offered her a couple of pennies — the cost of a call from a telephone booth at the time — and told her to call me when she turned 16. Charming. It must have been 1966, as by the next December, pence had gone and cents were in. Now as we talked on the phone, I wasn't speaking with a schoolgirl any more: she was nineteen now and a student at the University of Canterbury, studying English, living for drama and the theatre. She was also ill and needing to go for treatment; with my typical cheek at the time, I invited her to come over and stay. We agreed it would happen and she'd bring some actor friends. I was in for a shock.

A week or two later, a hot red Mini pulled up outside, disgorging Theresa, Edward and Paul after a speedy, cramped trip over the passes. She bowled me over straight away with her sheer confidence, a voice trained in the shadows of Ngaio Marsh and Mervyn Thompson, all five feet and not much else of her, but those luminous eyes. I made them all welcome, wishing she'd come alone. I sat there while Mum brewed tea and coffee: three confident voices, the generation that hoped to change the world on a fresh stage now, declaring the play had begun. "He looks like Sam!" Theresa declared to the other two, looking at me, as if I should know who Sam Neill was. I was nonplussed by this thespian invasion and probably

Rapahoe Hotel sign: Les Holmes, artist.

played the working-man role too defensively — but we got on well. She was beautiful and I wanted her. We took a trip in the Mini that night out to the Rapahoe Pub: blinding rain bucketing, a miracle the four-up sardine tin didn't slide off the road as Edward hurled it over slippery rail crossings, windscreen wipers virtually stalled. We stood and drank in the packed hotel bar, observed as curiosities by the miners and the wives and girlfriends, until it was closing time at ten. I was drunk in more ways than one.

A week later I was in Christchurch staying with Edward and visiting Theresa in hospital. I knew he had feelings for her so I tried to outflank the competition by inviting her to come over again to recuperate, once she was discharged. She agreed and duly arrived; I was smitten. We talked late and soon, slept later. Enough to say — as any lover knows — that in the beginning, it often as much the voice and the ideas that do the work of seduction. I was as hungry for the spirit as the flesh; in spite of all the books I borrowed from Peter Hooper in an ad hoc attempt at self-improvement, my mind was starving on the Coast. Had I stayed put, I'm sure I would have become one of those backwoods autodidacts the country threw up in the 19th century. I needed to test my mind and she could see this. "Why don't you come back to varsity?" was the challenge she put to me. I'd never thought that was possible, but she was telling me I should go and find out. Here was somebody with faith in my intelligence, something I'd not felt since I'd dropped out of high school, shadowed by shame. I decided to try.

About the same time as the confirmation arrived from Child Welfare that I had been accepted and my first appointment would be to Blenheim, I heard from the University of Canterbury I was still eligible to re-enrol and begin again. I had not failed my three dropped courses, which had been discontinued. The letter I had asked Peter Hooper to write on my behalf may have had some influence. His reference was a fillip to my low confidence: "As a teacher long familiar with the calibre of seventh form students," he had written, "I have no hesitation in saying that Mr Holman's ability to sustain degree studies is far in advance of that of the average undergraduate." Theresa and I had decided we would live together. I moved quickly to end my time in the Forest Service and my prospective career as a child welfare officer was called off (better for all concerned). I resigned prior to the appointment in Blenheim and gave notice to the Woodchuck. In the final months of 1970 we set up house in Christchurch, ready for my fresh start as a student in the New Year.

Soon after arriving back in Christchurch I met Theresa's mother Alice. She was a generous and resourceful woman, the widow of Ginty Newcombe, one of the nineteen Strongman miners killed with his mates in the explosion of 19 January 1967. Whatever she thought of our madcap romance and plans, she was diplomatic and gave us her help and support. Soon we were ferrying pieces of furniture and kitchen utensils from her flat in Armagh Street to one we'd found in Edgeware Road, piling high Theresa's tiny Mini. We'd secured the upstairs unit by fabricating a story at the agent's office: we were a professional married couple, with me starting a new job soon at the Christchurch *Press*. That much was true; I was going into advertising, running another line in pork pies when I'd told the paper in October I was available for the full-time position, all the while intending to resign in February to start my university course. Suddenly I was in the city, in a relationship, in a collar and tie — not quite who I'd thought I was six months before in the West Coast rain, planting pinus radiata on greasy burnt-off hills.

It seemed that my former madness had driven me into the world of physical work, into the power of the body; now, driven by love, I began a fresh attempt to enter the life of the mind. Formerly I had been like Hermann Hesse's Goldmund in my sally into the world; perhaps now I would be Narziss, wrapped up in the pleasures of the intellect. I would bring into the cloisters all my active and subliminal Goldmund hungers and flaws. We set up house and I went to work by bus, into the fabled Square, haunt of bodgies and bikies, once ruled by floods of evening cyclists pedalling home; now, since the relaxation of hire purchase regulations, by tides of cars. I became a classified ad collector, zooming around the city on a zippy 50cc Vespa that lived in the downstairs garage underneath the impressive colonial turrets of the *Press*. My new employer was a bastion of conservatism — in its own estimation, the *Times* of the South — and a playground of the privileged from Christ's College and other well-heeled schools.

I was meeting people I might have met earlier had I stayed at university in 1965: the burghers of a provincial city, tasked to provide news, advertising and of course, editorial profundities for the citizens of the Garden City. I began at the lower level of life in this august culture, slicing the ads of the local car sharks from the Cars-Sell section of Classifieds, gluing them to the pages of a jotter pad, then taking the result out to the yards. It was fun at first scooting around the Square and down Colombo Street or St Asaph to Moorhouse, dragging off the cars at the lights. Weaving its way to the front of the queue, a tiny Vespa could leave most sixes for dead. Arriving at Sydenham Park Car Sales or Ford Motors, the sheet of ads would be handed to the salesman in charge who struck off the vehicles sold, added new entries and made corrections. Collecting all the changes on my morning round, I would hare back to the paper and zap the copy in the Lamson tube, up to the typesetters for the next day's paper, for printing dummies and proofing.

The old *Press* building in Cathedral Square, 1977. Stuff/*The Press*

That was my daily round, with not a lot of demand made on my brain; some lunch hours, me and my mate Tim Glubb would grab the Vespas and whizz up the Cashmere Hills for light relief. The secret was to move fast and not get caught using company scooters for such hijinks. I needed some of that: things were getting complicated with my love life. It's enough to say that Theresa and I found our incautious selves facing the prospect of parenthood. Our brief and intense romantic daze broke down under that strain and we separated. I was faced with a situation beyond my control and my previous experience: heartbroken and confused, kicked off my former foundations, unable to decide what to do next.

Theresa moved out and I was alone in my professional couple's St Albans flat, facing a blank wall with the mocking lines of a Simon and Garfunkel song coming back to haunt me, replete with hyperbole and self-pity. I had played 'Kathy's Song' to Theresa not long after we had moved in together; prophetically, she didn't like it, thought it was unhealthy. She was right, but then, I *was* unhealthy, addicted to love and need. Years later I would stumble into the work of the American poet Jack Gilbert and these lines from the poem 'Steel Guitars':

> "   … The heart in its plenty hammered
> by rain and need, by the weight of what momentarily is." [16]

The weight of the moment became too much. I had to get myself sorted: going to work in a daze, trying to explain how confusing my life had become to my uncomprehending mother back on the Coast, all the while counting down to a second attempt at a degree in English. I wasn't even sure what for, except maybe for writing poetry.

In the middle of the whirlpool I found myself back in touch with my old school friend, Maurice Teen. We'd been sixth formers together and had stayed at each other's homes. I'd gone to see Peter Hooper with him one weekend from their house nearby in Paroa. When I'd dropped out in 1966, Maurice had stayed on at university working at a law degree; he'd become bored with it and gone selling insurance. Returning to study like me, he wanted to finish off the final year of his LLB and do something with his life. Over a few beers at Cokers in Manchester Street, I poured out my heart: what was I going to do? Maurice had an idea, suggesting I come in with him on his plan to buy a bread round. As well as completing his degree, he had a nest egg he wanted to protect.

Overnight bread deliveries to the suburbs in those days were handled in the same way milk vendors had their runs, before the overpowering rise of the supermarkets killed both trades. Maurice would buy the van and the goodwill from a vendor he knew who wanted to sell; we could set up in a flat together, share the work at night and study during the day. He couldn't do the whole round himself and I needed a job and a place to stay, cheaper than my flash St Albans flat. We shook on it. I became a midnight rambler bread van driver: a head full of Chaucer, Donne and Hopkins and a heart full of cracks.

In preparation for the coming year, we found a flat in Antigua Street and I gave notice at the *Press*, telling more lies about a decision to go back to study. I was leaving Tim behind, with his stories that he was related to Glubb Pasha, the soldier and scholar who trained and led the Arab Legion before and after the Second World War. We had gone together once in our lunch hour to visit a Great War veteran he knew, a survivor of a mustard gas attack eking out his final years in a dingy Linwood flat. Tim had a zest for life and a care for people; I would miss him.

We took our nightly delivery van lessons with Hughie Coyle, the owner of the bread round Maurice was buying, meeting him at Smith's Nutty Crust bakery in Ferry Road. He taught us how to load the hot fresh loaves from the busy ovens, slotted in the right order for delivery. We would ride shotgun with this dynamic little Scotsman as he showed us how to navigate from Sydenham to Halswell in the dead of night: leaping from the van's sliding door grasping a Thick-and-Thin or a Vienna, posting it smoothly in the bread tin by the letter box, while neighbourhood dogs went crazy and the citizens of Christchurch slumbered.

Bedford CA van, c.1970.

All the while my other life was running underneath: my heart baffled and confused, a prospective father, unable to straighten my life out as usual. I walked back into the old university quadrangles and became a student again. The place looked the same but I certainly was not. Wary of my last brush with Philosophy in 1966, I opted for two first year courses: English and American Studies, not quite confident to do the full three papers and work part-time. Courses then were year-long over four terms, with a final exam to complete a series of written essay assessments in the calendar year. The tuition was virtually free, with allowances, along with a full social life at a time the tides of world and New Zealand history were rapidly changing. Woodstock had happened in the previous year while I was still on my slow return from life in the country, Vietnam had turned into an open sore in the American psyche and protests here were hitting the streets.

The Woodstock film opened in cinemas at the same moment I was writing essays on poetry and history, trying to make sense of W.H. Auden, Henry David Thoreau and the robber baron capitalists of the American frontier. Auden's poem, 'As I Walked Out One Evening', hypnotic and seeming artless, led me into burrows and nightmares where Time coughed in the background as lovers kissed.[17] Even in the midst of my troubles — a plunge into another milieu, changed radically from that of four years earlier — I was like a starving man given real food for the first time in recent memory. At a showing of the Woodstock film I ran into Theresa again with her friends Bill and Donna Stalker: colourful figures in the student culture of the time, he with his tall frame, bullfighter's moustache and she slim and stylish in a long leather coat, seen bound together whirling around the city on his classic Ariel Huntmaster 650. They seemed like gods, bold harbingers of the new.

Recalling them brings back how inadequate and rustic I felt among these sophisticates with their drama society acting confidence, their ease with the music, the mood of protest — and the drugs. I was still in the beer-drinking mindset, not that I was drinking much. Mostly I was too hard-up, too busy or too tired, and parked my alcoholic tendencies for a rainy day that was coming. I could go through periods of control and

Anti-Vietnam War protest march, Auckland 1971.
Newspix.co.nz/*New Zealand Herald*

abstinence — not unusual with addicts — but my disease hadn't gone away, just to bed. There were chances to get wasted and sleep around but I never did; in my heart I was still with Theresa, in spite of my family's incomprehension at what was going down. My mother couldn't fathom our relationship, the estrangement, and it just wasn't worthwhile trying to explain. After all, she had a new man in her troubled life and some happiness at last. I kept going: lectures, readings, essays, keeping the flat ticking over and working with Maurice every night on the bread round. There wasn't a lot of free time for despair.

The night run around the city and inner suburbs was proving a life-saver, as it wore me out. Maurice would drive down to the bakery after an evening meal and load up, heading out to deliver the first half of the round. At midnight or so he would roar into the back yard, clamber up the stairs and pass me the key to the Bedford. I would hare off into the night and drive my four or five hours of deliveries until dawn, taking any returns back to the bakery, in bed by 6 or 7 a.m to grab maybe five hours sleep before my first lecture at eleven. Thank God that wasn't every day; on later lectures, I could sleep in. It was punishing schedule, but together we survived a year.

There were some strange sights on the night shift, out there with taxi drivers, milkmen and cops. A woman crying by the front gate in her dressing gown was one that haunted us both; she wouldn't tell Maurice what was wrong and the secret stayed with her. In the deep frosts of winter, the bread tins needed a good kick to get them open. We ran, we froze, we made the run work and Maurice at the year's end had his degree, had his nest egg and sold the business to his father. He headed up to Wellington to work as legal advisor to the wharfies at the start of what would become a brilliant career.

I still had some deep waters to navigate before that time. On July the fifth, Theresa gave birth to our son and I drove out to Burwood Hospital to see him, in Maurice's old blue Vauxhall. Nothing had changed; everything had changed. I looked at Timothy with his black wisps of hair. I put my massive index finger into his tiny grip and he held me.

Then I drove back to the empty flat. Crossing Moorhouse Avenue onto Antigua Street, I saw the neon sign on top of the pub, a massive bottle of Gordon's gin. I pulled over, walked into the bottle store and bought a bottle of the same, one of lemon squash, drove home, opened them up, mixed them, sat on the couch and drank most of the mixture. By the time Maurice arrived back at the flat from wherever he'd been, I was drunk as a sailor on leave and spouting rubbish. As I fell off the sofa he picked me up and dragged me to bed. The baby's head was wet and I'd fallen off the wagon.

17

When Hemi met Pablo

We all have a year, a time in a year in our lives when everything changes: for seeming good or seeming ill, from within or without or both, from a small event to a national disaster, a birth or a death. Ecclesiastes 3:1. To everything a season: mine mixed up poetry and paternity in unpredictable ways in the year 1971, when for the first time as an adult I entered into the study of literature and the journey of fatherhood. Neither beginning looked propitious. I can only talk about the paternity in riddles as it concerns two other people who have not asked to be in this sentence; the poetry was born in a time of emotional turbulence, that much is true.

I was still in touch with my old high school English teacher, Peter Hooper, and wrote a poem for him, as well as a few others. I plunged my sleepy head into books, struggled into the morning lectures after nights on the bread round, looked around me at the other minds and bodies and tried to steer my way through this whirl of new impressions and big ideas. I sat in Mervyn Thompson's lecture on Gerard Manley Hopkins, riveted as he dramatised 'The Windhover' with a reading that shamed the two airheads behind me, gossiping about nothing, as verbal magic was woven in our hearing. The theatre of the word had me hooked.

In American Studies, the history lecturer swept back a crown of luxuriant white hair and, like the eagle of American heraldry, mounted the podium with us as the prey. He told the same jokes every year, in the same place. The literature was different: Thoreau I could take or leave, but when David Walker took us through Whitman and Dickinson and on to Allen Ginsberg I was right there with him. He became my tutor and treated us all like adults. I had found my next mentor: David was a practising poet and critic, his work appearing in *Landfall* and our student mag, *Canta,* where I read his poems. I found the courage — maybe the desperation — to ask if he would look at my writing, and he agreed. After a tutorial session I handed him a few sheets of paper, handwritten efforts from that same faithful Parker 45 I'd used when I'd written those early attempts on the Coast.

When he came back with the result, it wasn't what I'd hoped for. Something craven in the human psyche is looking for love and approval when we court authority figures. What I got was a needful cold bath and it brought me up short. David handed me my poems with typewritten comments (that gave him authority right there — he had a typewriter!). I scuttled away like a kid with a stolen biscuit, to devour my report; pretty much, it was 'fail'. He'd been ruthless and unsparing: the rose in my poem for Peter Hooper was a cliché that needed "flushing away with last night's bath water"; he was put in mind of the Russian poet Mandelstam who spent a whole evening trying to persuade "a non-poet to non-poem". Ouch! Was I a non-poet? Then the killer blow, "If more means less, then less!" What hurt my feelings was actually the cunning stroke of a Zen master. The proverbial bamboo cane with which he whacked me across the rump actually woke me up. My writing was unformed, uninformed and hopelessly derivative.

Instead of giving up, I pressed him: who was Mandelstam? I made it my business to find out and David helped me with some of his books. In 1971 there was nothing of the enigmatic Russian's work in translation in the university library. I was not able to find any of his poetry until the first widely available English versions of his selected poems appeared in 1973, edited by Clarence Brown (Babette Deutsch, who wrote my beloved *School Journal* poem, 'Marseillaise' had been translating his poetry in the 1920s). Brown's book, a work shared with the American poet and translator W.S. Merwin, would become a talisman. With recommended works by Pablo Neruda and César Vallejo, this generous and cultured New Englander urged me on to explore more poetry. This was my second creative writing class, following on from high school with Peter Hooper. David gave me a boot in the arse to wake me up, with pointers to where good writing could be found.

The next helpful thing he did was to allow his students in their final essay assignment to write on a topic of their own choosing. It was truly exciting in that American Studies class. The later history sections took us right up to Vietnam, black and white on the TV news bulletins and the subject of regular street protests every Friday night. David obliged with lectures on the Beats, Ginsberg and company, quoting the howling bard's fruity lines from the poem, 'America', where the USA gets told point blank what to do with its atom bomb: "Go fuck yourself!"

This was potent stuff: back then lecturers didn't swear in front of their students, but this was literature! We lapped it up, pretending to be shocked. Prowling the library shelves, I'd discovered the work of Theodore

Roethke, a more conservative stylist than Ginsberg and a writer I grew to care about. Maybe I sensed his alcoholism calling to my own, another of Ginsberg's company of minds destroyed by madness, as seen in the opening of his epic poem, 'Howl'. I would write my assignment on the poetry of Roethke, his signature poem, 'The Far Field', from the book of the same name (for copyright reasons I am not able to reproduce it here, but it will reward any seeker).[18]

What delights me is how even today I can still write down an almost complete stanza from memory (missing out the opening line, "I learned not to fear infinity" and transposing the penultimate and the last). I dived deep into Roethke; again, there was not much critical material available to me in the library, so I took a risk and wrote about the poet's influence on my writing and the parallels in our work (if indeed there were any). It was a 'boy-meets-poetry and falls in love', confessing a growing addiction to reading and writing poems for their own sake — and for my sanity. Handing it in, I disclosed to David that I was working under "trying conditions" (this was after our son's birth and nights on the bread round). He gave me an A+ and wrote, "In spite of your difficulties, this is the best thing I've read so far on Roethke." I didn't cry, but my heart sang.

David was leaving. His time in New Zealand was over and he was heading back to Maine, back to the family farm and teaching at the University of Southern Maine. He invited me to his flat the night before he left, plied me with sherry and advice about the books I needed to find, including the South Americans Neruda and Vallejo, and the Russian novelist Goncharov and his opus, *Oblomov*. I dutifully noted all these and would soon be rewarded; we promised to keep in touch and until his premature death in 2008 aged sixty-four we did just that, in what he would later celebrate as "our years

Earth
Marriage

To end by weighing as nothing
pratings of those who judge you a lonely fool –
these rumours overrun by the rattling, endless
spears of your flax
the sea wind hones.

In acceptance, your mingling
grows ironic weeds –
when time frees thought
and love, you tend
a single, reaching rose –
speaking the colours
of sorrow, words
of another time.

Jeff Holman

The poem for Peter Hooper, complete with the rose. It became a title for his third book of poetry, *Fragments III, Earth Marriage, 1972.*

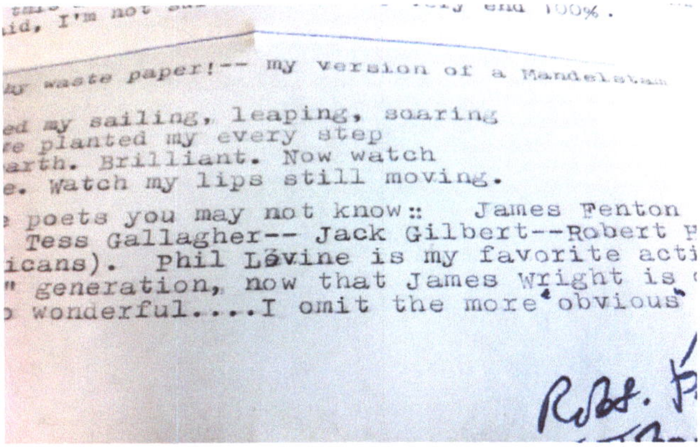
waste paper!-- my version of a Mandelstam
ed my sailing, leaping, soaring
re planted my every step
arth. Brilliant. Now watch
e. Watch my lips still moving.
poets you may not know:: James Fenton
Tess Gallagher-- Jack Gilbert--Robert
icans). Phil Lévine is my favorite acti
" generation, now that James Wright is
wonderful....I omit the more obvious

A letter from David Walker in 1985, suggesting poets "you may not know".

of stubborn friendship", inscribed in a copy of his 1976 collection, *Moving Out*. En route later to England in 1987 I managed to visit him and saw the bleak spring snows melting around Freedom, Maine. David Walker did for me what any good teacher would do: he made a friendship, pointed me in the direction of great poetry and left me to get on with it, all the while passing on remarks and feedback by letter until I grew able to stand on my own. We also shared a book together in 1974: this was my introduction to David Young and David Waddington, publishers of the poetry-meets-graphics series, *Fragments*.

I followed up David Walker's advice to find and read other poets and soon had myself a copy of Pablo Neruda's massive *Selected Poems*, a weighty 1970 Cape edition edited by Nathaniel Tarn. A complete novice in the work of this or any South American poet, I opened it and entered. Here was a world as full and abundant as any Amazonian rainforest, teeming with bilingual riches and completely foreign, alien, unlike anything I'd ever come across before in poetry. I'd been enclosed in an English language tradition written mostly by English writers; the few North Americans I was discovering were on the whole, urban. Neruda was from an entirely different world: a bloody and painful collision of Spanish colonisation with the indigenous peoples in the South. His Chilean native roots and his Spanish tongue produced a universe of poetry as varied and super-abundant as the surreal landscapes in which his works were born.

I had found another master and one whose frontier psychology and First People's consciousness melded with a healthy Marxist politics made him an ideal model for us here in New Zealand. We were not English, nor east coast North Americans; we were a southern people and those on a wild edge of the Pacific, sharing the same rim of fire and the vast expanse of water, the world's greatest marine dimension. I had crossed these waters with my mother to get here, sailing across the Equator to stand in the New

Pablo Neruda (Ricardo Reyes): the young poet.
Wikipedia Commons, Public Domain[19]
BELOW 'Algunas Bestias/Some Beasts', in Neruda's 1970 *Selected Poems* (Cape).

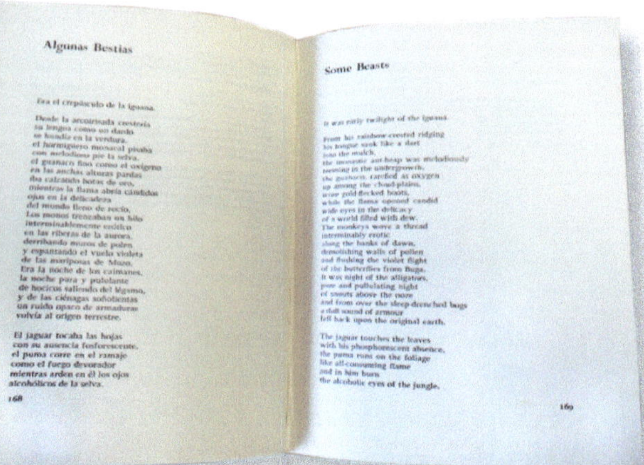

Algunas Bestias

Era el crepúsculo de la iguana.

Desde la arcoirisada crestería
su lengua como un dardo
se hundía en la verdura,
el hormiguero monacal pisaba
con melodioso pie la selva,
el guanaco fino como el oxígeno
en las anchas alturas pardas
iba calzando botas de oro,
mientras la llama abría cándidos
ojos en la delicadeza
del mundo lleno de rocío.
Los monos trenzaban un hilo
interminablemente erótico
en las riberas de la aurora,
derribando muros de polen
y espantando el vuelo violeta
de las mariposas de Muzo.
Era la noche de los caimanes,
la noche pura y pululante
de hocicos saliendo del légamo,
y de las ciénagas soñolientas
un ruido opaco de armaduras
volvía al origen terrestre.

El jaguar tocaba las hojas
con su ausencia fosforescente,
el puma corre en el ramaje
como el fuego devorador
mientras arden en él los ojos
alcohólicos de la selva.

168

Some Beasts

It was early twilight of the iguana.

From his rainbow-crested ridging
his tongue sank like a dart
into the mulch,
the monastic ant-heap was melodiously
teeming in the undergrowth,
the guanaco, rarefied as oxygen
up among the cloud-plains,
wore gold-flecked boots,
while the llama opened candid
wide eyes in the delicacy
of a world filled with dew.
The monkeys wove a thread
interminably erotic
along the banks of dawn,
demolishing walls of pollen
and flushing the violet flight
of the butterflies from Muzo.
It was night of the alligators,
pure and pullulating night
of snouts above the ooze
and from over the sleep-drenched bogs
a dull sound of armour
fell back upon the original earth.

The jaguar touches the leaves
with his phosphorescent absence,
the puma runs on the foliage
like all-consuming flame
and in him burn
the alcoholic eyes of the jungle.

169

World. Neruda wrote of sexual tides and luscious fruits, of vicious colonial masters and ruthless corporations, fantastic beasts in jungles and rivers, of restless oceans and peasants oppressed, the salads of summer and the wine of love. His deep humanity and his embrace of living leapt up off the pages at me. I was in love again.

The love poems — from his first and beloved 1924 collection, *Viente Poemas de Amor*, so perennially popular in his native Chile that they were known, en masse, by heart — would get any romantic by the throat as the poet cast sad nets into his lover's oceanic eyes. Even better, for one who knew no Spanish at all, was the chance to gaze across the page at the original and practise, alone and out loud, such voluptuous sonorities as, "Inclinado en las tardes tiro mis tristes redes/a tus ojos oceánicos."[20] I never learned Spanish but I absorbed Neruda and in this way taught myself that poetry was as much in the feelings and the sounds as in meaning and intent, the kind of emphasis I was learning in the academy.

Neruda saved me, in poems like 'Walking Around', where he sang of world-weariness, and 'Algunas Bestias/Some Beasts', which began with the iguana caught in the twilight.[21] The poem had no frills: just the plain perfect statement, a single-line stanza to introduce the exotic and terrifying denizens of the Amazon and their hypnotic non-human powers. From the ghostly jaguar, the alcoholic eyes of the jungle burning, to the fearful anaconda in the deep waters, coiled like the circular earth, consuming and redemptive — here was life's glory and its dangers. This was not just about humans in any one place and time: it was continental poetry, colonial history, the human heart opening up in agony, bewilderment and longing. Neruda was a stepping stone for me, before I came face-to-face with a local hero — James Keir Baxter.

I first encountered the confessional voice of the 1960s in Baxter. He in turn had earlier been influenced by Robert Lowell, whose work I would discover later. David Walker had seen this clearly and written about the Lowell-Baxter axis in a recent issue of *Landfall*.[22] Living in my upstairs Carlton Mill Road flat, with Gary Langford the poet and family below me, I was meeting writers on the page and in the flesh. Gary was working on his first book, *The Family*, a long poem as the introduction sets out, on "the position of the family founded on duty and work, the dark twins of colonial life". Meeting him put me in touch with other writers and their books. Ted Hughes was a world to explore, along with Sylvia Plath — but for me, it came down to Baxter. His public profile and his notoriety meant that for once, a poet was front and centre in our national life. His ongoing print spat with the muckraking *Truth* meant that even if he was out of sight up at the Jerusalem commune on the Whanganui River, the paper would dig up something on the capers of this middle-aged religion-crazed dropout to scandalise respectable Kiwis.

In 1970 Baxter had published *Jerusalem Sonnets*, a thin volume with its Ralph Hotere cover binding the thirty-nine meditations within, verse epistles, letters he had written to the priest, Fr Colin Durning. The following year came *Jerusalem Daybook* and in 1972, the year of his death, *Autumn Testament*. Another book of poetry, *Runes*, came out posthumously the year after that. All of these in some measure flowed into my life at this time, becoming models for my writing for many years. The elements were seductive: a confessional tone, an address to the reader that was personal and seemingly private; disclosure of hopes, dreams and contradictions in the here-and-now; quotidian realities spiced with declarations of love, madness, infidelity and faith; and a relentless self-mythologising tendency that could easily entrap you in its narcissism.

My copy of Baxter's *Jerusalem Sonnets*, 1970.

By permission of the Hotere Foundation Trust

In Poem 34 of the *Jerusalem Sonnets*, he wrote:

I read it in the Maori primer,
'Ka timata te pupuhi o te hau' —

The wind began blowing; it blew for a century
Levelling by the musket and the law

Ten thousand meeting houses — [23]

In 1972 Baxter came in person to Christchurch and declaimed to a bunch of curious students. He got under my skin, and much later, to make sense of that time, I wrote a poem, 'When the Broom Bursts'; an attempt to come to terms with the way I had absorbed his presence. The poem says more about me than him, as you might expect from a confession, but also charts one of his lasting legacies — the way he would foreground Maori values in an uncomprehending Pakeha world. What was he on about? We had the best race relations in the world, we were told; the soundings, the eruptions, the early seeds of brown baby-boomer protests yet to hit home. Many elders were still committed to gradualism, in resignation to a century of struggle and precious little gain. I wrote:

You came to the University like St Francis
in your dirty coat and bleeding feet
and spoke against abortion.
I saw you weaving spells outside the caff
in league with the PYM and God Almighty.

The story was of two women:
one white, one brown, both pregnant.
The white parents had the child
"cut out of her gut"
but the Maori kid was spared.

How? The tupuna took her.
Why? Because of arohanui.
Community: people over things.
You idealised tangata whenua
against the Pakeha bourgeiosie.

What shook me was your voice:
even now I hear you
like my dead lover's laughter
in tune with an unseen
existing order.

What strikes me now, at a thirty years' distance from writing this poem, is how I was still using his mode of address; that I was well aware of what he'd been saying at that time about the position of Maori. In 1972, as I sat in the student café that evening and ate my meal, looking across to the table where Baxter was with some of the Progressive Youth Movement's leading lights and other groupies, I wasn't able to get up, go over and thank him. Would it have been as in 'Ode to Auckland', a late poem where he sits in another varsity cafeteria with six Catholic acquaintances:

> One wanted to show me the poems he had written
> [...]
> Another hoed into his plate of cheese and camel turds.[24]

Was I another groupie, wanting the fairy dust of fame?

They all disappointed him in the end with lame excuses as to why they could not give one of his Maori friends a place to crash for the night. "Roimata ua, roimata tangata — /The tears of rain are falling, Tears of rain, tears of men."[25] Not long after this experience, tears were indeed falling: on 22 October Baxter died of a heart attack in suburban Auckland, on a stranger's doorstep. We held a memorial reading for him in Christchurch on 12 March 1973, where a host of big guns stood up and

Baxter and friends; a photo from the *New Zealand Herald.* The caption reads "Dinner and a discussion on religion. While Baxter is a Catholic, the topics include everything from atheism to Zen Buddhism."
4 January 1971, Newspix.co.nz/*New Zealand Herald*

read, save for Allen Curnow who did not come but wrote a poem to the dead man, excusing his absence, including the line: "Winged words need no crutch, /and I've none for you". I was delighted that my old friend and mentor Peter Hooper was a reader that day. I got up the courage to read 'He Waiata mo Te Kare', from *Autumn Testament*, Baxter's love poem to his wife Jacquie. I'm not sure if it was for them I chose that poem, or a form of de facto recognition of my own brokenness. My own Baxter poem ended like this:

> So, this is as good a time as ever
> to salute the living speaking still
> when broom pods burst in January
> black seeds over the dusty roads I walked
> to the swimming hole at the Blackball Bridge.
>
> This is as good a way as any
> to touch my hat like a boozy Dad
> weaving home at dusk
> past our nosy neighbour arms folded
> over her pinny at the gate next door,
>
> tweak the old felt brim
> like a true gentleman
>
> to a fellow dried-out drunk
> who outlived and outloved
> the grave of New Zealand.

Outside Te Papa, on the edge of Wellington Harbour:
lines from a James K. Baxter poem, 'The Maori Jesus'.

18

Inhaling

In a change of hearts meanwhile, Theresa and I had reconciled and married. Early in 1972 in a whirl of activity, we'd moved from Carlton Mill Road to a rental house shared with ten other hopeful urban lefties: students finishing their degrees, old friends and new, occupying a huge Edwardian villa at 368 Papanui Road. The effect would be to experience something of the counter-culture without buying into the committed lifestyle of a place like Chippenham, just around the corner in Browns Road. It was a cross between idealism and expediency, a mega-flat with all the opportunities for creative accidents and domestic friction. On the whole it worked well, with a cooking and cleaning roster that only occasionally broke down.

I was perennially broke: my few savings from the holiday job at Fletchers plywood plant in Riccarton were soon gone and it was down to scratching along on my morning job bagging potatoes at Market Gardeners in Waltham. I was doing three papers, including Japanese; the second-year American Studies lectures were in the morning at a time I was humping potato sacks in a dusty tin shed with two elderly chaps who plastic-bagged the spuds for the shops. Sadly, I couldn't continue with the course I'd enjoyed the most. I'd taken English again at level two and Religious Studies, a course where you could leave the lectures one week feeling like a Buddhist and the next, a follower of the Tao. The Japanese classes were a small revelation: it was like being back at secondary school, with an odd formal teacher-pupil relationship at variance with the culture of the university at large.

With a part-time job, I soon found the daily study workload a test in itself. I considered dropping Japanese after just a few weeks, which so distressed the head of the programme that I relented. Hearing of my financial straits, my teacher Kinoshita-san came back next day with a big bag of Japanese baby clothes, surplus now to his family requirements. They even included a pair of blue Little Leaguer bib overalls with a matching baseball cap (post-war, the American game had become big in Japan). I resigned from potato bagging, said goodbye to the foreman (an old West

Coast identity operating under another name, pretending he'd never met me) and became a full-time student, more interested in writing poetry than studying, persevering with the steady stream of Japanese homework and my essays.

The real excitement of the year came when David Young and David Waddington — also sharing the house at 368 — produced the third in the series of their *Fragments* poetry volumes: Peter Hooper's *Earth Marriage*, a collection of his poetry graced with Dave Waddington's haunting photographs of the West Coast where the poems were set — using my poem for Peter as the book's title. The house became the venue of the book's launch; for the first time, I was caught up in the excitement and the promise of publication. Peter was there reading his work, Mervyn Thompson and Gary Langford joining in, people coming and going, wine flowing. The buzz that fills a room at a book's delivery into the world hit me, and I wanted some of that for myself.

These events have little to do with the actual writing of a poem, but they are seductive and no honest egoist with a pen in hand can avoid the desire to be published one day, and their need — in most cases — to be admired. I had a few poems and showed them to David Young, who said he liked some of them. As a journalist he knew about writing, and encouraged me to keep going. I kept him on file, as relationships with potential publishers are always attractive, especially to poets (poetry being a hard sell, always). Writing though was mostly on the side: I'd taken a job as a university library assistant in the evenings, giving out the reserved books.

When my father was admitted to Christchurch hospital early in 1972 with a diagnosis of lung cancer, my life came under increasing strain. He was discharged after a course of chemotherapy and sent home to die, except he had no home to go to after my parents' divorce. In Greymouth, my long-suffering mother agreed to take Dad back under her roof and nursed him until he died in October. I had a nervous breakdown in the last days of his dying, all my unresolved anger over our fractured relationship knocking me sideways. My own shaky marriage too was under stress through all these changes, and before the year's end, we parted. Now a solo parent, all the stress of the past twelve months flooded my life, driving me crazy. I was a mess.

I couldn't think straight: photos at the time show a wild-looking individual with a manic aura. We had a steady stream of visitors: people wanting to crash for the night and usually, someone with a stash and a joint to hand. I'd held out against marijuana when it came my way until then, without knowing why; now, I suddenly had no resistance and took the offered herb. Until that moment, I didn't know how tense and uptight I had been; not since being prescribed Valium earlier in the year, then throwing it down the toilet when I realised how it made me oblivious to fear in my job at the plywood factory in the holidays. I could see myself getting injured or killed while in the soporific state it induced. This marijuana stuff was different.

I doubt that anybody can truthfully say forty years later what the effect of a drug was, that first time. I do know it had me lying on the floor in a state of induced relaxation as the Moody Blues blasted their way through 'Knights in White Satin', as if the words and the music contained the secret of the universe to be absorbed unimpeded into my anaesthetised nervous system. I was hooked. Nobody was going to tell me this stuff was evil. It's hard to know now whether my domestic meltdowns or discovering Sweet Mary Jane and Sixto Rodriguez crooning 'Sugar Man' on his high-rotate album, *Cold Fact*, had rendered me unable to concentrate enough to sit my end-of-year exams. A visit to my doctor at Student Health was enough to get me an application for aegrotat passes. I couldn't get my life to stay still in one place; by the time Christmas came in the year of Baxter's death, my life as a student was over for the second time.

The original members of 368 Papanui Road had broken up and we reformed as three solo parents, a couple of psychiatric nurses and a mentally ill transient who soon had to be ejected because of his dangerous outbursts around our children. I quickly fell for one of the solo mothers, Lee Drury, walking into a new relationship before dealing with the wreckage of the past. Love, or need, or both — who could tell? The landlord turned up one day and told us he was selling the house and we had a month to move out. We found another rental property not far away in Rugby Street and moved in. By early 1973 I was a copy holder

Kids party time, 114 Rugby Street: poet Greg Jackson looks on.
OPPOSITE Semi-crazed, at 368 Papanui Road, 1972.

on the Christchurch *Press*, the literary editor of the student magazine *Canta*, an itinerant declaimer of poetry and a confirmed smoker of dope. My part-time evening job on the paper introduced me to another side of newspaper culture, a very different crew from those in classifieds where I'd worked two years earlier.

Some workplaces attract those who can't fit anywhere else; the *Press* reading room in 1973 was like that. They needed people with a good command of English who were happy to work night shifts, along with some part-timers for the busy Saturday edition. So far, so normal, yet this place had more oddballs and eccentrics per capita than anything else I'd struck in the country thus far and I must have been one of them. There was a certain cachet in belonging to this strange band, charged with ensuring that the paper hit the streets every day minus grammatical blemishes, aberrant house styles, or errors in advertising copy.

Proofs would *whoosh* down the Lamson tubes from the printers to reading room chief Chris Neale's desk; he would then distribute these to readers and copyholders who sat at sloping desks facing each other. The proof reader would correct errors using a time-honoured code of symbols that told the printer what needed fixing, from *dele* (delete) to *stet* (let it stand). One person would read aloud while the other checked what was read; with the flood of classified material on Friday night for the Saturday paper, we would race through the car ads and the property sells as if running a commentary on the Melbourne Cup. A room packed with twenty or thirty people chanting these same rhythms was like a cross between revivalist prayer meetings, noisy parties and the mental hospital wards out there in the gulag that existed at that time.

Since made redundant by the advent of personal computers, workstations and the internet, such newspaper reading rooms probably performed a public service: housing the otherwise unemployable and offering a day job to writers who had a novel or a bunch of poems going on elsewhere. My reader complained to me one night that he had to stop, he was having acid flashbacks. It was that kind of place: with a classic motorbike junkie who could do the ton on his ancient BSA 500; a stand-up comedian; a follower of Subud (an Indonesian spiritual movement) and several others like me with developing drug problems. But it meant I could write poetry and run around during the day when openings arose, giving a reading here and there — once even to a bemused group of trainee teachers at training college. What they made of renditions of Voznesenksy, Neruda, E.E. Cummings and a few of my own efforts is lost in space, along with the *Press* reading room and its cast of heroes.

My next trick was to get arrested. In March 1973, a series of demonstrations against US bases in New Zealand and "the militarisation of Harewood" took place in Christchurch. On Saturday March 24 I decided to go and join the protest at Harewood, borrowing my flatmate's blue Vespa and putt-putting out to the airport car park in my long leather coat. I arrived before the police had managed to set up their barrier on the road and was parking the scooter lawfully when a policeman charged up to me shouting, "Clear off, I'm sick of you pigs!" He was grumpy, maybe one of those who'd been called in from out of town and required to do overtime (there were over 300 cops there that day). He didn't seem to know that we were the ones supposed to be shouting, "Pigs!"

I left the scooter and took to my heels. Back down the road, a barrier went up as Air Force choppers — employed for the first time at a demo — swooped overhead, massed ranks of police assembled and German shepherds strained on leashes. The loudspeakers barked, "Leave now, or you *will* be arrested!" After a decent interval chatting with my new friend, the veteran protester Keith Duffield, seeing that top cop Gideon Tait and his men meant business, I joined the crowd and began slowly to leave. As I walked away on the footpath, a cop grabbed me from behind, pushed me over, then frog-marched me back to a processing van parked just outside

Under arrest: Harewood demo, 1973.
Michael de Hamel

the Caltex station. I was cuffed, fingerprinted, photographed and carted off with seven others to the bowels of the new Christchurch Police Station.

I spent the night with Keith explaining to me we had to get our stories to match, as the police would be upstairs doing the same and preparing to perjure themselves. He was right; at the trial some months later, the cop who nabbed me stood up and lied about my refusal to move and my obstruction of a footpath. I came away with a $25 fine and a renewed distrust of authority. I wrote some pretty angry poems that winter, as well as a few that would make it into my first book with David Walker in the following year. Rugby Street allowed me a space to begin a writing process addressing the grief over my father's death: from the first serious attempt in the 1973 poem 'Father & Son', to what would become 'As big as a father' in the 1990s.

> I do not want another father: old man, now
> dead, that cancer faded
> and swelled you, speechless
> at the door, yellow
> feathered fingers ...

No longer enrolled to study, I spent time on the campus editing the literary page for the student magazine, *Canta*. This meant trying to find a few poems that were worthy of space. The role had once been taken by Baxter himself, back in 1947–48 when he was reluctant to publish his wife-to-be J.C. Sturm's work — arguably better than some of his own that saw daylight in *Canta* at the time. Once, while he was away, Bill Pearson, editor in absentia, published her work; if only she'd chosen to step out of Baxter's considerable shadow. Baxter had also been a copy editor on the *Press* at the time, in the same reading room as me; there was a literary whakapapa in that building that included Allen Curnow and many others.[26] For *Canta*, I also wrote some self-important manifestos about the type of poetry that would make it into the magazine, best-forgotten examples of ignorance and arrogance.

I did manage at least one scoop. On 11 September 1973 a vicious right-wing coup encouraged by Henry Kissinger and the CIA toppled the democratically elected socialist government of Salvador Allende and installed the fascist regime of the dictator, General Augusto Pinochet. Allende died in a contentious suicide; just over a week later, Pablo Neruda — hospitalised with cancer — was injected by a doctor believed to be acting on the orders of Pinochet and died on 23 September. Thousands of shocked and mourning Chileans defied the army and Pinochet's denial

Salvador Allende at Palacio de la Modena, 11 September, 1973.
Wikipedia Commons

of a public funeral and broke the curfew, crowding the streets to weep for their poet. The Left across the world was shocked and disgusted at events taking place in Chile; those who cared for Neruda and for poetry mourned him with his people. Six days later, on 29 September 1973, W.H. Auden died in Switzerland at the age of sixty-six; in one week, two of the 20th century's major voices had fallen silent.

I got busy and contacted Rob Jackaman, an English expat poet and lecturer in the English Department, to see if he could give me a few words on Auden's significance, for the Lit Page in *Canta*. We had a short timeframe to get the copy in but Rob agreed; while he got to work, I wrote an appreciation of Neruda to go with his piece. It felt like we were honouring the mighty fallen, that this was real journalism, writing to a deadline about things that mattered, writers who counted whose work would live on. We did not know then that the Chilean coup was the harbinger of a neoliberal revolution arriving here ten years later, an ideology New Zealand would embrace in the guise of freedom and personal responsibility.

The page came out for the last *Canta* of the year, 5 October, and it was a little beauty. Rob was hard but fair on Auden, "Beginning urgent, he wound up in detergent", ending his piece with the observation that his finest poems were "a fitting enough epitaph to Auden without anyone else really needing to say anything." My brief obituary for Neruda — accompanied by four of his poems in translation — opened with the title, "WE ARE MANY", his credo for the dispossessed.

"Two weeks back in the rubble and blood of the broken dreams he had traced, Chile's prolific and revered son, Pablo Neruda, died in his home far from the mighty rivers he had so often celebrated in his torrential flood of work." I noted the circumstances of his death, its significance not just for Chileans but the "small and the weak everywhere". Grasping a Maori proverb from somewhere, the obituary ends, "It is to the people and the earth that his life and art is now deeded: a great tree has fallen." That was my last column for *Canta*.

19

The bin man and the bin

The job at the *Press* and Lee's work as a photo retoucher at Standish & Preece kept us going financially, until the reality of her pregnancy pressured me into finding something that paid better. We were on the move again, the Rugby Street experiment breaking up as we downsized to a cheaper part of town, Sydenham. Between the two us we had Lee's Honda 50 Sport, my BSA 350, a few bits of furniture and of course, books and records, the urban hippie set-up ubiquitous in the 1970s, along with a grunty stereo and freely available drugs. Somebody suggested I try the city council depot for a job on the rubbish trucks: work half a day and then be free to write or hang loose. Within a week I was a professional bin man and freelance writer, about to rediscover — as I had on the shearing gangs — that pain was an unremitting teacher.

We settled into 143 Huxley Street and I turned up for my first day as a rubbish man. The culture then — before the advent of paper and plastic bags and the present one-man automated bin pick-up system with organics, rubbish and recycling all separated — was "a kingdom of stinks and sighs", to quote Theodore Roethke. Each truck, flat-bed or hydraulic crusher had its own dedicated team who followed a pattern of five daily rounds over their allotted patches of suburbia. We began each day with a thirty-minute slot from 7 a.m. in the inner city collecting the trash from

Rubbish day in a Christchurch suburb, c.1960.

Christchurch City Libraries (1716) PhotoCD 11, IMG0050

OPPOSITE The old style of bin that died in the 1970s.

business premises before heading out to the homes of the waking city. We were not allowed into residential areas before 7.30 a.m., mostly starting around eight. Residents left a metal bin on the kerb and the runners (two or three) ran to the groups of cans and emptied them with a crash into the groaning crushers of the Bedford — or threw them up to a 'shaker' guy on the tray of a flat deck truck.

The flat decks were mainly used as back-up trucks for when the hydraulics on a crusher burst and a new hose had to be fitted out on the job, or back at the depot. This happened most weeks; you could never be sure if your truck would survive a round, meaning long delays and curses from crews who just wanted to finish and get home to their other lives. Many bin men were by nature and calling transients, or unemployables elsewhere: students, fitness freaks, alkies and wanderers, with a few noble professional garbos who made this their career. Most of us were passing through, or looking elsewhere: I'd never run so fast, stunk so high, or discovered as many muscle groups as I did in that first week, not even as a shearer.

For the first few days I was on a flat deck crew with a wreck of a man who looked like he could barely shuffle and a couple of lithe young Maori guys who loped along like greyhounds on half throttle. The human wreck staggered and shambled while these two artists performed a kind of ballet. We took turns running and picking up bins, then swapped, up on the truck to catch and empty the flying cans, firing them back to the runner in one smooth motion. Every physical job has its secret, its dance, a series of moves repeated by rote so often that any thought of beauty is lost in the repetition. I had seen this embodied in my shearing experience; now I was watching it again in these Maori greyhounds.

The runner would hit a group of bins like a bird of prey, flip the lid off with one hand and with the other, grab the handle, swing it head high and as it travelled, give a last flip. The full bin flew to the hands of the shaker on the truck, who bashed it to unleash the fetid cargo of ash, eggshells or whatever festered within — and with the same smooth choreography, flipped the bin back upright and fired it down to the runner below. They repeated this all the way down the street, halted only by a bin so heavy it needed a two-man haul up and over. This was the dance of the bin men: the poetry of trash collection. It had its own presence and beauty, silhouetted in a stinking reality that most people naturally avoid.

It was sobering to discover that some of those same citizens whose rubbish we were removing had difficulty in treating us differently from the refuse. We were often abused and in one case, threatened by a loser with baseball bat. He'd got the fingers for some dangerous driving near my new crew, Paddy and Arthur; after passing us, he parked, then lay in wait with a baseball bat. Advancing down his driveway, he changed his mind when he saw the three of us. I was the white weed of the crew but Arthur, a tall sinewy Ngapuhi, fearless as they come, and Paddy, a stocky Fijian student, made up a pretty convincing front row, loping from street to street in little more than cut-off shorts and singlets. By now we had moved from Bedford crushers and bins to plastic bags and open high-sided Fords: two guys running ahead and stacking to limit the number of stops, one inside the Ford tramping the bags as they flew in like bombs.

With Roy, our driver, we made a tight team: that bonding, the sense of completing a job, the physical burn of a muscular fitness was a temporary release from my inner world. This was a Maori world too in many ways; they made up a high percentage of the workforce. If you liked fish heads for breakfast, there was always a kai on the go in the smoko room when you arrived each morning (one look at the eyes and my appetite was gone). There was plenty of joking and kidding: Arthur found a set of knackered chest expanders in the trash as we motored down Lincoln Road one winter's morning. Next minute, there he was on the mountain of rubbish, splendid in his shorts, running a series of faux fitness moves for the entertainment of the morning commuters.

At home, things were changing: Lee was getting near to term in the new year 1974, I had the chance of a book with *Fragments* — and my drug use was accelerating. I was writing again: mostly confessional poems based on my circumstances, some of which would end up — prematurely — in *Two Poets,* the book that came out near the year's end. I was plagued with a sense of dislocation and a simmering anger I couldn't access or deal with. I smoked more dope, drank and dropped acid. Pregnant, Lee had an ongoing custody battle with her ex-husband over their son; a winter survived on the rubbish trucks gave me notice that there was no long-term future in picking up after other people. Others were persuading me I could do something better with my life.

Alcoholics have a genius for self-sabotage and I was no exception; a deep lack of self-worth and a paranoid marijuana ego don't make for the best of partners. I couldn't understand why sometimes I would just explode and punch a hole in a cupboard, or, in one case, a glass sliding cabinet in the kitchen. I was the one needing help; instead, I was about to join the

Babes in the wood: Lee, Lex, Timothy and me, 1973.

helping professions as a psychiatric social worker. The rescue mission I passed up with Child Welfare in 1970 was back on the agenda; the flipside of addiction for many users is co-dependency, the helper-rescuer syndrome. I was primed to go down that road, and it would not end well.

Even before I took the LSD with a poet friend I was becoming unhinged; a couple of acid trips fooled me into thinking I could access the keys of creation by self-administering unsafe chemicals of unknown provenance. It was as if I just didn't care; with a few cans of beer on board to dull the rational sites in the brain, dropping a trip seemed like a good move. It might have had some nasty results. Fortunately, after two attempts at flying, the supply dried up and I lost interest; it was too unpredictable. I could see the shimmering lyrics of Jefferson Airplane in the air of the room. There seemed to be a living personality in the wallpaper patterns. My flatmate's boxer dog turned into a raging rabid monster and I found myself in the bath, minus the water, eating carrots. I thought I could see for miles and gaze into the atom. When I gave Greg a ride home on my Beezer, all the way out along the causeway to Sumner I could hear the valves in the cylinder head opening and shutting, the wheeling gulls crying inside my head as the door of the world seemed thrown wide open.

Except it wasn't. I needed to go to work the next day and found myself lurching around the city in dark canyons, trying to pick up rubbish bags and look like nothing had changed. Fijian Paddy took one look at me and shook his head, "Boy, I feel really sorry for you."

I stared at him, hung-over with mystical intuitions: "Not half as sorry as I feel for you, Paddy," I intoned, intimating that now I knew where it was at, but he never would.

That wasn't true either; he was hardworking and straight up with a good sense of humour. He could see I was a wreck and I couldn't, but that's the old story of the alkie and the addict: everybody else has got it wrong except you.

I came back to my saner self on a night in May as Lee woke me and said, "Let's go!" Staying with her through the labour and seeing my daughter born was far and away the superior trip. I can still feel traces of this in the poem I wrote to celebrate her arrival —

> stunned
> by all that made you look at least
> ten million years old, from your
> mother's softened vitals to
> your female mammal sleeping eyes.
>
> Praise the being here.

The poem would soon appear in print: David Young agreed to go ahead with a first book of poetry, to be shared with my former teacher, David Walker. *Fragments 5: Two Poets* arrived in a cardboard box on the table in Huxley Street in late 1974. I could hold in my hand a book that held my work. Probably I should have waited, taken more time; some of the poems were slight and others needed revising to bring out the best in them.

I didn't know about anybody else, but I needed that book, if only for the affirmation that somebody else believed my writing was worth enough to place in the public arena, that I might keep going and develop through this first step. It bandaged and splinted my woeful self-belief and kept some hopes alive. It would be twenty long years before another book would follow, but for now I had copies to sell at readings and give to friends, a sliver of evidence that I could write poetry.

Instead of pressing on with my writing life, my next move was to apply for a job as a psychiatric social worker at Seaview Hospital in Hokitika. To grow as a writer and heal as a human being, it was probably the exact opposite of what I needed to do.

Fragments 5: Two Poets included my series 'Strange Children'— image by David Waddington, 1974.

20

A demon at my table

Snatches remain of the interview that got me the job: the long drive over to the Coast in Alan's borrowed Holden wagon; the confident nurse waiting with the other applicants, sure the job was his as he winked at staff passing by; the board member who asked me if the Religious Studies paper from my abandoned degree meant I would be proselytising; and later, my genuine surprise when they wrote and told me the job was mine. I was the only applicant with any tertiary experience, so I assume they saw me as teachable, able to go on and do the necessary qualification later. Back then, provincial areas like the West Coast couldn't always be too picky; had they seen my life over the past few years, my real life, not the one on the CV, they might well have hired that nurse.

One more time, we packed up to move house. I hired a truck and drove our worldly goods over the Lewis Pass, depositing them at the nurses' home where we would have temporary shelter, and then drove back to Christchurch. We loaded the few remaining bits and pieces into our old grey Commer van, complete with cats and chickens, and wobbled off into the teeth of a pelting rainstorm in the Lewis that swamped and stalled the windscreen wipers. The rain was so fierce and thick in the dark, it was like drowning in a whirlpool. The cat growled, the chooks warbled; we sang to keep our spirits up as darkness and rain swallowed us. Unseen forces were howling all about me on this return to the source of my childhood wounding. So, the memories mocked me, who are you going to save this time?

After a short stay at the nurses' home in Hokitika, we found a rental house at 47 Sale Street. We moved into a large wooden bungalow fronted by a low concrete wall with those typical rising sun cutouts, and a line of rata and magnolia along the drive to the garage where the Commer would live. Timothy and Lex were enrolled at school for the first time as we set about bedding in and meeting the neighbours. Old Alec Rae became a source of endless tips on vegetable gardening, as did his wife on the flower beds. At long last I was attempting something of a suburban

Being normal: Raine (10 months) and Lee, Hokitika 1975.

accommodation with middle New Zealand — job, house, schools, the whole nine yards. I was bringing along a bagful of hand grenades too: the adult child of an alcoholic and compulsive gambler, a co-dependent with a bunch of addictions, from nicotine to dope.

The hospital board at Seaview had never hired a social worker before and I'd never done social work, nor had I any qualification. We had to feel our way into this. The first priority was to get an office with a filing cabinet, a pot plant, and of course, a painting. I got to choose and for the next two years, every time I looked up and stared at the wall, there was the print of John Constable's iconic image, 'Boat-Building near Flatford Mill'. There sat the craftsman crouched on a stool in front of the half-finished hull and a river visible behind the trench dug out for the work, held back now by a lock. The channel would later be flooded and the new boat float away for a lifetime on Britain's waterway network. It was a meditation that had little to do with what I was there for, but government offices at that time were often decorated with such irrelevant but worthy examples of romantic art. Maybe they were onto something.

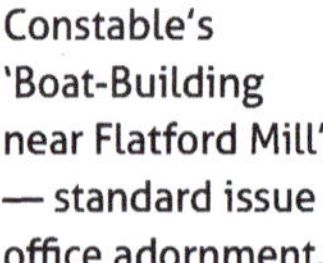

Constable's 'Boat-Building near Flatford Mill' — standard issue office adornment.

When heading over to the main administration block to join my new workmates for morning tea, in my loud yellow check lumber jacket and purple flared trousers, I discovered that if I slotted a file under my arm (even if empty), it made me look purposeful. Tom Lee, the pharmacist (who also ran the chemist shop in town), saw through that ruse: "Ha, he's got the idea!" he snorted when he saw me looking as if I knew what I was doing. I'm sure most of them didn't know what to make of me either, but the medical superintendent and the two doctors (one the superintendent's wife, the other a GP from Sri Lanka) were keen enough to put me to work. Paddy Davison, the head shrink, was a tall Irishman with a raffish wit, toper's veins, and a history, I was told, as a commando in the last war.

Paddy sat me down and gave me a list of people I needed to meet: medical social workers and the head of the Department of Social Welfare in Greymouth and various others in Hokitika, district nurses and policemen. It was a whirlwind tour of my fresh importance: the mayor's wife even came knocking to welcome us. I went along with it all and adopted the role, all the while feeling it was just that: a part I was playing, winging it. Next, I was off to Wellington for a three-month social work training placement at Tiromoana in the grounds of Porirua Hospital. Having just moved my family to a new life in a new place, I was buggering off and leaving Lee to it with the hope of just one return trip home at the end of six weeks.

Phone calls and letters would have to do, as I settled in to making friends with a brand-new group of social work inductees who I would share my life with for the next eighteen weeks. The course was run by Ruth Manchester and Agnes Brabin, experienced social workers and tutors who soon had us into bonding exercises of the milder encounter group mode, where we discovered and uncovered ourselves. This was too much eventually for at least one person from Probation, who pulled out and left after a few weeks. It wasn't easy being far from home and family; some of the locals went home for the weekends, while the rest like me hung around and explored the limited charms of Porirua.

I got to know Chris Harvey, who had a brother up the Coast Road back home, and Jude Dore, a former nun who had left the cloister and was a now a committed social activist. We were shepherded around the city, touring state housing areas and visiting Whitby, a flash suburb around the corner which just showed how easily money could keep people apart, a harbinger of the approaching '80s. Never the twain would meet. We were driven to borstals and taken to see patients about to receive ECT in the hospital next door to our quarters. With shock treatment, I only got as far as hearing the doctor recite the litany as to why it had to happen to this woman lying nearby; as he tested the injection to knock her out, the sight of liquid spurting from the needle was enough and I fainted to the floor.

Lying there, all I could hear were distant voices and the sound of a jet flying low over the hospital; panic struck me that they were going to give *me* the ECT. Ever since that moment, that empathetic bond with a woman about to have her brain shocked, I have never been able to stomach the whole idea of electroconvulsive therapy — an oxymoron if ever there was one. Even rationalisations from previous patients, the minority who feel it has helped them, have never been enough to shake my conviction that it is a torture of last resort.

Ask Janet Frame: she is one of the frontline literary witnesses of its potential to destroy much of what makes us most human, our memories. In her memoir, *An Angel at my Table*, she wrote, "Electric shock treatment may turn many grim memories out of house and home; what is certain is that it invites as permanent tenants the grim memories of itself, of receiving shock treatment." [27] I wrote a poem about it all, the first line reaching up to catch my terror: "The metal jet is overhead …". From that moment on, I was never going to make it as a psychiatric social worker. This whole experience caused me to change sides: become the client, the patient, become in some strange alchemy, an artist. The shock was everything I was running away from: poetry and the mysteries I needed to explore.

Lee and I survived the separation, and by the time I got back to Hokitika to start my work officially, she had made more friends and got involved with the local playcentre. We set about building a more permanent chook house, with the help of Kevin, a long-time Seaview resident who suffered terribly from a cripplingly low self-esteem and chronic anxiety. He would retreat to the asylum for periods of rest, in between roaming the night and climbing to the top of giant metal power pylons. Today it would be unethical to have a patient come to your home and work for you without pay, but then it was common for the patients in this small town to mix and mingle. For some, Seaview was both home and refuge. We fed Kevin and treated him like one of us; it was a sense of family

Konvulsator electroconvulsive 'therapy' (ECT) apparatus in use in the 1970s and '80s.
Erlend Bjørtvedt (CC-BY-SA), Wikipedia Commons

that he lacked and never found, but for a moment, we were dependent on each other and so equals.

He will be dead now, almost certainly, along with the lost tribe of the abandoned and unloved who still populated the psychiatric gulags of the mental health system in the 1970s. This was especially true in 'dumping ground' facilities like Seaview, where many — having lost contact with their families, shut away into madness over the previous thirty or forty years — had been ghosted from other more crowded institutions like Seacliff, a Gothic horror twenty miles north of Dunedin. This house of pain was granted literary immortality through the pen of one of its better-known residents and almost victims — Janet Frame. I was discussing with Wattie Campbell, the head nurse, my recent reading of her novel *Owls Do Cry*, when he proudly affirmed that he had "nursed" her in Seacliff — neglecting to mention how close she had come to being lobotomised while in the darkness of the gulag.

I was reading books recommended to me by some of my tutors back in Tiromoana: a kind of anti-psychiatry brew including Thomas Szasz, the radical Hungarian psychiatrist known for such provocative works as *The Manufacture of Madness* and *The Myth of Mental Illness*. With my deep distrust of authority, this iconoclastic stuff was meat and drink. Instead of inculcating myself with therapeutic models of psychiatric normality, I was more likely to be reading *If You Meet The Buddha on the Road, Kill Him!*, Sheldon Kopp's book about the pilgrimage of the psychotherapy patient. Kopp was eminently quotable, as in "All of the significant battles are waged within the self." I was as much in need of help as any of the patients, while at the same time at war with the system I was serving. All that was required was that I would meet my nemesis: a figure who would arrive and blow my cover, reduce me to a mutual level of nakedness and drive me back into whatever primal calling it might be that I was avoiding: Lear and his Fool, twice over. It wasn't long before he appeared: bipolar, wild as his beard and shock of black hair — the brilliant West Coast jade carver Bill Mathieson, who would unmask me as surely as the extremes of feeling and chemical surges were doing to him.

Bill Mathieson: jade carver, artist, explorer, 1980s.
Image © Te Papa MA_1320049

21

Thai Buddha, New Zealand Green

Complete with my three months of training and a bright new Honda Civic that in those days was the closest thing a government employee could get to driving a sports car, I was set loose to visit those discharged and their families, to "support the patient in the community". This was in the era when — as a reaction to the downsides of long-term institutionalisation — care in the community was the rising catch-cry. Seaview, as a large employer and a vital link in the town's economy, was not the most likely to embrace these changes. Possessed of sufficient zeal and an early dose of programming from my alcoholic family, I climbed into the white Honda and sped off to Reefton, Greymouth, Ross, Harihari and Karamea to do my home visits.

It worked like this: one of the doctors would call me in and give me the background of the patient ('clients', in our social work culture, I'd been told in Wellington). Sometimes it would mean a visit to the family to interview them at home; more often a call on someone recently discharged. I was a cross between a spy and a priest: checking out the home environment and its inhabitants for any signs of contributing factors to the patient's problem, right through to hearing confessions, with no power to absolve anyone. A typical case was in my follow-up visit to a patient in Karamea, when I was advised to check in with the local GP before calling at the patient's home. The GP turned out to be a locum, the radical psychotherapist Jack Ballin who was slowly dying of cancer. He had gone to this northern outpost of the hospital board's range to pursue his fascination with native plants, especially ferns, doctoring on the side as he declined to inevitable death.

Jack had visited the family himself and had made his own diagnosis: she wasn't the problem, he was, the husband who sat through the entire visit reading *Time* magazine. I was wasting my time, it seemed, as the real patient was not open to treatment. As Jack was giving me his considered opinion and regaling me with tales of his group therapy sessions in Sydney — "People would jump out of the windows to avoid the truth" — he was showing me around the rare miniature ferns in his greenhouse and sizing me up. As we wandered outside to the car, he looked at me and said, "You know, when you walked in here, I thought, this man's a façade. But I was wrong, you're a bloody charade!" With that deathless diagnosis, he turned away and left me to make of it whatever I willed. He was right. I was putting on a false face to the world, pretending to be somebody I wasn't. I was an addict, playing out my role as helper when I needed the help myself. Jack Ballin's well-aimed arrow stuck in my heart and stayed there until I was ready to do something about it. He died a few months later, having set me up for a meeting that was to blow me out of the water and out of social work.

Bill Mathieson came across my path as a routine follow-up assignment from Dr Desaram, the tall Sri Lankan GP based at Seaview to gain psychiatric experience. A delightful man not averse to sharing his own stories of encounters with drugs, I will never forget his tale of life as medical student in Ceylon when his flatmate would concoct a delicious meat dish that always left his fellow students feeling mellow. "Ganja, Jeffrey!" he chuckled, "He was spicing our meat with ganja!" I stopped short of telling him I was smoking as much as I could get. It was hard to crack down on the trade in his home country, he told me, as the growers hid their plots deep in the jungle where the police and troops would not venture. Why not, I asked? "Tigers, Jeffrey, tigers!" If only he'd known what jungle he was sending me into.

Bill was one of the country's finest jade carvers, a prolific genius who had learned his trade alongside those who had begun the revival of interest in working this stone so precious in Maori culture. Named pounamu by tangata whenua, it was abundant on this thin strip of coast that had always drawn those who admired its strength and lustre. For Bill, an incident where a horse was run into and killed on the road near the motel in Paroa managed by his wife Pam, triggered a psychotic reaction; for the next many years, he would be in and out of hospital, hounded by a bipolar personality of extreme highs and lows, troubled all the way by excesses of drug and alcohol abuse that would kill him in the end. Setting out on a road to help, I ended up joining him in the clouds of home-grown marijuana, the beakers of wine that would undo me and throw me off the helper's horse.

It began so well: visits where I would sit in the South Beach Motel office with the two of them, then drive off down the road after a cuppa and chat, to make my notes for the hospital files ("Your reports read like stories," Dr Fergusson would observe, astutely; this, of course, because I was just a frustrated writer). I found myself calling in at the motel with Lee and the kids on the weekend just to say hello, breaking all the rules of professional engagement, the kinds of things I would be discussing during the week with my supervisors in Greymouth, Jean Trowland at the hospital and Alan Campbell at the Department of Social Welfare. I found that with Alan I could discuss my growing entanglement with Bill in some detail, without judgment. It didn't stop me from crossing over, as if everything in my unconscious seemed pre-programmed to identify with the brokenness in people I met, to revolt against rulers — and seek relief in the herbs of oblivion. It was a short step from visiting him to sharing the herb and smoking dope together.

That's how it is: you're talking, having a drink, a pleasant time, when somebody pulls out the weed and there's a decision to make. For me back then, it wasn't hard. To say no would have put me on the other side (the side that was paying me, the side critiqued by people like Szasz and Kopp and Alan Watts and other writers I was devouring in my search for meaning). The other side was the authority figures of this world: the power brokers, the ones who could drug you and lock you up, who could shoot jolts of electricity through your brain, all jailers and healers together. Better to choose your own poison, your escape.

As the joints were lit, the familiar departure from the comforts of reason began afresh: the THC took me away from all of that into thought trains which jumped the rails, sentences that trailed off, backtracking and backtracking on the backtracking, until there was no clue at all as to where you had begun, the people with you losing track too, laughing and crying out of nowhere, hunting for something sweet. I wasn't a social worker any more; it's taken until I wrote this paragraph right now to see it with such clarity. Jack Ballin's words were coming true, the mask was slipping and I was on the road to something else entirely.

The day the line was crossed began with a visit to the motel to see how Bill was doing; finding him not at home, Pam asked me in to wait, he was expected soon. We were chatting over tea when Bill's white Cortina raced in, braked to a halt, the door blew open and there he was wearing only brown roll-up pants and flashing a machete. His hair was wild, his eyes were wilder, it was scarily filmic: "The cops are coming! He dobbed me in! We have to get rid of the dope!" he declared, then turned and fled. Not knowing what else to do, I followed; I knew he wasn't a danger to me, as it all became instinctive. He'd gone to the greenhouse at the end of the motels, uprooting plant after plant in a frenzy, stuffing them into a large suitcase. When every bucket was empty, he looked and me and demanded, "Well, Mr Holman, what do we do with all these?"

Without thinking, I said, "Put them in my car, they won't be looking there!"

The consequences of my being found in a West Coast Hospital Board car with a bootload of marijuana stuffed into a large green suitcase were not to be entertained — I just did it. He was in trouble, I was helping; it was all in the moment, swept away by his paranoia and my need for acceptance. I told him I'd hide the dope at home and he could come and pick it up later. To avoid the oncoming police raid, I sped south to the hospital, slowly sobering up and wondering what kind of corner I'd painted myself into. There was no turning back. I wasn't quite *Fear and Loathing in Las Vegas*, but it had that potential.

The police never arrived; there were no police coming, except in Bill's fevered mind. Nobody had dobbed him in, he was in the grip of his own extremities. He turned up a few days later at our house in Sale Street, and saw how much I had helped myself to the dope, as instructed when I left him. "My god, Mr Holman," he cried in mock horror. "You've been very generous to yourself!" We lit up, drifted away and departed normality. When he was flying high there was no rest for Bill; he left, reversing down the driveway as fast as that poor Cortina could travel backwards.

Many roads criss-crossed over the next two years: old friends came back into my life, new people arrived, more booze and dope, more Bob Dylan albums that soundtracked the intensity of the booming surf on the dangerous beaches, fossicking up on Blue Spur for Chinese ginger jars left behind in the bush by long-dead miners, and of course, the unresolved issues in our relationship and each other, masked by a drug intake that kept us both wrong-footed. I'd crossed the line so many times in my work that it was only a matter of when something would blow.

Two things happened: Bill was admitted for another spell under lock and key and I decided it was time to move on and look elsewhere. A 'geographical' is what alkies call it, when the pressures of addiction and its consequences persuade the user that a change of scenery is required.

Bill's wife Pam was visiting him in one of the secure villas at Seaview when he wriggled out of the toilet window, hotwired their car and headed north to Greymouth. When we realised he'd made a run for it, I rushed to the rescue and found him on the bed back at the motel in Paroa, spouting random chunks of César Vallejo from a book I'd loaned him. "The secret of the universe, Mr Holman!" he declared, waving the poetry at me, a naked West Coast William Blake, mad with knowledge and desire, as if he was staring into the atomic core of DNA. "The secret of the universe!" I heard a noise at the door and two policemen entered quietly and stood there, regarding the two of us. "It's okay, he's not hurting anybody," I reassured them, not quite knowing what Bill might do next. They wrapped him in a blanket and with the two of us in the back of a Holden, drove us down to Seaview. On the way, I told him a story about tigers and strawberries that I'd read in a book by Alan Watts, the Zen philosopher and one-time priest.

A man is walking along beside a cliff above the sea and suddenly two tigers appear and charge; he's trapped. He looks over the edge and sees an old tree root extending, so he scrabbles down and grabs it. The tigers, enraged, loom above and swipe at him but can't quite connect. He waits, hoping they'll get bored and leave; suddenly, the root lurches and begins to work loose. He can still climb back up but the tigers await; he looks around and sees something else growing on the cliff face — wild strawberries. The root loosens some more, a spray of gravel spills down the cliff face to the rocks below. He has a choice: fall to his death when the root gives way, or reach for the strawberries, letting go of his grip on life. What does he do, I asked Bill in his handcuffed poetry-saturated pounamu-shattering bipolar world — what does he do?

Given Bill's nature, a grab for the strawberries would be fitting. He was a man pursued by tigers, a shooting star of profound beauty, out of control and burning up.

I'd had enough. I had to escape from myself. I applied for a job at Waikato Hospital, flew up there, did the interview and got accepted — again. I must have brought off the charade well: I was way sicker than at the Seaview interview two years earlier back in 1974, but they liked me. Back in Hokitika we made our plans to move. Lee was happy, as she would be nearer to her family in Tauranga and the grandparents would see more of the kids. We were invited to a farewell party by some friends, just us; halfway through, half cut, I drove home and picked up some more music and had the brainwave of collecting a female friend on the way and taking her back to join us.

Wrong move: Lee was not pleased and the atmosphere chilled. When we got home and fought about it, I threw my hands in the air and wrote a letter to Waikato saying I'd changed my mind about the job. The underlying instability that I was masking, by playing the role I'd learned at my mother's side, was showing its cracks. So, there we were, having resigned my job, given notice on the house, with nowhere obvious to go and nothing to do. Lee was going to leave me and I'd run out of answers about what came next. My mother had been living in a bach up the Coast Road at Punakaiki; right at that point, her application for a state house unit came through and she was moving into Cobden, near Greymouth. I talked my way back into reality and we managed to persuade Mum's landlord to give us the bach. Instead of the shift north on promotion and access to an urban world, the next move found the five of us and the dog crammed into a tiny holiday home surrounded by nikau palms, musicked by the eternal sea, and a welcoming community of marijuana-laden hippies. No job, no prospects and no plan: welcome to mañana.

Lee with Bill Mathieson with the kids, Punakaiki, 1977.

22

Death is a shepherd

People we knew, and others we were meeting for the first time, began to turn up and embrace us; locals gave us vegetables and others brought whisky and books. We took walks on the beach, met up with Bill again once he'd been discharged. I felt huge relief that I was once again unmoored. That couldn't go on forever, though; another old client from my Seaview days gave me a part-time job in his toy factory in a back street of Greymouth at the Holy City. This was the old Catholic working-class area near to where my mum had moved when we got her out of Blackball and my father's influence, ten years gone. Two nights a week I would stay with her in Cobden and work for David, making parts for his steam trains and talking about life, anxieties, drugs and whatever else crossed our minds. In an ironic reversal, I was being nursed in my dark valley by the people I had been paid to help. It was salutary, a proof that we're never far from falling, Dylan's "How does it feel, to be on your own, a complete unknown, like a rolling stone?" ringing always somewhere in the echoes of my mind.

We got the kids into the school at Barrytown and spent more time around my youngest sister Beth and her husband Ron on their nearby farm. I picked up some shearing with a hippie farmer from up the Coast and slowly we reintegrated, got back onto some kind of level. My train-maker employer David had a cousin in Dunollie with a house to rent nearer to town, so we packed up and moved again. No 54 Herd Street was an old miner's cottage, built over a one-time rail line to a long-closed mine; you could unearth fine chips of coal by digging in the garden. I was back in my Blackball world, this time with the benefit of THC to calm my system. Bill would turn up with hard-nosed drug dealers and share Thai Buddha sticks thick with seeds that popped as they burned. I'm sure now it was laced with something else, and it knocked me over more than once. They drove a big brutal American car and there were whispers of weapons in the boot. Pleasant as our situation might have looked, it was still thin ice.

Raine and Lee, Nile River Festival, 1978.

The landlord came to collect the rent one time and noticed what we were growing in the garden among the carrots and peas. It wasn't long before a surprise police raid announced itself on a weekend we had friends visiting, out in the back garden on the hill drinking and spliffing up. A police Land Rover hurtled up Herd Street spewing dust, overshot our address and reversed madly back our way. We had plenty of time to pick up the young plants in their buckets and throw them all into the overgrown section next door. "Who, me?" was all the police could get out of us, so they left grumpy after searching the house. I figured it was time to look elsewhere, and maybe buy a place. We found a cheap alternative, a dilapidated deceased estate for sale in Runanga, just around the corner at 9 Walker Street. In the last days of State Advances loans and the capitalisation of the Family Benefit, we were able to buy a house for $6500 and move in. As I left Herd Street I stole the landlord's copy of Robbie Burns' poetry, just to show him he couldn't get away with dobbing me in.

The house had belonged to a widow whose life had been tragic: bashed by her alcoholic husband, she had seen her son jailed for shooting his sister, mistaking her for the drunken abuser as he lay in wait for his father behind the door. On a late-night trip home from the pub, wandering down the railway line, the old man was later killed by a train. To some it was a house of horrors, but to us, shelter from the storm. Yes, it needed a new roof, the paint was peeling, the grass knee-high, the coal range in the kitchen rusted out from roof leaks; there was a toilet in one of the front bedrooms, the closest point to the sewage system down the hill in the cul-de-sac. The old outside dunny, rendered obsolete by this modern amenity, was full to the gunwales with empty bottles, as was the shed. We set to work to make it livable and I talked my way back into another white-collar job in social work, needful by now of a steady income.

Alan Campbell, my old supervisor from Seaview days, wanted to run social work training for community volunteers in the Department of Social Welfare in Greymouth, so I was given a part-time job. Back in a collar and tie it felt weird, but I did my best to readjust. I was in the government building there in May 1978 when the latest news, gossiped and tutted over around the tea trolley, concerned troublesome "Maori radicals" up in Auckland. A peacetime army of over 800 police and soldiers had forcibly removed the Maori occupiers and their supporters at Bastion Point, citizens protesting the proposed private sale of land gifted to government in the 1880s. This was early in the Muldoon era and there was little sympathy among my colleagues for the protesters. I hated the way clients of the agency were often disparaged. It wasn't the most promising career move, and our involvement with the local foster home was also unfortunate. Lee took issue with the way some of the kids were being handled, when we had no mandate to say anything.

We were trying to straddle two cultures, two changing views of the world, where statutory authority and idealism collided. Lee had a magic instinct for attracting and identifying with broken-winged seagulls, both of us in the wrong place for maybe the right reasons. We were both using alcohol — and in my case, plenty of marijuana — to medicinal effect. Given our personalities, it was a volatile combination. A few years earlier, Dylan had sung in 'Tangled Up in Blue' that "when finally, the bottom fell out, [he] became withdrawn" — my tactic exactly, passive aggression I'd learned from my mother. It blew up in my face on Queen's Birthday weekend that June. After a gathering up the Coast Road on a Sunday where the wine flowed and the herb was inhaled, we arrived back home in Runanga drunk and still stoned and argued over something trivial. I said enough to enrage Lee, who walked to the bedroom, packed a suitcase and drove away into the winter's night. It was happening, she was leaving. I just froze.

The 5th of June 1978 is a day that has never left me. Overnight, Lee had taken off for Christchurch in our old Austin van, driving the Otira-Arthur's Pass road at the most dangerous time of the year. The van hit black ice not far from Aickens: she lost control, left the road, was thrown out and killed. Early after daybreak the accident was discovered and by 8 a.m. there was a knock on our front door and two policemen on the step. They broke the bad news and asked if I could go with them to the hospital mortuary and confirm it was Lee. They were kind, firm, respectful, deserving of compassion themselves in their grim work of announcing doom.

We had a friend staying who offered to look after the kids and I rang my mother, asking her to come as well. I entered that shock zone where a cushion of unreality surrounds us and the moment becomes all there is, swamped by chemical waves of emotion that will return as grief in the hours and days and years ahead. The dead are different: they are no longer us, they are them — it was her and not her. Somewhere beside that icy road under the gaze of the stars, that animating magic Lee possessed had left her. I had seen death before, seen my father die, but this was different. My life changed in the moment the sheet was lifted from her face. Her death stared back at me, as if I was seeing a vision of my own end. There was no way to reply, for either of us.

The next few hours and days live on as a series of stories: there was shock and there were tears, but you can't truly describe grief and mourning. We can only feel it: it is embodied, it is anything but words, it shakes and trembles our whole being, which is why the bodily embrace of the bereaved one is the only useful resort of the comforter. I was hugged and held, as were our children: many people came to the house to mourn with us, themselves in shock and in need of comfort. Family, friends, Lee's parents, brother and sister, her ex-husband, my first wife Theresa — and of course, Bill Mathieson. Our friendship had survived my defection from the mental hospital culture and he was at my side quickly, stricken in his own deep way. My co-workers from Social Welfare appeared too, letting me know I was off duty on full pay. I would never return.

In conversation with the funeral director, we clothed Lee for her final days in our sight with a long black dress I had bought for her, outlined with poppies. As she lay in state like a queen of Egypt, you could be forgiven for thinking the dress was chosen for that moment. On the day of the funeral service, the undertakers brought her in the morning to the house; we carried the coffin up the steep path and placed it in the sitting room where all and any could come for the remaining hours and make their peace and farewells. Funerals can be wildly eclectic gatherings, bringing together people from all times, places and cultures on life's journey. This one was no exception, with everyone from a conservative Christchurch accountant, Lee's parents from the Depression and Second World War generation, right through to dreadlocked alternative lifestyle veterans straight out of *The Whole Earth Catalogue*, reading and chanting over the open coffin from *The Tibetan Book of the Dead*.

I wasn't of a mind to shield our three children from the reality and they were all able to see their dead mother, albeit privately. It is something I have learned long since: Maori navigate this passage from life to death with far greater wisdom and skill than Pakeha, in the ritual of the tangi. Kids are included here, learning that death happens in life and is part of the process. Not all of those around me approved my handling of Lee's departure, but I followed what I felt was human need. I had made contact with an old Anglican minister from my childhood, Les Morris, the man who had paid my dad's gambling debt in 1955 to shorten his prison sentence. He'd been a padre at Seaview while I was there and we'd reconnected; a phone call to Christchurch and he was on his way. He took the service in the packed funeral parlour, leaning down to me in the front row and repeating, "Look up, Jeffrey, look up!"

Bill was among the mourners too, along with Theresa. Overcome with emotion he was laughing, apparently, giving others reason to wonder what the joke was. Overcome, it was just his way of grieving. It poured at the cemetery as we hugged each other beside the grave. Back at the house in Runanga, the locals had come in to help with food and drinks and my family were there too, looking after the children. The house divided itself pretty much along cultural lines: mainstream and alternative, the former down the back in the kitchen, the latter in the lounge up the front, legal drugs and suits at one end, ganja and Bob Marley braids at the other. Lee's family and her ex-husband, in their own world of shock, were unlikely to mingle intimately with people living along the Coast road on the proceeds of pottery and weaving. I shuttled between my adopted tribes and tried to keep myself together.

Copious amount of ganja lit up at the front of the house. I had to run around telling my hippie spliffers to cut it out. I had good reason for not wanting my suitability as a parent to be questioned. In the end, I left them all to it and went for a drive down to the beach at Rapahoe. It was Bill Mathieson who got hold of me that night and told me straight I needed to

Logan Baty

mend my fences, then and there, in the loss of my fiery lover who he too had loved. He knew it was possible to love more than one person at the same time, to love many; he knew it because that was how he was. He was pointing out to me that Theresa was there, she had come out of love into the eye of the storm.

When I saw Lee dead in the Grey
Hospital morgue, was she pounamu
on the beach because
the broken wave was spent? No matter
how long or how hard I'd held her
she'd never warm to me the way
this jade heats up in my grip.

Lay it back on the desk
and it keeps what's left
of my touch for near ten minutes.
The woman I loved lay stiff
when I kissed her brow, cold
as the frost she skidded over
into the broken-backed abyss.

('Holding Pounamu', from *As Big as a Father*, 2002.)

Lee's headstone, Karoro cemetery, Greymouth.

23

At the Jordan

For the second time in my life I was a solo father, this time with three children one of whom was subject to a custody dispute. Before he left after the funeral, Lee's ex-husband Ian asked when he could take his son to live with him, now the boy's mother was dead. I told him that wasn't going to happen — she had expressed the wish in her will for me to retain custody. His response, naturally, was, "I'll see you in court." It was hardly the best start to dealing with three grieving children who had lost a mother, while daily surviving in my own sea of feelings. Having to care for others, especially children, after a death is a blessing of sorts. You have to keep going and retain a sense of daily life in the midst of death's unreality. I gathered them to me and, with the help of family and friends, navigated the early days.

Once alone, I was ambushed again and again by grief: overcome in the middle of doing the dishes or hanging the washing in the back yard. In the evenings, after I'd put the kids to bed, surrounded with images of Lee in the front room, a coal fire burning and incense curling, I would medicate myself with wine and marijuana until sleep gave relief. Friends would come and help: some would stay over, cars were loaned and even given. Two friends from Hokitika arrived with a 1962 Rover 100 and gave me the keys; he owned a garage, she had been one of Lee's close friends. "Pay me when you can," was the response to my protests. Abel, a Coast Road friend raised upright by his evangelical family, arrived with his truck and helped me get a load of coal in from a local private mine; then making tea laced with ganja, keeping an eye on me, he poured out his own troubles.

I had a wad of cash people had slipped my way over the time of the funeral: that West Coast habit especially in mining communities of making sure there was something to tide a family over in death and disaster. They were well acquainted with mortality, these people, the men facing dangers every day underground, the women living with threat of accidents, injuries and worse. I was a newbie in Runanga, regarded by some locals with suspicion. The knowledge of my Dunollie dope-growing habits would have done the rounds, but when it came to a neighbour

Raine, Lex and Timothy, with Oats, Punakaiki, 1977.

losing a loved one, they rallied to my aid. I was on a sickness benefit at first and then managed to pick up some shearing here and there; later in the year, occasional work came on the Greymouth wharf unloading the tuna boats when the season opened. The case with Ian went on: lawyer's letters, my contacts with Social Welfare and social workers assuring me I had a good chance of retaining custody. My genius for getting myself into unplanned and unscripted situations was alive and well.

With the boys back in school, I was taking my daughter to the local Playcentre, and ended up on the committee. The hardened wives of the miners looked askance to begin with, but slowly they accepted me; not so much their husbands and sons, I'm sure. I would cycle through the twinned villages with my untamed hair and multi-coloured kaftan flowing in the breeze, carrying my precious cargo in a child seat behind me. I can still see the faces of the men in the miners' bus passing me one day on their way to the afternoon shift as I rode home: not amazed, not even hostile, just dumbfounded at whoever, whatever it was that had come among them. Miners tend to be conservative when it comes to daily life on the surface, radical when lives matter underground. I was a weird anomaly.

The small-town mind had shown its hand in 1974 when the Kirk Labour government, in an attempt to domesticate the counter-culture, had gazetted areas of marginal land in the Ohu Project. The state would support certain community groups — communes — to farm these areas. A kind of homegrown kibbutz scheme, ohu had a poor survival rate, falling foul of local authorities and bylaws, Runanga being no exception. A plan to site one on the scrub land north of the rail line near Rapahoe met with strong opposition from the mayor and the council, with fears of an infection in the borough by the drug culture that would surely accompany such a close proximity of taxpayer-funded hippies. Whatever it was those miners saw when they looked out of the window of their bus at me, it was not an especially welcome sight, not least because of the gender politics

Rescue Service miners, Strongman Mine Disaster, 1967.
Les Holmes, artist

that were radically changing the urban centres of New Zealand at this time, leaving areas like the West Coast and its tough miners, sawmillers and fisherman mostly unmoved.

Out of time and out of place, I tried to find both, often on days when I wasn't sure any more what made sense or where to go next. Trying to keep up a conversation as the year rolled on, I was writing to the Gosdens, Lee's parents, people I barely knew, having met them only once before she died. They had been left out of any discussion about where their daughter might be buried or how the occasion was managed; having driven all the way down from Tauranga after getting the terrible news, they were as numb as I was. I wanted to include them in what was happening and how the kids were doing, but it was like writing to strangers. Lee's mother replied graciously but we were all still in shock: their Carole was gone and there was no redress. The woman I knew as Lee was someone they had seen little of after she left home and married Ian. After that marriage broke down, and in her involvement with me, she was moving in another world.

I was also writing to Theresa; as well as caring for the Gosdens' grandchildren, I was caring for our son. If you had wanted to design a complicated set of relationships to deal with, in the midst of the grieving process, this would have been a good place to start. I owed fealty to the dead and the living: what Lee would have wanted, what the other parent and grandparents needed, what I needed and most of all, what was right and good for the children, one four and two seven-year-olds, vulnerable and dependent on whatever choices I might make. My mother would come and spend weekends helping and supporting me but there was no way her surrogacy could make up for their loss. Lee was an active and committed mother and her sudden dramatic absence was a deep wound in their lives.

I found myself writing to Theresa weekly, needing to talk to somebody who I trusted despite our earlier falling-out, who cared about me and the children. Within the year, she had come back to the Coast and moved in. Not all of our friends approved but I was past caring, more than a little deranged with grief and guilt. I hadn't given up on dope, having installed a hydroponic nursery of plants in our roof. I would circle outside the house in the dark, checking if the lights that were hot-housing my little plot of green were shining out through the eaves and the rust spots in the weathered iron roof. I was paranoid. Smoking the herb that had contributed to my bust-up with Lee, I was still lacking any real insight into my troubles.

What happened next was a bolt from beyond: an old friend of Theresa's got in touch and came to visit. He'd been down to the bottom with a bad drug habit and now, like a new man, he was changed: born again. I offered him a joint but he wasn't taking; lit up within by another magic, he was definitely not the same man, and put it all down to becoming a Christian. We talked and asked him questions, what had happened to him and how come he'd made this U-turn. We'd had another old friend from student days visit recently and she had made the same commitment to this Jesus that I'd long ago given up on.

Yes, I respected Jesus Christ as a kind of sage and martyr but had no real belief that he was relevant to me, or that humanity was salvageable by divine intervention. There was too much evidence to the contrary and yet, this guy was different: kinder, more considerate and humble than I'd known him to be before. He was working for Radio Rhema, the Christian radio station in Christchurch, and he said he knew a few people who could answer the questions we fired at him. He'd put us in touch if we wanted to know more. After he left, I just went back to my Dylan records and my diet of ganja — the *Street Legal* album had just come out and was getting a thrashing. But the visit had affected me.

The sequence of events is hazy now, but we discussed the Holy Spirit, after references to the third person of the Trinity kept leaping out of the New Testament which Theresa had begun reading again. Some of the conversations I'd had with our born-again friend came back at me, like the cost of following Jesus. According to him, it meant everything. One night soon after he'd gone I found myself in the bedroom on my knees, talking to a God I hardly believed was there, in a prayer that included the less than trusting words, "… if you're there". The Methodist preacher Charles Wesley once wrote that he had been "strangely warmed" as he read Martin Luther's preface to St Paul's Letter to the Romans, at a moment when the Holy Spirit opened his heart and walked right in. With me it was as if a net of stones was slowly lifted off my shoulders and I stood upright; that old knot in my gut broke loose in a mysterious flood of peace. I can't call

I got down on my knees and prayed to Jesus.

On my knees to Jesus: Nick Williamson, artist, 2017. BELOW Church door, interior, St Anastasia, Verona (detail), 2013.

it less than that, the moment when I finally knelt and invited this Jesus in.

The effects were almost immediate and quite unbelievable: I hadn't expected anything, but underneath it all, I was desperate. Lee's death had left me naked on the shore without an answer; death — remorseless and impassive — had beaten me up and walked away. I believe now that what I experienced in that encounter was the power of Jesus' resurrection from the dead. When I submitted myself by faith like the thief on the cross, I was raised with Jesus, on the third day.

Theology, like history, is retrospective; but as this was happening, in the moment I wasn't analysing anything. This is the problem today for a beloved atheist friend who analyses everything and explains away my "culturally conditioned psychological experience" as something that lets me believe in a fairy tale akin to teapots orbiting Mars. Reason revolts at the resurrection, and why not? Even St Paul writes of the foolishness of God and the cross. All I can say is that since then, the reality of the One I met on my knees that night has been borne out in subsequent experience and all the trials of life.

I walked out of that room smiling; it wasn't long before we were both on the same hymn sheet, as Theresa had been making her own journey of faith. We broke open the Bible and started to read the New Testament again; suddenly, the literary creation of Jesus in the book began to walk off the pages, speaking to both of us, as if He were in the room, inside our heads. The cross made sense now, the resurrection and all that followed; it explained why, a few weeks earlier when we'd driven to Christchurch and ended up in the back row of a cinema watching *Jesus of Nazareth*. As Robert Powell playing Jesus hung on the cross and Anne Bancroft as Mary Magdalene wept with his mother Mary below, we ended up weeping too, as if we'd lost a family member. The Hound of Heaven had tracked us down and nothing now would be the same.

Most conversion stories end up in the loop of Christian-to-Christian: Christian bookshops, songs and testimonies, the newly converted speaking to the long-time believers. Yes, in the orbit of secular literature, we have Augustine's *Confessions* (the first modern memoir), Dante's *Divine Comedy* along with Donne's poetry and sermons, C.S. Lewis's *Surprised by Joy*, works known and read by many of those outside the churches. For the most part though, my bet is that in the minds of those with no experience of such events, the image of what I'm about to relate is redolent of cults, brainwashing, the harvesting of weak-minded, gullible recruits by persistent doorknockers like the Jehovah's Witnesses. This was not my experience. At the moment I knelt, I was still as against Christ as Saul on his horse, riding off to Damascus to arrest and kill any Jews there who had decided to follow this Jesus. The book of the Acts of the Apostles tells us how God knocked him off his steed, blinding him with light. As St Paul he would change the entire trajectory of Western history.

Converted around the same time, Bob Dylan was singing on *Slow Train Coming*, the album that cost him wave upon wave of former fans, "I'm gonna change my way of thinking, get myself a different set of rules." He was used to defections when jumping ship; for me, it was a joy to think my hero was on the same road. Making that record, he drove the Nashville album producer Jewish atheist Jerry Wexler mad with his constant chat about Messiah, until Jerry told him to leave it out. But that's what happens. You can't keep it in. Neither did I, and the effects were obvious: like the Man said, "I come not with peace, I come with a sword." Some people listened to my ravings, others ran a mile (I don't blame them). I felt I'd been saved from drowning and thought — naively, it's true — that people would be happy for me and would want some of the same.

I went to see my mother and declared, "I've found Jesus!" — at which she replied, bless her, "That's lovely, dear, I've always thought you'd go into the church." I had to put her right, "No, Mum, it's not that, I've been saved, I've met the Lord, it's got nothing to do with churches or buildings." From long practice, she humoured me (I was known to her as an enthusiast, in my various past manifestations). But she could see the changes happening in my life.

My brother and his partner were next to hear the good news. He came around to see me and I declared my new-found faith. As we talked I recalled the stash of marijuana I had hidden in the house (we'd smartly removed the plants from the roof). I grabbed the plastic bag and threw the weed into the fire. Eric nearly leapt in after it. "You could have given it to me!" he groaned.

"If it's bad for me, it's bad for you, brother," I told him. He shook his head. Was his brother going mad? He wasn't convinced I'd made the right move, but his partner Bev was. She was coming around and joining our nightly Bible studies, when we sat down after tea and pored over my grandmother's ancient King James version. Bev gave her heart to Jesus and Eric wasn't far behind.

Next came a friend who lived across the road and within the month, my mother. We were on the cusp of a revival, one of those series of moments when an individual, or small groups of people — often well outside the established churches — are overtaken by undeniable experiences of God's presence in their lives and things happen, hearts are changed. Whole communities can be revolutionised at times like this, as it was in the beginning of the early church. One sign is that consciences are daily tweaked by past wrongs needing righting. In my case, it meant finding the address of my former landlord in Herd Street and returning that copy of Burns's poems I'd nicked from him, with a written apology and an explanation of why I'd had a change of heart. The news was travelling around the town: the hippies were into some crazy stuff and the proof was, they'd killed all their chickens.

That much was true, in part: we had hens in the back yard and a rooster that in the early hours drove mad those living next door. He was indeed sacrificed, not in any blood rite, but as a result of our awakened conscience: love thy neighbour, as it is written. There followed a whole host of changes (some of which were extreme), a cleansing of the stables: books, records, Buddhas, anything that seemed inimical to faith in Jesus and associated with idols was doomed. The *I-Ching* and the sticks I'd thrown with Bill and other friends from the counter-culture ended up in the fire. We were serious.

I was serious too about my responsibilities towards my children, especially Lex. The legal challenge from his father hung over us and I was deeply troubled about my position. I was now the guardian of another man's child and he had both legal and moral right to dispute this. We had been together as a family for five years and Lex was now a son to me, as was my own boy; my daughter was his sister. Theresa and I talked and prayed over what was the right thing to do. Unexpectedly, with blinding clarity, it came to me — Lex had to go back to the father who had kept up their relationship with regular contact over those years. It was the hardest decision I had ever made. There are no winners in a situation like this and I would not wish the same choice on anyone. I broke up my family and we drove Lex over to Christchurch to be with his father, leaving him there with our own heartbreak and that of our two children. He had lost a mother, a brother, a sister, a whole family in the space of a year.

The next thing I needed to do was to get a job and stand on my own two feet again; it was time to get off the sickness benefit. I went down to the wharf and asked about getting something more permanent than the seasonal work unloading the tuna boats I'd dabbled with earlier — and they took me on. For the next two years I was a knifehand, forklift driver and tuna chucker: cold, dangerous, monotonous at times and a million miles away from what I had ever wanted in life. For now, it was God's will that mattered and deeply, sincerely, I took this on; after all, weren't most of the early disciples fishermen?

We had some help turn up from over the hill: a teacher named Graeme Carlé and a friend arrived and before long had persuaded us that those who had repented needed to be baptised. This was nothing to do with the sprinkling of babies' heads that mainline churches offered to the believing and the unbelieving alike: this was full immersion as adults, aware we were undergoing a symbolic burial and resurrection in the plunge underwater and the lifting up again. The old life was dead, Graeme told us: the new

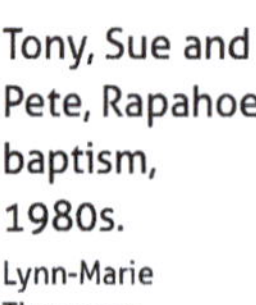

Tony, Sue and Pete, Rapahoe baptism, 1980s.
Lynn-Marie Thompson

began as we arose with the living Christ. It was there in black and white in the scriptures and we agreed; a trek through the bush behind the town to the Coal Creek Falls led us to our watery grave and one by one we went under and arose, shocked and breathless in the freezing winter waters. We sang, shivering, to a freshly learned chorus, "I have decided to follow Jesus, no turning back, no turning back!" The bridal veil of the falls cascaded behind us: it would have been hard to find a more Kiwi Jordan to have crossed.

Papatipu kissing me

Ancient rivers wake me with whispering.
They know I'm home, they call you too.
Invisible, you move beside me, sleep in my heart
like the lie of the land. I can feel my
rhythms return from beyond: we

rumble through the mountain pass,
again the suction of being born, again
the chorus of buried bones, and liturgy
graven by the weight of the stone.

I have dreamt, like a pope, of
kissing this land: papatipu, papatipu.
And now I bend to so kiss you.

Te kuku o te manawa!
The pincers of the heart!
Te kuku o te manawa!

As Big as a Father, Steele Roberts 2002

My well-worn annotated study Bible, its pages all but thumbed to death.

24

God on wheels

This was a time when I said goodbye to a few old friends and made some new ones. It wasn't unusual to see people in town cross the street when they saw me coming, in case I buttonholed them with my gospel. I went to see Bill Mathieson at the motels and gave him the news: I belonged now to Jesus. Lucid as ever, he looked me in the eye and said, "Well, Mr Holman, this is the parting of the ways!" I loved him for his honesty and his perception: he knew what this was all about. He took two pottery goblets and opened a bottle of white wine, pouring mine until the wine flowed over the rim, not stopping. "Thy cup runneth over!" he laughed, jester and sage as always. Bill would follow his own star to the end, and this symbolic act was his way of saying he understood what I was doing — but wanted no part of it. He was an extremist, and in that moment, in that mode we were one. Bill Mathieson had it all: insight, honesty and a skin too thin for this world. When he laughed he was crying: I knew that from of old, when he had sobbed uncontrollably with sounds like laughter at the funeral service for Lee.

Life developed a new rhythm: waking early, lighting the coal range, praying and reading my Bible before making porridge, mounting my Honda 50 in the dark, whizzing the few miles into Greymouth and down to the wharf for my day's work. Unloaded from the fishing boats, albacore tuna we dropped into huge vats the size of swimming pools, full of freezing saline solution. Frozen overnight, the brick-hard fish were hauled out one-by-one by hand into bins the next day, forklifted up to containers on the wharf and hurled inside until the container was full. These fish had swum all the way from Canada in their yearly feeding and breeding cycle and now, caught on lines off the West Coast of New Zealand, they were about to be shipped all the way back again to California to be canned for the US market.

It was hard yakka and no kind of rubber glove could ever keep the freezing brine of the tanks from soaking your fingers as you hauled the fish out. Nor could the woollen inner gloves keep out the cold as we picked up the rocket-shaped tuna by the tail and heaved them into the container. I sang Christian choruses as I did so, driving my mate Tom mad: "What the fuck are you so cheerful about?" He probably wanted to punch me. My shoulders ached, my hands froze, it was hard and monotonous, but it was a job. It meant I was a responsible adult again, something my drug-induced torpor over the past few years had helped me avoid. In the evenings after we'd prayed with the kids and sent them off to sleep, we would get together with a couple of newly converted friends, listen to Bible studies on tape and pore over the scriptures like bees on flowers, hungry for truth and revelation. Our Christchurch contacts had recommended books and Bible translations and given us music as well. We became the owners of a New American Standard translation on 14 July 1979, Bastille Day, a gift on the day we were remarried in the old Wesley Hall, Greymouth.

Our new friend and adviser Graeme officiated and gave us the news that there was a local Anglican vicar who was in the charismatic movement; it might be a good idea if we joined a church and avoided the dangers of becoming a sect without elders. Gingerly we took his advice, which led to a necessary, yet problematic, bonding with an older conservative cohort in the Cobden-Runanga parish where Neil Struthers served as vicar. He welcomed us aboard and we shared a couple of years in fellowship, getting involved in crusades, seminars, street preaching outside the Greymouth Town Library on Friday nights and generally living the gospel as we saw fit. Our attendance at the small Runanga church was a novelty to begin with — here come the hippies — but we soon connected with the wider community. We graduated from drug barons, and then holy rollers, to a guarded measure of respectability. There was, however, a problem: as we continued to grow and attract new members, our habit of full immersion baptism rubbed some of the older conservatives up the wrong way and we were dobbed in to the bishop in Nelson.

I was invited to meet him with Neil on a subsequent episcopal visitation, to be informed that we could no longer be permitted to 're-baptise' people. No amount of appeals to the New Testament could convince the bishop that we, as disciples, were commanded to do the same by the actual boss: Jesus. This was an old quarrel that went back to the Protestant Reformation in Europe and England, when reformers arose — Luther, Calvin and others — proclaiming the authority of the scriptures over the traditions of the church. Members of Anabaptist sects (re-baptisers) found themselves bound with ropes and thrown into rivers and down wells. So, you want to be baptised? Take that! These people took threats to their traditions seriously. We were not at all in the same danger, but we were told we could no longer carry out baptisms. The vicar sided with the bishop, and the writing was on the wall for a parting of ways, not water.

It finally came to a head over the issue of Bible studies in the home, something we had been happily doing before our Anglican link had developed. Neil started telling us what we could and could not do, which resulted in my informing him that the Lord was my shepherd, not him. It was another ongoing issue of church history: who had authority in matters of doctrine? For our fresh-faced group of the saved, it was a matter of conscience above tradition. That ended our time with the vicar telling us what to do, although we kept up relationships with many of our friends in that church.

Not long after we quit the Anglicans, we were in the home of one of the new believers, having a spontaneous session of praise and worship. Some of us spoke about what we were reading in the scriptures, and there was prayer and a shared meal. It just happened without any drama: in a mutual agreement of the like-minded the Runanga Christian Fellowship was formed, a name we gave to a network that already existed. We were re-inventing the wheel, perhaps, but we were happy to make a start and share all we had. For us, it was possible to see that the early church had grown through the demonstration of spiritual transformation, in hearts open to change, through love.

It wasn't hard to organise the hire of the local school hall and run services, which would end in shared meals. Midweek Bible studies went from house to house with new people just showing up, curious, hungry, some sticking around, some not. We took part in community outreach, like

Nile River Festival, 1980s — our free food tent.
Lynn-Marie Thompson

OPPOSITE We had fun, too: with Theresa at a rock'n'roll night at the Runanga school hall.

the time when we built a food tent out of old timber and corrugated iron at a Nile River Festival up the Coast Road. We provided free hot meals, creating the opportunity to talk with people wondering what these Jesus Freaks were doing there, giving away literature if anyone was interested. There were a few people having bad trips on whatever they'd been taking and so we became a place of refuge for people like us: outsiders, addicts, the wounded and the seekers.

Back in the town, things had changed. By early 1981, I'd had enough of life on the wharf and put my name down for a job at the post office in Greymouth. Shortly afterwards they got in touch and said the postie's job in Runanga was coming up: was I interested? Enough said, I put my name in the hat and got the job. For the next five years I would cycle around the town delivering the heavy volumes of mail that existed in those pre-internet days: talking to the locals, delivering wedding telegrams on Saturday mornings and the sad ones that spoke of a death; making friends with the lonely elderly who relied on my turning up at the same time daily to orchestrate their routines; praying over the letterboxes come rain or shine and singing the choruses that soon got me the name — almost affectionate — of 'God on Wheels'.

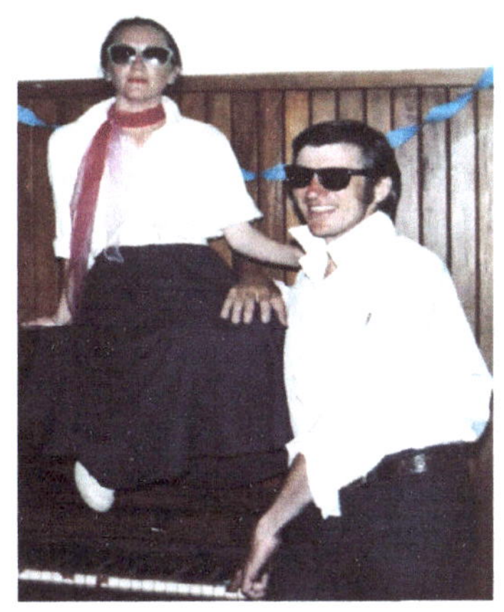

We built relationships with other Christian groups: a music ministry in Christchurch called Judah and people from Faith Family Fellowship, a group of mostly young, urban Maori and Pacific believers who would visit us and share in the life of our community, turning up for camps we organised in the old school out at Kokiri, near Stillwater. It was through this connection that we met people like Jim Doak, a psychologist and gifted teacher and Wally (Tetaki) Tairakena, a dynamic street preacher. Wally had been with Nga Tamatoa in his early days and was now working on the rubbish trucks in the morning, then every afternoon duelling with the Wizard in Square. These preaching competitions amused, befuddled and entertained the passers-by, while converting a few of the listeners. We were visited by travelling elders (Milton Smith, a former Brethren man, gone charismatic) and Roy Hood (a Congregational pastor who had become an effective social worker with a heart for all comers).

With all this help and support, caring and non-authoritarian, we got on our feet and grew: we shared what we had, sold cars and drove the ones left over, worked on each other's houses, raised money for anyone in need, got involved in the local community, took in those without a roof to call their own, helped get kids who had dropped out back into education, got into home-schooling, while some of us adopted kids and others fostered the unloved and abandoned. Our homes were open to overseas travellers: hitchhikers we picked up and gave a bed for the night; Israeli backpackers with stories of war service in Lebanon; and a Japanese cyclist who insisted on taking my picture in the postie's electric blue tracksuit of the day, quaint exotic peasants that to him we seemed to be.

We lived our faith and let the walk be the talk; this was a genuine revival of early Christian life in a West Coast backwater, as New Zealand slid slowly to the end of the Muldoon era and what was coming. These days were the last gasp of any kind of socialism, our past about to be amputated in the Götterdämmerung of Rogernomics and later, Ruthanasia. My eyes were very much on the moment, not the slipperiness of politics — it was all about change on a personal level. I was busy making friends with some of the older Runanga residents, who would stop and chat to me as I slipped the mail into their oddly assorted weather-worn letterboxes.

I slowly realised my arrival was an important part of what were often long and lonely days, especially for those living alone: the widows and widowers, the never married, the lost souls of everywhere. Thus I met Roy McGlashan, a retired miner, a single man who lived down the end of Ross Street in Dunollie in the old bach he'd built himself. Roy tinkered with his cars in a garage near the letterbox, and we got to talking. I tried bringing up the subject of Jesus and that set him off: he'd had a bad experience in a Catholic orphanage as a child and resented the nuns who had caned him. Inviting me in for a cup of tea (made with condensed milk on a table shared with the cat who scoffed his tucker beside us), Roy would produce scrapbooks filled with newspaper cuttings from *Truth* and other sources, all damning evidence of flawed popes and abusive priests. Time would reveal him as far-sighted.

Roy was one of life's walking wounded, and over the next few years we became firm friends. I stopped trying to convert him and he gave up on trying to convince me of Catholicism's perfidy. My witness to him was giving him a chance to tell somebody of the hurt he was carrying, and to be believed. I became a kind of de facto counsellor on my rounds, hearing out the gripes and troubles of many. My old social work training in listening skills stood by me and I loved hearing these stories.

One of his neighbours took to timing my trips up and down the cul-de-sac and phoned the postmaster to say how long I'd been at Roy's place. The town had a few curtain twitchers, and I was duly hauled over the coals,

Roy McGlashan, miner and friend, Punakaiki, 1967.

promising to mend my ways. When I told Roy that I couldn't come in for a cuppa on the round, he said he knew who the spy was. I told him not to get annoyed; instead I would come after work and have a chat. That was how it went thereafter: I got to hear him play his violin for me, to hear more of his heartache, and later, given the prize of any photo of him that I liked, my choice taken from an old biscuit tin full of pictures he kept under his bed. The one I picked, taken by a friend out on the Pancake Rocks at Punakaiki, would one day grace the cover of a book of my poetry (an art I'd almost lost but was beginning to rediscover).

I'd also tried without much success to interest my old teacher and writing mentor Peter Hooper in the Jesus Road; I'd continued to visit him and show him what I was writing. "Peter," I'd declared to him one day on a visit, "what I really want to be is a writer." He looked at me as if I'd missed something out. "But Jeff," he replied, "you *are* a writer!" I never forgot his patriarchal blessing; it was years before I could fully believe him, but his words were the balm of Gilead. We were also having experts in various fields come along and give home seminars to our growing fellowship — music, art, anything creative — and it struck me that Peter was an ideal choice to run a writing retreat at one of our homes, for all who cared to come.

He agreed and we met at Pete Bell's place, its large remodelled living area packed out with would-be scribes. It was a roaring success. Peter brought one the handouts he'd developed from years of teaching; he used them now with his own small private writing groups. From that one meeting in 1984, a burst of creativity in the following year produced a small booklet full of poems that we all had written in the months that followed: *Out of His Treasures*, a reference to Jesus' saying in Matthew 13:52 that "Every scribe who has become a disciple of the kingdom of heaven is like the head of a household, who brings forth out of his treasure things new and old."

Thirteen voices, including mine, appeared in this small stapled booklet, a chance to see something of ourselves in print. My contribution was 'The Retired Miner', a poem about our neighbour whose daily routine I could see from my vantage point on the hill, on days when I was off sick or on holiday and my stand-in delivered the mail.

By 8 o'clock he's limping down
to get the milk, a stranger
in the Monday morning sun.

He stops and stares
at the coal heap
and wonders what to do.

At 11 o'clock he's back
to get the mail and kick
a red ball to his old black dog.

Twelve will be dinner time:
there's no smoko this morning and
there'll be no smoko again.

A lifetime spent in the dark
and now in the light of day
the hours hang heavy.

I still have the yellowing cyclostyled printout of Peter's notes for that day: 'On Being a Writer'. They hold up today: writing about what you know and understand; comments on mood, feeling and tone; words that fit together; imagery; what happens once the first rush of inspiration runs out (editing, revision); and some helpful advice on magazine publishing. Best of all, he included a copy of a handwritten poem with revisions, then a typed copy with further changes and a request for suggestions. He was pointing to the need for craft and showing how he worked at that spindle. Peter Hooper was doing in provincial backwaters what Bill

3/4/78

It's as the Autumn came today
and lay down in the field
her empty haunches
husked of her seed
fulfilled
quiet sky wrapped her
in dove-coloured cloud
all trees were stilled
a grass-blade held its drop of rain
a single cricket piped
a silver rill
dark pines
above their sleeping boughs
within the pond
drowsed into dark.

Peter Hooper's revision exercise.

Manhire would in time parlay into a university programme and a school of letters. He was also busy writing a trilogy of novels, *A Song in the Forest* (1979), *People of the Long Water* (1985) and *Time and the Forest* (1986). I was privileged to proofread the first of these, and it was a testimony to his "craft or sullen art/Exercised in the still night" that *People of the Long Water* won a national book award in 1986.[28]

By this time there were a good many more involuntarily retired and redundant government workers making that same trip to the mailbox every day. The new Labour government, its back now turned on the class that had created it, slashed and burned their way through the debt mountain of the former Muldoon regime and began to privatise everything in the state sector that wasn't nailed down. Around that time, Theresa and I had both been reading books about the American theologian Francis Schaeffer's project after World War Two, building a community in Switzerland where the battered souls of the young could come, to question and test the relevance of faith and the very point of existence after the unspeakable horrors and inhumanity that had overtaken the world since 1939. We felt a calling to go to Europe and do there what we had seen God do for us, and with much trepidation and prayer we made enquiries about going to

Switzerland. I'd begun learning German with a friend of mine and the initial plan was to go to L'Abri (The Shelter), study with the Schaeffer community, then try and go to Germany.

Schaeffer had died the year before but his work was ongoing; we wrote to the Swiss address and were told there was another L'Abri-style community in Hampshire that would be a better option for us. We made the call to leave our newly minted world and started planning the journey. Not everybody was on board: it meant a huge wrench, selling the house and uprooting our kids again (now only two of them since Lex had long since gone back to live with his father). The brothers and sisters in the fellowship were nervous too. We'd been together for five years and, as the older members, were among the founders. We prayed and committed the journey in faith. Things began to unfold: L'Abri in England accepted our application to come for three months and we quickly found a buyer for our extensively refurbished house on the hill, the sale of which was to fund the airfares. Ken, an old friend from the fellowship and Blackball days, said he wanted to spread his wings; he signed up to come with us.

The days of March 1987 went by in a blur: I found it hard to sleep and my thinking went into an overdrive of 'What ifs?' Runanga had been a shelter, under those almighty wings spoken of in the ninety-first psalm. L'Abri in rural Hampshire was a complete unknown. Farewells began in a long succession, including a big send-off in the school hall where we'd been singing and praying and teaching for the past five years. We had a concert where anyone could do an item. As my final contribution, I dressed up in my original grey postie's uniform (a smart suit replaced in the early 1980s by a shapeless trackie that was functional but ugly). Looking like an Austrian railway porter from the turn of the century, I rode into the hall on my old red postie's bike and read my piece, a poem entitled 'God on Wheels'. I'm never going to cap that performance.

Reading 'God on Wheels' on my NZ Post bike in 1987.

Saying goodbye to the old Blackball Bridge, 1987.
Noel Saxon

25

Back to Blighty

The 'God on Wheels' poem, perhaps mercifully, has long since disappeared, but as a historical item, I wish it back; not, however, the tearing up of our roots and the long goodbyes. I made a farewell trip up the Grey Valley with a friend and stood by the gorse garden the once magnificent bridge to Blackball and its mines had become. Our tickets and passports were due to be picked up on the day we left, which made for a stressful trip over the mountains — no room for error. The passports, stamped in Wellington on 25 March 1987, were couriered to Christchurch, to be uplifted with our travel documents. That night we boarded a flight to Los Angeles, via Tahiti; the US immigration stamp on the visa entry page is for the following day, right-on-time delivery, the Japanese call it.

The tearful farewells at Christchurch were later capped with a thunderous take-off from Auckland, the shuddering DC-10 opening a few of its overhead baggage compartments as we tore down the runway and climbed into the starscape, leaving our known world behind. Tahiti was humid and uninviting on the stopover, with no time to leave the terminal while the jet refuelled and picked up more passengers. Over the long stretches above the Pacific I would look down at the ocean, scattered convoys of clouds almost stationary above the waters, and think of my father and his wars, fought over those vast turquoise tapestries of liquid light.

Los Angeles was an awful way to wake up. The meandering lines of exhausted travellers, the immigration checks, stumbling out into the foyer, getting grabbed by a taxi man who knew just the right motel nearby. Too tired to argue, we found ourselves sleeping through an all-night pool party, right under the flight path of roaring jets that began landing early at one a minute and finished late. We hired a car to see the sights; I was too wiped out to make the most of it all but we walked downtown LA, drove through Watts past African-American churches with names like Holy Fire and Temple of the Lord, and goggled at the massive portions they brought us in the diners and restaurants. Next stop was New York with our kids and Ken on the big bird, crossing a snow-spattered vista of the Rockies to the lights of Chicago and on to JFK.

Our trip on the subway to Grand Central Station and out onto a rain-drenched street, struggling with fat suitcases down to the YMCA made for another shell-shocked arrival. Awoken early again, this time by the bashing of trash trucks seven storeys down, we were up for a bite of the Apple. Our sightseeing ended when we hired car a few days later, heading north to the farm of my old friend and mentor, the poet David Walker in Freedom, Maine. Ken had arrived back from Avis with a white Chevy European and we crammed ourselves in for the 400-mile journey, darn near to Canada. Getting lost in the Bronx on the way, we fluked our exit in driving rain right onto Route 95, crashing for the night in a motel.

Stopping briefly in Boston, we pressed on into what became Maine's worst flood in decades; the spray from the big rigs passing us made it almost impossible to see the highway, as if we were driving underwater. Following maps, we made it that day at dusk to the aptly named Maine town of Waterville, only to be told the road was flooded and we'd have to take a backroad route for the next twenty miles. We got lost: it got later, darker and wetter. Coming to a crossroads, we found an old-style country store still open, with a clerk way down back under dim lights. Opening with a line somewhere between Hitchcock and Stephen King, I enquired, "We're lost, can you tell us how to find Freedom?"

His grunts and gesticulations were almost indecipherable, but I nodded my thanks and reported back to Ken the way I thought we should go. We were still driving blind. A providential turn here and a backtrack there saw us an hour later pulling into the yard of the Walker home, received with amazement by my old friend and his wife, Frances. He just couldn't get over how we had made it: "All the roads in here are flooded, we're cut off!" We couldn't explain either, exhausted and famished. Homemade spaghetti never tasted so good, then collapsing into sleep surrounded by Russian novels and Colombian poets in the book-lined loft. The next day we toured the neighbourhood, took a trip to Portland, the lobster town where Peyton Place was shot on location, and came home to a Thanksgiving turkey dinner with cranberry sauce, "A late one," Frances insisted, "to celebrate you making it here in that flood."

With David Walker, poet and teacher, Freedom, Maine, 1987.

It was hard to say goodbye after a few short days and head back to New York and our next abode: we moved to the Chelsea Hotel for the sense of proximity to vanished giants, as befits a pilgrimage. This leg of the journey included a visit to the White Horse Tavern in Greenwich Village where Dylan Thomas checked out terminally, believed then to be the effects of another heavy drinking bout; that opinion is now contested, with death likely the result of undiagnosed pneumonia. Whatever way he died, he was dead and we drank to his genius. A final fling was the tickets to the Bottom Line Club scored by Ken, with Kris Kristofferson a few feet from our seats singing protest songs about Nicaragua and the Sandinistas.

As we queued up to enter, an oceanliner-long black limo pulled up and a hunched figure slipped from a side entrance and into the car. Ken was onto it: "Hey, that was Johnny Cash!" Ken went on to write one of his best songs about that moment, the kind of glance at fame New York can so quickly give and snatch away.

We had a plane to catch the next day out at JFK, so we said goodbye to the Chelsea and its ghosts, and a weird and wonderful bunch of tenants who cooked their meals on open flames out on the balconies. We hopped the train to the airport. Next stop, Heathrow: a return to the place of

Concert ticket for the Bottom Line Club, New York, 1987.

my birth, a land of story and myth that had left me no recoverable memories at all. Whatever was waiting in London, as Dylan had sung back there somewhere, I was "blown out on the road", a prime candidate for the culture shock when imagination meets reality. That would be in the vicinity of Hackney Wick London E9, in the grim and gritty towers of the council estates waiting to greet us.

III

Age: in bed with the muse

I see myself, but from the outside.
I keep trying to feel who I was,
and cannot. Hear clearly the sound
the bucket made hitting the sides
of the stone well going down,
but never the sound of me.

— from 'Summer at Blue Creek, North Carolina' by Jack Gilbert,
in *The Dance Most of All*, Knopf, Random House, 2009 (see Endnote 16)

Manor House, L'Abri Fellowship, Greatham, Hampshire.

26

To the manor borne

Touching down late at night, burned up with travel and jetlag, we waited at Immigration while Ken was grilled on his New Zealand passport by an official who asked him why someone with 'Labourer' as an occupation would be going to a Christian community in Hampshire. Welcome to England and the class system. With our nine suitcases and his guitar case, it was off to Hackney Wick in two black cabs, one or both of which robbed us on the fares. We peered out into the darkness all the way in from Heathrow, to lights and roads and traffic with no sense of direction until we pulled up under the Colditz towers of twin council blocks on the Homerton Estate. One of our old friends from the Runanga fellowship was living in London, sub-leasing a two-bedroom flat from another Kiwi guy on an entirely illegal basis.

This is how immigrants from all over the world make landfall: one comes, more come, five, six, seven, eight, nine, ten, until rooms burst at the corners and another place is found; eventually a community builds and maybe even a ghetto. Jews from Europe filled the slums of the East End late in the 19th century; as they prospered, generations moved out to North London, Finsbury Park and other locales; families from the West Indies sailing over on the *Empire Windrush* after the Second World War were herded into a park near Brixton and spread out from there in South London. After the war in Bangladesh, refugees flooded in; from Uganda in Amin's time and later, the Kurds, wave after wave. We were one more group of hopeful pilgrims on Albion's shores.

Cups of tea made, toast and biscuits, lots of chat and heads beginning to nod, it was time to crash. God knows how Robbie fitted us all in but we were out to it in no time. Waking disoriented and drugged from wonky body clocks, we were fed and watered, taken for a stroll around the area in daylight — gray light would be a truer description. The lift on the fourth floor was broken, the rubbish chutes packed with evil-smelling stuff, the stairwell a gallery of graffiti; the atmosphere in the run-down brick tenements ominous. As we walked around Hackney, down to the corner shop to get milk and papers, many of the figures passing seemed bent and broken: sallow from lack of sunlight, sunken into themselves, like those northern wraiths the painter Lowry would introduce to me later. That was where my depression rose from its depths, in the condition V.S. Naipaul has described as the "enigma of arrival".[29]

Whatever my parents had bequeathed to me of English culture and however much Britain's media had soused my childhood and growing years with a sense of my natal land, nothing could prepare me for the shock of seeing it for the first time. What might have been for me as a two-year-old mere colours, shapes and sensations became a film set with real-life actors, the sensual assaults of a tired city moving into spring with the winter-weary populace of its poorest quarters passing me in the grimy streets of the East End. I began right there to hate and reject it: not even to turn around and go home, just to be not there in that bleak environment. I found things to do and say, to put on my parent face, my husband's

'Going to Work', L.S. Lowry, 1943.

Public domain[30]

role, my friendly persona — but deep down it all felt like a mistake, a bad dream. For the next ten years the shock of return would never quite relent, never allow me to feel at home in my own skin in England. None of this was the country's problem, it was all mine.

History has plenty of stories of disillusioned immigrants, some who boomerang back to wherever their hopes and dreams had urged them to leave; then others who have no choice but to accept whatever the new host country is and does, the refugees. Church history has examples of missionaries who folded under the pressure of alienation; New Zealand had its share, with one or two who 'took the blanket' and instead of converting Maori, slept with their women — the madness of sending single men to the ends of the earth unsupported, soon apparent. We had plenty of support externally, that wasn't the problem. It was our internal baggage that would test us.

After a few days scouting the tourist charms of London — the Tower, pigeons in Trafalgar Square, the buses, the Tube and the corner pubs — we turned south for L'Abri in Hampshire and our home for the next three months. The sun was out and it was spring. As the city vanished behind us and a countryside of oaks and rolling fields opened its bookish pages, it was hard not to feel joy rising. We were heading down on the A3 to an old manor house near Greatham, twenty miles north of my dad's old naval base at Portsmouth in the heart of Mother England's Home Counties. This area was as other to Homerton and Hackney as Wiltshire chalk, say, to Wensleydale cheese. It was from rural miles like these in the north and the west that the drift to the city had begun in the Industrial Revolution: poor villagers moving off the land into slums and factories, and finally, into the grim high-rise estates that were built in hope after the devastation of war. My grandparents, who I'd left behind me as a toddler, had ancient links to this land.

These were the inklings of the extremes of English society that would force themselves on my attention in the next few months and years that followed. The Thatcher revolution was hard to see in the green lanes around Greatham and Liss — bluebell carpets in their shocking glory under the elms, oaks and beeches — but it was here nevertheless. The manor house itself stood on a feudal site that had been occupied since the collation of the Domesday Book by the invading Normans in the 11th century. As we crunched to a halt on the pebbled driveway, the flint walls and red-tiled roof of the three-level house with its rook-roost multiple chimneys, was a storybook vista. No more lord of the manor, this manor was now the Lord's.

Francis Schaeffer's disciples had spread out from his original home base in the Swiss mountains in 1955 and established satellite communities worldwide, staffed by a range of professionals from other fields who shared his evangelical and intellectual bent. Schaeffer taught and argued philosophy, the art of Christian apologetics, or explaining the faith; his aims were wide and deep. He sought to promote and defend an objectively true Christianity in community, with open debate and embodied example of gospel truths. Questions were welcome, almost obligatory, as well as communal service; you came, you challenged, you dug the garden — that kind of thing. He encouraged a fully rounded experience of life, including artistic productions in all fields, and did not shy away from the social sciences and grassroots initiatives. This appealed to my restless need to write again and that reflexive helper gene: a social gospel and a manifesto for creative work. Here was our beachhead for whatever England would come to mean: a ragtag, hippie-cum-surfer invasion straight out of Runanga took root on English soil.

We met the elders — Schaeffer was, after all, a Presbyterian — and discovered that English Richard was a psychologist and American Barry, an actual rocket scientist (he'd been a physicist on the Apollo Program). Everyone had come from somewhere else in the world, geographically and professionally, students and staff alike. Our job was to make the community work and seek the reality of St Paul's words, "Christ in you, the hope of glory."[31] For the next three months, we ate, argued, sang and prayed together; for us, it also meant continuing to home-school our two early teenagers on material that came all the way from the New Zealand Correspondence School. There was a rich cast of characters: a Jewish accountant from Andorra who made his living playing the stock market; Jim, a Canadian cartoonist who sold us his Hillman Avenger when he left; Debbie, a New York photographer; Chris, a tortured escapee from apartheid South Africa; Mary, a dancer from the midwest; and Richard from Chicago, a poet.

This was the church you're having when you're not having church; but whatever else it was, it wasn't what we'd left behind in Runanga with its loving anarchy and freedom. I mourned that loss. I attended discussions, listened to the cassettes in the tape library, majoring on apologetics, which fascinated me. I loved a good argument and there were plenty to be had around the meal table. I should have spent more time talking to Richard, the psychologist who lived on site with his family; he was a counsellor and an expert on depression. He'd written a pamphlet, *Perfectionism: The Road to Hell*, which made perfect sense to me, an unwilling slave to obsessive-compulsive disorder. Many of the students would spend time with him but I avoided any intimacy, suspicious as always of authority figures, in denial about my own need for radical healing. One seed L'Abri did plant before we left was in an AA pamphlet I picked up from the foyer. It was a series of twenty questions for those who had grown up in families where alcohol was a problem. If you answered more than half with a yes, they suggested you more than likely had been affected by somebody's excessive drinking. I scored on almost every point.

As the three months and a glorious Hampshire summer came to an end, what next? Richard Winter and his family were leaving for America on a month's holiday and needed a house-sitter. We offered to help and gratefully took the job. That meant more live-in time to plan the next step, a move further south to Poole to stay with my aunt and her husband while I looked for work. In the meantime I took a two-week ESOL crash course in Guilford just north of Greatham, in hopes of maybe getting a job as a teacher of English to foreign students. There was no firm plan as to how we might live; the money from the sale of the house in Runanga, to travel to these fields of glory, was fast running out. The friends from the fellowship at home had supported us all along the way, but now we had to find income in England. It would need more than a wing or a prayer: we'd had the former, now it was time to wait on the results of the latter. They came, but not quite as I expected.

27

Breaking down

We loaded the old Avenger right up to the cheap-and-cheerful roof rack, aimed her maroon body with its black vinyl roof towards Petersfield and points south, waving an affectionate farewell to the Winter family whose house we'd shared and to L'Abri, our shelter, with its scattered community of new friends. Some we would stay in touch with and see again, others never. The experience, the proof that *konoinia* and *agape* were real and could co-exist among strangers, was energising and reinforced the values we had learned in those seed years in Runanga: God is love and only love, made visible in genuine care of, and commitment to one another. We were heading to Auntie Pat's place in Broadstone, Poole, to spend a couple of weeks house and job hunting in the lap of my father's family. Turning forty, I was discovering what it was like to have blood relatives outside your immediate family — comforting, but strange.

Pat and I had met when she'd come out to New Zealand in the 1980s, but husband Les was a new person to embrace. An MS sufferer, a retired electronics engineer, he was a witty companion and they both made us welcome. A childless couple, they had married young: both working, they had done well, having moved from their London working-class roots to a life as comfortable but un-showy bungalow-owning members of a rising middle class. They were the type of voter Thatcher aimed to capture and often did; not in their case. They were *Guardian*-reading Liberal voters deeply embedded in a Uniting Parish church. Carrying wounds from her wartime evacuee experiences and the Depression that had also shaped my father, Pat was a nervous, warm heart; Les, in slow decline from his condition, could be quite demanding. It was obvious we couldn't prevail upon their kindness for long.

After a few days sightseeing, taking in Brownsea Island where Baden-Powell got the scout movement started, the chained Bibles of Wimborne Minster, Corfe Castle and John Lennon's one-time millionaire mansion looking out over Poole Harbour bought for his Aunt Mimi in 1965, we were able to rent a caravan in a windswept seaside park while the hunt for a holiday rental went on into bleak September. This type of short lease was common over the winter and we found a flat in the Poole Old Town in a mews just off The Strand. By now we were all but broke. Between searching the vacancies at the Job Centre and scanning the Wednesday *Guardian* for openings, I found myself lining up to apply for a UB40 benefit down at the Department of Employment office. No, UB40 wasn't just a band.

Fortunately, they agreed to pay me: my British birth certificate and UK passport meant I was entitled to an unemployment benefit even though I had left the country almost forty years before. I celebrated turning forty in November of that year in a seaside holiday home, on the dole just as my grandfather had been, reliant on social security during the hunger years of the 1930s. In his case, it took four years before he could find work again. I had no plan to wait that long, despite slipping slowly into a depressive phase. Strapped for cash, needing all the state was providing to pay the rental and manage the food budget, we would walk the town with the kids. It was hard not to wonder if maybe, just maybe, I'd made the wrong move coming to England after all.

Sharing a Mars bar became a treat. We would count out the slices of bread for the day's meals. It was at this low point I saw a job in the *Guardian* that would be life-changing — but not in the way I would have chosen. The vacancy was for a care assistant at a home for homeless men in Kent, run by a trust with a street outreach in London. Kenward Trust — named after the manor house they owned and had turned into the base for a therapeutic community — was a Christian charity that took alcoholics and addicts off the streets. For those who wanted more than soup and bed for the night, a shelter and a home were offered among the hop farms and oast houses in the Garden of England. I applied and made the shortlist.

My trip to London and the successful interview opened a door that would give us work, a base to move on from and accommodation on the job — I was hired. We packed up again, said goodbye to Pat and Les and drove the 140 miles north-east to Yalding in the darkness and rain of late

Kenward House and grounds: our former flat is visible, second balcony, left.

December, celebrating on the way with a meal at a roadside Happy Eater, Britain's low-rent answer to McDonalds. We had gone from one manor house to another, from one Christian community to a very different one. We were met with a warm, overwhelming welcome on the eve of Christmas. Once decanted into our upstairs flat, we were whisked off to a party to celebrate our arrival and admission into the Kenward family.

Overpowered and exhausted, I wanted to run away from the sudden blaze of kindness and attention showered upon us by the manager Godfrey, his wife Carol and all the staff. Unaware of how frayed at the edges I was, I'd signed up to a live-in job house-sitting thirty damaged men. We'd been through a year of major changes: needing security and stability, deracinated and feeling weird, I was close to burnout before I even started.

We had a couple of days to bed in, meet the residents and sort out schools for our teenagers as the home-schooling option came to an end. I was initiated into the compulsory evening Bible studies: a tradition begun by the founder in the 1960s and a requirement of the men who agreed to come and take part in the life of Kenward. I soon discovered that these gatherings, which took place at six every evening barring Sundays when church attendance sufficed, were endured by most of residents as part of the price of coming to Kenward. They were a cross for the men to bear, hanging out for their medication doled out afterwards when the lesson ended. Even before I started work in earnest, this culture of compulsion provoked misgivings. Jesus attracted, never compelled his followers.

As usual, my nose for authoritarian contradictions would get me into trouble. I was always suspicious of the misuse of power and sensitive to its application, a lifelong bequest from the bullying in my childhood. These were good people doing God's work in their own way, but no matter how hard I tried, I couldn't help crossing the lines as I'd done at Seaview when I changed sides in the '70s. As a family we needed the safety and security of belonging, of having safeguards around our own weaknesses, but I couldn't identify with the Kenward way of doing things. I could see the good — the care, the provision of shelter, a place of work and recreation — but could never accept the downside of requiring another person to listen to your beliefs expounded as the price of belonging and receiving that care.

These were addicts and alkies, dry drunks, men on the run, ex-cons, broken somewhere back there down the road, all with their stories of disappointment, damage and abuse. I had stumbled into my own worst nightmare (nothing to do with what the Trust was attempting), of nursing and covering for thirty different versions of my alcoholic and gambling addicted father. This was a condition I knew had a name: co-dependency. Over the following year as this built to a head, I was also finding a few literary charms in the area, shoots of hope for my writing dreams. The nearby village of Yalding had been the home of the Great War poet Edmund Blunden, and his brother still lived there. Aware of my literary bent, a staff member told me that Siegfried Sassoon had lived in a house on the nearby road to Brenchley, insisting, "You simply must go to the village, their cream teas are to die for." In a land of letters, something else began to waken within me.

Raymond Carver, 1938–1988.
Sharon Murdoch

As 1988 moved through winter and my conflicts wore me down, one day in August I picked up the *Guardian* and read an obituary for the American short story writer, Raymond Carver. His background mirrored mine: abusive father, sawmill town, dropping out, alcoholism — except, he'd got up off the floor and become a literary success. The obituary was headed, "The American Chekhov". I made up my mind to seek out his work. We were having some of the residents come up into our flat, something we'd been advised against. One or two were quite demanding and manipulative, but my identification with the broken-hearted was too strong. I always went the extra mile. Instead of supervising Irish Sean — a long-term resident going back to the beginnings of the Trust in 1967, a regular and embittered stirrer at Bible studies — I would work beside him on the road or cutting wood and tiling the roof. It was Kiwi-style, getting stuck in, but I was told that as a house manager I needed to delegate. It was becoming obvious the mix was not a good one.

The glories of Kent in the summer could salve many wounds: cricket played in whites along the banks of the Medway heading in to Maidstone, the regular hop vines and wizard-hat oast houses, the county's symbol. Seeing a Spitfire one day low over the oaks on the horizon, it was H.E. Bates all over again, the 1940 of my boyhood dreams. Pete, another Christian friend from Runanga, arrived to stay. On impulse, I drove him to Brenchley for that fabled cream tea. On the B2160 from Yalding, a wooded back road we stopped to view the house where Sassoon had lived. As we stood on the roadside and stared, the door opened and a woman called out, "Would you like to see where Sassoon wrote?" Amazed, we accepted, honoured with a brief guided tour of this celebrated war poet's one-time home. The woman kindly pointed out the location of the nearby cemetery where his aristocratic mother, Theresa Thorneycroft, now lay. We drove there to pay homage.

The cream tea at Brenchley afterwards completed a storied afternoon: a thatched roof and an open fire, the tearoom dog sleeping at our feet. Back at Kenward, the next pair of visitors, recovering alcoholics both of them, were to change everything. As I poured out my troubles to Val, he looked at me and said, "You should go to Al-Anon. These guys are driving you crazy." He told me this was a companion organisation to AA, set up for those in relationships with alcoholics, loved ones affected by the drinker. I took his advice, getting myself along to a regular meeting in Maidstone. I'd already blown my top at one of the Kenward staff members, burned out like me. He was making cruel remarks about a resident's eating habits (we often shared meals in the dining room when on duty, and there were a good number of eating disorders in evidence). I felt this surge of anger: it was like my dad and his extra helping of sarcasm at the embattled mealtimes of my childhood.

I stood up, snarled at Steve, picked my plate up and smashed it on the floor. That eruption had been brewing for years and had nothing to do with him, poor man. I would stay a while longer under Kenward's roof after that night, but as pieces of the plate flew across the floor and food splattered the lino, I'd just offered my resignation in the most emphatic way. I'd blown up, given notice on my chaotic, repressed inner life. I was crashing out and it was time to go.

28

How to sell a book

But where? I was stuck. I could see the situation was getting out of hand, surviving most days by getting up early and writing for an hour before my shift began; at lunch times, retreating upstairs to the flat where I would lie on the floor and practise deep breathing-slow release relaxation exercises to keep my sense of panic under wraps. The dawn writing exercise was one of the recommendations of Dorothea Brande, whose multi-million-selling advice manual, *Becoming a Writer*, I'd picked up in my travels. Since its first publication in 1934, her recipe for writing success had sold way more copies than those of the writers who bought the book. I was following one of her recommendations, to get up and write straight out of bed, just face the blank white sheet and start.

It sounds crude, but the idea was good; writing is a habit as well as a craft and this was about the former, not the latter. I wrote page after page, none of which I have ever revisited, but something changed. I tried her other handy hint — drinking yerba mate tea — but soon forsook that and backslid into coffee. None of this changed my issues with emotional burnout and in the end I had to visit the GP in nearby Wateringbury. He was a wise head, used to dealing with the residents and staff at Kenward. He took one look at me and asked half a dozen questions, designed to test whether or not I was suffering from depression. I replied to each of them and he then pronounced sentence: "You're depressed. You're suffering from stress-related burnout and I'm writing you a sick note. You have to resign and get out of Kenward."

I felt relief as much as fear: here was my get-out-of-jail-free card. I quibbled that we had nowhere to go, it was tied accommodation and other such anxieties, but the good doctor was not fazed. "I'll write you a note for the council in Maidstone, saying you've been rendered homeless on medical grounds. They'll put you on the emergency list. Just go back to work and resign." He'd done this kind of surgery before. I placed myself in his hands, at the mercy of Kenward and the local council; once more my UK/EU passport was giving me an ironic advantage. As a citizen, I was entitled to such benefits, notwithstanding having lived outside of Mother England for most of my life. I went back to Kenward and sat down with my manager, Terry, a compassionate ex-army man with business experience, and a committed Christian. I showed him the sick note.

Terry didn't hesitate: he already knew I was in trouble and that something had to give. He was genuinely sorry to lose me, he said, and of course we could stay on in the flat until we found somewhere in Maidstone. I said I'd be available for light duties and we shook hands; my short career as a residential social worker was over. Leaving was another wrench for us all as I'd made some genuine friendships, particularly with the men under Kenward's care. There were characters like Titch, a five-foot-nothing Cockney of advanced but unknown age who looked after the pigs, fag glued to his bottom lip as he discoursed in an impenetrable dialect and questioned everyone's sanity, most often in the queues outside the dining room. His eyebrows were as thick and as tangled as the hedgerows he slept in on his springtime walkabouts to London, when the weather warmed and the road beckoned again. He got too old for that in the end, did Titch.

Titch with a sow and her litter, Kenward, 1989.

Who could forget old Fred, a French artist of distant English birth who had lived almost all of his life in Paris and returned to England as an elderly man, to end up in Kenward's care? My job was to get him into the bath on occasions, something he resisted with a deathless rebuff — "*Une maison de fous, maison de fous!!*" — expressing his conviction he'd been sent to a madhouse. There was Scots' Alex, a needle man who would sit at the bottom of the stairs leading to our flat, advising me as I sped around the place in my driven state, "Just keep taking the Valium, Jeff!" My favourite staff member was another Scotsman, Hugh, ex-Royal Navy, who through his knowledge of naval networks put me in touch with three of my father's old wartime shipmates on HMS *Illustrious.*

As well as doctor's orders, I'd taken Val's advice and found my way to an Al-Anon meeting in Maidstone. That's where I met Jenny and later, her husband Dugald who would become my sponsor (not their real names, obviously). Many people have strange ideas about Alcoholics Anonymous

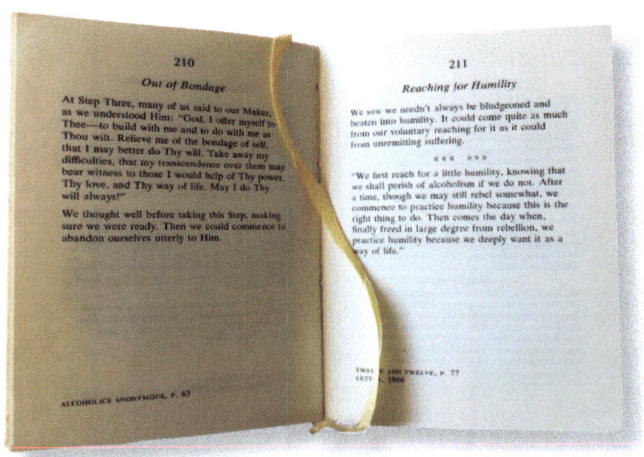

210

Out of Bondage

At Step Three, many of us said to our Maker, as we understood Him: "God, I offer myself to Thee—to build with me and to do with me as Thou wilt. Relieve me of the bondage of self, that I may better do Thy will. Take away my difficulties, that my transcendence over them may bear witness to those I would help of Thy power, Thy love, and Thy way of life. May I do Thy will always!"

We thought well before taking this Step, making sure we were ready. Then we could commence to abandon ourselves utterly to Him.

ALCOHOLICS ANONYMOUS, P. 63

211

Reaching for Humility

We saw we needn't always be bludgeoned and beaten into humility. It could come quite as much from our voluntary reaching for it as it could from unremitting suffering.

<<< >>>

"We first reach for a little humility, knowing that we shall perish of alcoholism if we do not. After a time, though we may still rebel somewhat, we commence to practice humility because this is the right thing to do. Then comes the day when, finally freed in large degree from rebellion, we practice humility because we deeply want it as a way of life."

TWEL[illegible] AND TWELVE, P. 77
LETT[illegible], 1966

AA literature: pages on humility, from *As Bill Sees It.*

and its offshoots — the 12-Step programmes, including Al-Anon where I now found myself with a roomful of alkies' wives. Ignorance, suspicion and bad press have all conspired to create a negative view; even for a drinker whose life is in freefall, or a partner who is being driven mad by a user, it's hard to swallow your pride and walk through the doors into a meeting. There and then, it was my best career move. I did know of AA from my time as social worker at Seaview back in the 1970s, but not much about Al-Anon. This partner group exists to support those whose lives — like mine, and those of my siblings and my mother — have been affected by living with an alcoholic, or addict.

It was here I learned more about co-dependency, where the child, and later the adult, is habituated to co-existing with a damaged and damaging parent. There is usually an enabling partner who hangs in there "for the sake of the kids" as my mother had done. The child imbibes the unhealthy relationship model at a deep level and goes on to replicate it. My caring role at Kenward was like my childhood home, times thirty — "an emotional Turkish bath", as Dugald would describe my choice of employment. It was at a monthly combined meeting of AA and Al-Anon at our usual venue that I got to meet him. Here I began to accept the advice to new members, that they get the help of an older person to start working the programme, reinforcing their decision to quit drinking.

I wanted a confidant and knew it had to be a male, so I went for Dugald, which was the best of moves. A nuggety Liverpudlian — a former docker and later a chef — he was kindness and brute truth in the one package. He was, I soon discovered, a shrewd psychologist, a student of human behaviour and need. Invited to his house, pouring out my troubles, it wasn't long before he nailed me down, not about my relationship issues but my former drug and alcohol use. He persuaded me that it just might be in my interests to go along to AA meetings and listen, to ignore the differences and see if I could spot similarities to my own story in what I heard shared.

I followed his advice. It took a few meetings, but it stuck: I soon knew I was one of them, and thirty years on I still belong among the drunks who have found that AA works for them. Dugald would take me for long rides in the country and we'd end up in some thatched picture-perfect Kent country pub, having a lunch minus the obligatory pint or three that was at that moment reducing the afternoon productivity for hundreds of thousands of English workers. He became in this way a surrogate: a father figure, a man who had once been sectioned under the UK mental health legislation and was now living proof that you could recover from alcoholic madness.

On the road to recovery, first things first; all I needed now was somewhere to live — and a job. A visit from an old L'Abri friend, South African pharmacist Chris Wüst, pointed me towards employment. We'd kept in touch after leaving the community and he arrived for a weekend. An offhand remark that he'd always wanted to try bookselling gave me an idea: maybe there was a bookshop in Maidstone I could try? One of the Kenward staff told me there was a Dillons branch in town, so the next working day, I went and enquired. Entering this temple of literary commerce in my fragile state was daunting. I didn't feel very employable: I was filling my diary with writing never to be published that revealed — as Dugald had encouraged me to do — my life in the raw, resentments, wounds, the whole nine yards. Books in bookshops like this with their shining shelves and stacks of new work looked to me as if they had emerged complete from another world, one where the authors spoke among each other in the same kind of polished Home Counties' accents in which the woman behind the till at Dillons was speaking to me, replying in the negative to my request: any jobs going here?

She did, however, point me around the corner to a new branch of the Waterstones chain that was fitting out an old granary store, soon to open as a competitor — they would be looking for staff, she told me. I made my way as directed and found a gutted shop with workmen inside installing retail furniture, and on the window, a sign: "Waterstones — opening here soon. Staff wanted, apply within". I found my way to the back of the store to Stephen, the manager, up to his ears in boxes of stock, invoices and general mayhem. I told him I wanted work, but I had no direct bookshop experience. He looked too young to be managing a bookshop. He gave me an appointment — "Meet me tomorrow in the mall for a coffee and we'll have a chat" — then rushed off to some other shop-fitting crisis.

I took the train back to Wateringbury with more hope. I was writing long lists in my AA fourth and fifth step work with Dugald, and getting my conflict out in the open: follow a dream and write, or go back to caring for life's broken-hearted? It seemed too much to square but at least this gave me an option, even if only a temporary relief. I met Stephen the next day and we sized each other up. He was not at all bothered that I had no retail experience; he asked me what books I'd been reading, and when could I start? He must have liked me. Whatever I told him about my literary life (I certainly didn't mention the Bible or the *AA Big Book*), it worked.

Ironically, I later became the buyer for the spiritual section (Waterstones gave its staff considerable latitude and the responsibility to run various sections and keep up stock levels). I could breathe easier now and nourish the hope I could manage some writing, along with selling books. I'd been reading the eminent poet Stephen Spender's biography *World Within World* and slowly he became a sponsor of another kind. In August I'd written a poem for him, 'The Swing Bridge' (it was not up to much) and another soon after, 'The Weaned Child' which, while it tries too hard in places, contains a pretty accurate picture of my state of mind at the time, on waking:

> I grab my hair by force of will
> and toss aside ambivalent sheets,
> as light makes white the window sill.

Writing again, about to get close to books. All we needed now was a house.

In the years that followed I would fill spiral-bound notepads and workbooks with daily reflections and drafts of poems that were never going to survive, but I kept at it, as if by chipping and grinding away at living blocks of language, a poem would emerge. I wrote love letters to Raymond Carver, and a homage to David Walker, my American mentor, in a poem called 'Moving House' that showed signs of life, a dream song of leaving and seeking a place to stand, where I

> keep trying to find the road
> back to the bare rooms
> and the cardboard boxes
> and the last look back
> at what was home.

I practised metre, wrote poems to friends and to my nightmares, addressed John Donne in sonnets, read Brodsky on Auden, wrote and wrote and wrote. I was learning that every poem that survives is only the tip of an unloved iceberg yet to be.

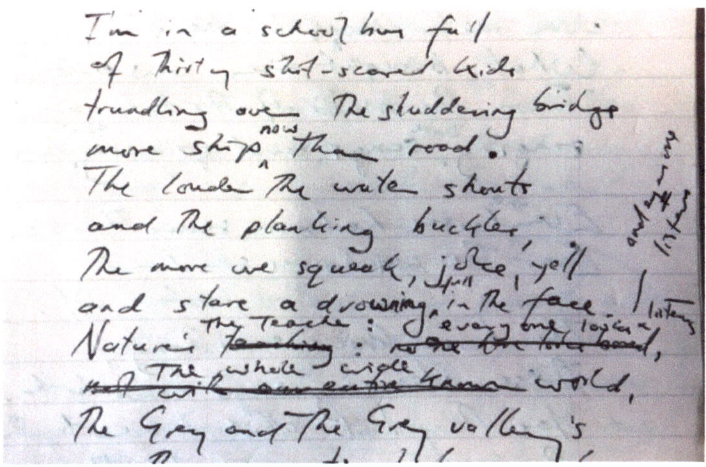
I'm in a school bus full
of thirty shit-scared kids
trundling over the shuddering bridge
now more ship than road.
The louder the water shouts
and the planking buckles,
the more we squeak, joke, yell
and stare a drowning in the face.
Nature's

Second draft of 'The Flood', written in July 1990, since sunk.

29

Janet, Jim and Te Whiti

Travelling by train the few miles from the station at Wateringbury to Maidstone East every day was a chance to read and reflect. Once in town I would use my phone card in the British Telecom box outside Waterstones to ring Dugald and listen to his words of comfort and encouragement. "You're all right you know, don't you?" he'd say (that was the last thing I felt I was, but I'd agree). It took a long time before I realised he wasn't saying, "You feel good"; it was more like, "Deep down, you're okay and all will be well." I arrived on my first day, a Saturday, opening day of the new branch with hordes of eager book buyers pressing on the door while a bunch of booksellers, many of us newbies, worked the tills.

It was nerve-wracking and frantic for a while, but with Serena, our trainer and advisor moving from till to till helping us with sales, we made it through and slowly got the hang of it. She was a former WH Smith bookseller who knew the business, unfazed by long queues and the stuff-ups of her trainees. A fair sprinkling of other staff had sold books before, so the branch was a good place to work. They paid well and once you left the shop, the day was over — unlike the whirlpool of emotion that Kenward could stir on any given day. I would walk to the chilly station in the evening and wait for my train, reading for comfort Janet Frame's memoir, *An Angel At My Table*, marvelling at her struggle to stay sane and write.

The gods of council bureaucracy were smiling on us: my doctor's note and our loss of tied accommodation meant we were eligible for a council house in Maidstone. Saying our goodbyes, we packed up and left the Kenward adventure behind. We moved into 11 Beaumont Road, a pebble-dash semi-detached two-storey council house in a row of lookalikes, with a small garden and even its own allotment where a share in a gardening space meant homegrown vegetables. Britain had dug its way to victory in wartime by offering community spaces like these. It was a lesson in urban living for colonials who longed for personal plots on huge sections. City living in Britain was all about making the best use of the available space.

The English, it seemed, could turn any hole-in-the-wall into a shop, as Napoleon had once quipped — to his loss. Our teenagers were settled into local schools and Theresa was soon volunteering as a tutor in adult literacy classes — a move that would open up a whole new career. The home-schooling experience was proving its worth, and we were all moving on as best we could.

Te Whiti. Nelson, 1883.
PUBL-0113-01 ATL

I was enjoying the job and exploring the charms of Maidstone, including its libraries, one of which had — surprisingly — a small New Zealand section. It was there I stumbled onto two change agents: Dick Scott's *Ask That Mountain*, a history of Parihaka and the prophets Te Whiti o Rongomai and Tohu Kakahi, and *The Fifth Wind*, by Robert Macdonald. Macdonald was English, had grown up in New Zealand from 1946, shipping back to England as a young man in 1958. In the 1980s he returned to political turmoil in New Zealand and gave a progress report on the nation from the hikoi with Tainui to Waitangi. Hearing his voice in Kent, I was waking up to racism, to who I was and who I was not. I set out to discover more about the land I'd grown up in and left behind, a loss I was silently mourning without confronting the homesickness. Dick Scott shocked me harder: was this our true history, had we truly behaved that badly? Between Janet Frame escaping the mental hospital gulag and Maori prophets speaking old truths, I was challenged, affirmed, even transformed.

I picked up more 'how to' books on writing, including one in a series that gave some good advice on getting into poetry. As a bookseller, I had some time to suss out these titles; books came often across my path that I might otherwise have missed. In mid-1990, this included a book about my grandmother's brother, the naval expert and spy, Hector C. Bywater. I spotted the eponymously titled *Bywater: The Man who Invented the Pacific War* in a publisher's catalogue of upcoming titles.[32] As kids, this was the man Nanny had always talked about and had us half believing. The bookselling trade was gently moving me towards books and writing and away from social work; a necessary cure.

The book on writing poetry suggested concentrating on one particular visual item and writing about that, giving a long list of suggestions, anything from medieval manuscripts to chimneys. I began to notice that England was exceeding rich in chimney architecture, and wandered the nearby streets examining the fluted variety of these brick-and-tile stacks.

They brought back visions of the busy jackdaws nesting in the high chimneys at L'Abri. I wrote some chimney poems as way of keeping my hand in, and discovered from this exercise a more objective way of honing in on a subject. It was a salutary alternative to angst and confessions. I also did some local history research on Maidstone in the Blitz and discovered that on a night raid in 1940 a German Heinkel bomber had been shot down a few streets away from Beaumont Road. I found the actual house where the bomber's tail had ended up in the garden, lined up from the photo in my book on the war and its effects on Kent.

I learned that the crew was buried in the Maidstone cemetery, so on a midweek day off I drove there and asked the sexton for help. He pointed me to the war graves section and, noting my accent, asked if I was Australian. When I put him right, he told me Kiwi aircrew were buried there as well, men who had died in the Battle of Britain. I found my way to the Commonwealth War Graves section and walked along the rows until I found the unmistakable silver fern inscribed on a New Zealand airman's grave. I felt something give way inside me and broke down on the spot. The loneliness of their faraway death was almost unbearable, and a reminder too of my distance from home. I walked over and found the graves of the Luftwaffe aircrew who had died near where I now lived. There they all lay, equal in death, Germans and New Zealanders shadowed by the tall cross and its sword.

My heart was turning south, back to New Zealand. I'd made a decision to return to my real home. My wife and son wanted to stay on in England; my daughter and I made plans to leave as soon as we could. There was only one problem: I'd travelled to the UK on my British passport. When I applied to the high commission in London for my Kiwi one, I got some bad news. I wasn't a New Zealand citizen and would have to apply for citizenship. This was a blood-runs-cold moment: what if they refused me? I was shaken: it turned out my brother and I had sailed out to New Zealand in 1950 on our mother's passport and had never needed to get one

German aircraft being dismantled for scrap, Britain, 1940.

of our own. We had both gone over to Australia in an era when passports were not required; returning to England, I'd assumed it was fine to put off applying for the New Zealand one after my arrival in the UK.

I took a few deep breaths and consulted the high commission in the Haymarket. They gave me a list of things I would have to do, to prove residency in the past and show that as a 'new citizen' on my return, I would have supporters to house me and help me find work, all so I would not be a cost on the government. It felt very, very odd: here I was, having to establish my right to live in a country where I'd spent most of my life. I was just inside a couple of boundaries to do with legal changes over time that meant I qualified to apply — so we got to work. I approached family and friends for affidavits: my mother, my siblings, my mother-in-law, friends, church members, former teachers, a whole range of people who gave proof of my residence from 1950 onwards, my school reports, tax details and a host of references.

Once that was done, it was a waiting game until the high commission asked me to come to London. At that point I would be required "to make the declaration and take the oath of allegiance, prior to the consideration of your application by the Secretary for Internal Affairs" back in New Zealand. The letter dated 13.10.89, from Mr K.R. Hitchcock, a consular officer, I still have with me. Having travelled there and met the requirements, I took the train back to Maidstone to endure a six-month wait. I carried on at Waterstones and kept writing.

In April 1990 I got a call from the high commission in London: my application for New Zealand citizenship had been granted. Hallelujah! All I need do was come to London, provide a photograph and the document would be processed and issued. I breathed a deep sigh of relief: the fear that I could not go home as a New Zealander was probably the result of irrational thinking, but until that moment it troubled me deeply. Like never before, I realised where I belonged: the pull of the land and the people came over me. We travelled up to Haymarket and on 11 April 1990, after signing up as a certified Kiwi, I returned with my new treasure: citizenship, belonging.

It was around this time I wrote that long, seventeen-stanza poem for James K. Baxter. There are some moments in the piece that still touch me, including one about Lee's death,

> What shook me was your voice:
> even now I hear you
> like my dead lover's laughter
> in tune with an unseen/existing order.

It was all about voice: absorbing our parents speaking, the soundscapes of family and friends, way back to those formless hours before speech and ideas could take shape, into the time of the child, the teenager and the awkward adult pierced by a song, stopped still by music. In England in 1990, the next poet's voice to ring in my ears was completely out of left field — the Czech immunologist, Miroslav Holub.

I'd never heard of this major 20th-century writer; had I stayed in New Zealand, I might have waited much longer to come across him. My luck was in: my manager Stephen asked if I wanted a trip to London to hear a poet he also knew little about. Head office had sent him tickets to a launch by Faber & Faber of Holub's new book, *Vanishing Lung Syndrome*; he wanted company for the trip to the Charing Cross Road branch. Holub was an unknown quantity — I didn't understand at that time why Ted Hughes and Seamus Heaney had him right up there on the pantheon of modern greats. I had been reading and enjoying the novels and stories of his Czech compatriot, Ivan Klima, so this would be an adventure in discovery. In the flesh, Holub seemed grey and unimposing, a figure from a Kafka tale, anonymous in any Prague street — until he opened his mouth and began to read.

English was not his first language, of course — nor was poetry his everyday profession. He was a scientist, but between the language of that discipline and his native Czech tongue, he transfixed me with his reading of the poem, 'What Else?' It would be patronising to try and fix here the sound of his voice in some kind of phonetic pidgin; the accent that filled the room was so thick, each word so deliberate, it sounded like a slow pronouncement of Time's imminent end. The room slowed down. He brought me to a standstill; it was as much the crackling of Czech vowels and consonants working to emit an English sentence, as any readily accessible meaning. As the poem ended, I was in love with words all over again and his surreal notion of poetry as akin to the hysterical barking of cats.[33] Cats? Yes, cats: you just believed him.

Holub was a master of disguise, overturning expectations. He has another poem, 'Fish', comprising the scientific names of fish, their skeletons stacked up to the ceiling for the purpose of embalming a dead Chinese emperor, Qin Shi Huang-ti. The poem ends with the terrible stench of all manner of rotting fish reaching high heaven, fish whose only function is "of stinking clear up to here".[34] This had little to do with fish or China: here was the rotting corpse of the Czech state under the Communists. Holub had survived the Nazis, the Soviet occupation, the Prague Spring of 1968 and here he was in the West after the 1989 Velvet Revolution. He

Miroslav Holub, poet, 1923–98.
Bloodaxe Books, UK

was free to declaim his truths to an audience that had little idea of how to write the kind of poetry that could live with dignity under such oppression. Holub's oppressors were simply unable to comprehend the inner freedom he possessed and few of us in the West had lived under the constraints of totalitarianism, save for refugees and émigrés.

This freedom is the reason Stalin had the poet Osip Mandelstam murdered, but only after he had telephoned him personally one night to listen to the sound of a poet's blood running cold. He toyed with him, just as Mandelstam had written the tyrant did with his sycophants, in a brave and reckless poem that signed his death warrant — 'The Stalin Epigram'. Writers like this, writers of witness, have given something back to us from the endless unfathomable butchery and cruelty that flooded the world in the 20th century: modern psalmists preserving human dignity and the sheer mystery of existence. I rode home in the train on air, an echo within me of another way of being. In Holub's slim book, I had in my hands a way of writing that had little to do with English, American or New Zealand traditions. This was the voice of silence, made audible. This was a different order of truth.

First draft of 'The Boy', 31.5.1990, published later in 2002.

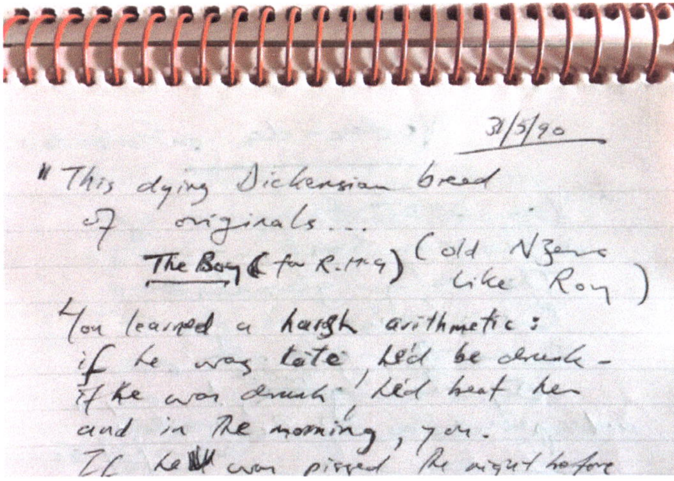

31/5/90

"This dying Dickensian breed
of originals...
The Boy (for R.[illegible]) (old NZers
like Roy)
You learned a harsh arithmetic:
if he was late, he'd be drunk –
if he was drunk, he'd beat her
and in the morning, you.
If he was pissed the night before

30

On Charing Cross Road

My struggle to find a place to stand was within and without; the need to return to New Zealand was entangled with my need to write. Somebody who understood that was my old teacher, mentor and friend, Peter Hooper. He'd written to me a long, tender letter earlier in the year in response to one I'd sent after hearing he'd had an operation for cancer. I knew I had to see him again. He confirmed he had undergone major surgery for cancer of the bowel and was slowly recovering at home in Ahaura, up the Grey Valley we both knew and loved. Anxious he might die and I would never see him again, I'd written him a poem and declared my love for him and my need of his blessing.

This contact — and the poem — had moved him to write a long, thoughtful and appreciative letter, still treasured. He wanted to reassure me and himself too perhaps, that I should not fret. As usual, he spent much of the letter reinforcing me; he was delighted I'd left Kenward and committed to paper that I'd made a decision to work towards full-time writing. He was sure that my "poetic impulse had not been stifled by other claims", evidenced by the poem I had dedicated to him. He continued, saying "after the emotional impact of it had subsided", he had tried "to read the work with some detachment" and concluded, "How firmly it sets me within my worlds — literary, the natural world of the Coast, the greater mystery of life itself."

Literary criticism was fraught with emotion for me at that moment, to read that my poem meant so much to him. He wrote that it had, "another value for me … because my life has been deficient in the usual commemorative and celebratory occasions natural to family groups. I value highly the rare spontaneous recognition from another that I am passing/have passed a significant mile-post on my way." Such an elegant way of expressing what the loneliness his life choices — and his sexuality — had meant for him. This was the closest I ever got to hearing him say he missed never having had the joy of a family of his own. He had me instead and a legion of others he had tended — and now one of us had declared that love and appreciation at a moment of mutual vulnerability.

The Coast we both knew: Reefton residents crossing paths, 1986.

My poem — 'Peter's Song: a celebration (1960–1990)' — confronts the reality of his possible death and uses that shadow to open a conversation. A quarter of a century later not all of it works for me, but it retains enough charge to bear partial citation, opening, "I can hear my voice now as it rises./Can you still hear yours?" I speak next of my own father's death from cancer, name the shared ancestors Peter and I had discovered together — Theodore Roethke, Pablo Neruda — and then take off my mask.

> Peace old father, father two.
> Did you ever know
> I was a son to you?
> When you're taken, my life will shrink
> like the Big Grey's mud bank
> in flood loses an acre a minute,
>
> / … /
>
> and the great sea seen
> from heaven stained with blood,
> as the deep is grey-haired
> in the Book of Job.

I took some liberty in the last stanza, having long since prayed that Peter would come to share the faith I'd found, and did a little proselytising — for which I know he forgave me, for the love intended.

Cross over with me, father!
Open your eyes and baptise
what remains of your body —
somewhere between Ngahere's
watercolour millsmoke
and the desolation of Totara Flat, enter
the brown snake of Grey's coiling water.

I spoke to him from where I was and I know it affected him. He returned the favour later in the letter, speaking of his own struggle to write, to teach, to live, to find a way of saying what he needed to say. "My stories were echoes of Sargeson and not until I began *A Song in the Forest* did I find my own voice. That's the problem for the writer — not 'What influences can help me?' but 'Who am I? What is my unique voice?' "

At seventy years of age, here he was, still working on finding his way. In saying this, he wanted to reassure me that I had what was needed to take the journey. "I'm convinced (1) that you are by nature one who observes and records life even while acting out your own drama; (2) that you will find your own voice; (3) that the road, as always, may prove bumpy and tempt with by-ways — as Eliot says in so many words, 'Every fresh start is a wholly new beginning for which you can't rely on the language of past successes'." I did not know it then, but this was the final written blessing of the patriarch.

Meanwhile, I continued with plans to return to New Zealand, as I had promised him earlier. "I'm thinking of coming home in a few months in (maybe) July-August. It won't be a permanent return; well, probably not. But a lengthy sabbatical, at least. I'm getting tired up here on the European Front."

We left in September, my daughter and I, flying south over the Middle East, just after Saddam Hussein's invasion of Kuwait and the arrival of US troops in Saudi Arabia. By the end of November, the UN Security Council's ultimatum to Iraq demanded his withdrawal by 15 January 1991 or face military action. It was a volatile moment in the geopolitics of oil; I just wanted to get my feet back on Aotearoa, flash my new passport, hear that "Welcome home" as we entered Customs and feel for a moment that I belonged somewhere. The land and the people worked their magic. I got a job in Greymouth in a small residential centre for addicts, bought an old Ford Anglia and began to rewire all my family connections. It took about two months of that healing wairua before I would realise I needed to go back to England, to finish what I started there: "One life, one writing", wrote the master, Robert Lowell.

Before that could happen, I had a mission to complete: find Peter and see how he was. I wasn't home long before I'd called and arranged to visit him in his latest home at Rutherglen on the road to Shantytown. The Ahaura experiment had not worked after his move from Lostwithin at Clough Road, Paroa, the purpose-built house he'd always wanted, with its recycled church windows and stable door rear entrance. I loved that place and while the new residence was beautifully sited and secluded in regrowth manuka and rimu, it did not seem as much his as Lostwithin. Paroa seemed to call him: this was the fourth home he'd had in that area from the time I'd first visited in 1965. The paintings that had intrigued me then — the Woollastons and the Chinese prints — were on these walls now and that sense of silent contemplation, felt those years ago, still reigned.

The old Anglia: Raine and I enjoying the moment, 1991.

Had he been conventionally religious, he would have been our Thomas Merton, a spiritual guide and confessor. With the love of Thoreau and Emerson as his scriptures and a transcendentalist/green philosophy, this was what he'd become, to other seekers. I thought I could feel his ribs as we embraced; he was noticeably thinner and paler, but full of talk and that habitual quiet delight in living that always drew me to him. We got to talking about my time in England, and his too, years ago; about writing and our mutual friends. He agreed to let me turn on my Walkman and record him (a new toy at the time and thank goodness, as I probably recorded his last thoughts on the writing life). He was working on a family history of the Hooper line in New Zealand, back to the Isles of Scilly and the Channel Islands. It was a healing balm to be once more in the presence of his loving acceptance. I never felt judged by this man.

I left with a sense of relief that he was still standing on the earth here with me; he'd survived a dice with death and there were the limitations imposed by the colostomy surgery, but he was alive and content. I got on with my life and work, making sure my daughter got back into education, and keeping up with family: my mother, my mother-in-law and her husband, my brother and his wife and a visit to my sister Beth recently moved to Nelson.

Peter Hooper at our last meeting, February 1991, Rutherglen.

Gradually, the reassurance of this homecoming worked deeply enough to release me for a return to England and we made plans to turn around and go back. I'd seen my friends and family, breathed the good air of the Coast and watched another failed attempt by the Labour Party to get back into office. The Gulf War was raging and I felt a pressing need to be back with my family in England, to deal with some ongoing obsessions that could not be confronted where I was.

This meant I would have to go and once more say goodbye to Peter. I made my way out to Rutherglen in the faithful Anglia; we enjoyed a glorious afternoon inside and out, wandering the property and talking books. Peter believed that there were so many being published, fine New Zealand writers like Owen Marshall and a host of others, that he simply could not keep up. He found himself at his stage in life going back to read those who had meant so much to him early on and through his journey. We spoke of love and loneliness and he recalled relationships that might have been; of missed opportunities and the meaning of friendship, the adoptions he had engaged in, informally and serendipitously with the lame, the halt and the blind — like me.

It was not an easy goodbye but, as always, we lived as if there would be a next time. Blinking in the bright afternoon sun, he stood out in the garden in front of a young rimu, a seed from the stately forest giants he had loved so deeply and worked so hard to preserve. He had lived long enough to see the Forest Accord, an end to the logging of rimu (my first job in the mill) and a revolution in the national response to our environment. He was there to see the creation of the Paparoa National Park in 1987. He was a poet but also a seer, one who could stand back, take in the view and divine what could happen to our world if we did not change course. Peter

Hooper was our Thoreau and it was my good fortune to be his pupil and friend.

I was back in England only two months, having moved from Maidstone to London, when the news of his death reached me in late April. It was raining at the time as I sat down and wrote for him and to him. The title and date on the poem read simply "Peter Hooper 24(?).4.91"; I had tried to work out the date of his death from a friend's letter, when it finally reached me. Far from home, for the second time, death had ended a precious relationship with someone deep in the roots of my West Coast identity. First it was Bill Mathieson in 1988, now Peter. The poem was dated as written on the 29th of April, 1991. It was many years later that I discovered he had died on the third day of the month; living alone, he was not found for some time.

I keep looking at
the good shot I got
of you in your grey
sweater, understating
an observation, your
light voice trailing off.

That sunset rimu over
your shoulder ablaze
with copperish fire.

31

Equal ops, homophobia & the class at City Lit

Set up now in our London council flat in Islington (we did a house swap with the tenant on the run from an abusive partner, happy to shift to Kent), with a good reference from my Maidstone boss Stephen, I walked into Waterstones Booksellers on Charing Cross Road and sat down to an interview with the manager, Paul Baggaley. Same deal as before: he read my reference, asked me what I'd been reading (Raymond Carver) and gave me the job. I'd tried — and failed, thankfully — to get a job with the Scripture Union bookshop. No doubt I was too far off their radar, my theology left-wing and charismatic. I was about to start a new life as the reference and language buyer in the basement of 121–125 — next to Foyles.

There would be many times in the months ahead when I would save the sanity of frantic foreign language students, wanting EFL and ESOL texts. They would approach the till in my basement dungeon with the plea, "Excuse me, ees these Foy Lays?" Dispatched from one of the English language schools that peppered Oxford Street just around the corner, with a list of books they needed to achieve some proficiency in our fiendishly irrational mother tongue, they were lost sheep at the mercy of booksellers who could load them up with a nice fat sale. If we didn't have the book in stock, I would generally direct them to Dillons on Gower Street, a massive emporium selling into the University of London and School of Oriental and African Studies. Never, if I could avoid it, would I direct them to that mazy bastion of biblioholic madness and mismanagement, our neighbour and the stuff of legend: Foyles.

As my family found their own ways into work and education, I dug deep and reacquainted myself with the intricacies of the bookselling trade and a gallery of colleagues in this busy London bookshop. The premises actually belonged to Foyles, a corner site on Manette Street, Soho, a vibrant intersection of history and present culture. A short walk away west was Soho Square with its park for summer loungers and t'ai chi exponents from Chinatown, with publishers' offices and restaurants galore on hand.

There were three churches in walking distance, including St Giles-in-the-Fields overshadowed by the massive Centrepoint Tower, home to pigeon-hunting kestrels, and St Patricks where I would later go on many mornings to light a candle and be hit up for change by beggars who prowled the aisles.

Denmark Street, a music shop mecca, was just over the road and St Martin's School of Art, a hop, step and jump away south of Foyles. Next to St Giles was the delightful, anarchic Phoenix Garden, an oasis of sanity, an absurdly human domain slavered over by high-rise developers. Many of us would eat our lunches there in the better weather of late spring and summer. The fumes, the traffic roar and the crush, all leavened by this restless crossroads of creativity and expressiveness. As well as having a job next to books, I soon came across a select band of authors who arrived almost weekly for book launches and events. Most of all I was free, whenever I could find the time or make it, to write myself.

I soon realised that almost none of the people I worked with had ever set out after high school or university to become a bookseller. They had blundered or wandered like me into the trade: on the way to, in the hope of, going somewhere else. There were actors, musicians, artists, DJs, small publishers, philosophers — and yes, writers. Ray Monk, who wrote a biography of Wittgenstein, had recently been employed running the philosophy section and, as I soon discovered, there was a Kiwi graphic artist working in the History section upstairs — Dylan Horrocks. We became good friends, both involved with the company union and working away at our crafts in the lunch hour. Dylan could be seen in Battistas Café next door drawing his early Pickle comics, while I sat across the road in the Café Dante writing poetry and downing coffees the texture of diesel oil as buses, taxis and delivery vans bustled past.

We were in the business of selling stories and information: fiction, poetry, encyclopedias, dictionaries, language books, travel guides, histories and latterly, computer manuals (in the sunset years of the pre-digital age when such massive tomes were eagerly bought by credit card- wielding business types who needed to know the secrets of MS-DOS and spreadsheets). I soon became aware of the real-life stories of those I worked with: the nervous newbie fresh out of university who had developed a bad sex-line addiction and would spend his lunch hour sliding phone cards into British Telecom boxes outside; he had a breakdown and fled. There was Jelena, an older Serbian woman who ran the travel section; her father had been killed by the Nazis in Yugoslavia during the war while she was still a child, terrified of going to prison with her mother, "locked up with the mice".

Waterstones Charing Cross Road staff, c.1995; I'm top right.

The ongoing bloodshed in her homeland during the 1990s would see her arrive at work inconsolable, distressed and angry at the demonisation of her fellow Serbs.

There was also the slow realisation that there were two groups of people pressing in on my consciousness: one seen, one unseen. Waterstones in London had a high number of gay staff; they could fit in there without the homophobia of many other workplaces. On the other hand, there was a notable absence: there was nary a black or Asian face in the shop when I started and it became more salient to me as time passed. When Dylan left to return to New Zealand, he passed on to me the baton of shop union rep and soon afterwards I was asked to be the London/M25 delegate at the national meetings, negotiating with management. A way had now opened for me to raise some of the wider issues in our workplace.

Light shone on me to address my own homophobia, a kind of cultural residue from childhood and adolescence I had never questioned; and an acute awareness that I had grown up in a colonial culture where racism was part of the structure of thought. Seeing it in action here in Britain drove home my need to address and challenge its manifestations. Friendships and embedded relationships both at work and with my involvement in Alcoholics Anonymous (I had become the sponsor of a gay woman, a colleague of my wife) were the re-education I needed to start dealing with wider questions of human sexuality. With the issue of race, it was more complicated; simply to bring up the question with

Waterstones' management during our discussions was to be met with blank incomprehension.

"How could we be seen as unequal?" they would respond? "Anyone can apply, we have no barriers at all, if you're qualified." By this they meant university-educated (for the most part), with a love of books. What I came to see, educated further by some of Theresa's black workmates, was the inability of these bosses to see the world through black and Asian eyes. How could they? They had no experience: inoculated by class and privilege, their liberal good intentions did not extend to an empathetic identification with the Other, no matter how many books they'd read. With the support of our national secretary Paul, a tough operator who had been through the bloodletting years of Murdoch's assault on the print unions, we began a campaign of education and moral suasion.

We asked the Waterstones bosses how they could have equal opportunities if they did not advertise. "We don't need to," was the answer, "People come to us, we have more applicants than we can possibly use." It was down to branch managers to hire, in the same way as I had been hired: a walk-up granted an interview, someone referred from another branch, or a CV lifted from the pile. What was missing in all this was how the culture looked to somebody walking into a shop: if you were black or Asian, you saw white faces everywhere, and often it was a white face — if you were still willing to ask — who would inform you, "Sorry, no vacancies." In other words, the chain was unfriendly and unwelcoming, unless you were "one of us".

When Waterstones were finally persuaded to create a new equal opportunities policy, things began to change. The manager's delegates who met with us and attended national conferences came on board and with buy-in from the company, with the union's input, equal opportunities requirements were written into their agreements with the Retail Book Association. Waterstones were now under an obligation to work towards educating staff and management in the culture and practice of equal ops and to start advertising vacancies in public media like newspapers, not just notices on shop fronts. As we had argued, the wider you canvassed, the more likely it would be to find quality applicants. Head office people from W H Smith — which owned the Waterstones chain — were later heard to be upholding this "definitive recruitment policy" at a meeting with the chairman of the UK's Equal Opportunities Commission, who was keen to cite it as a working model for other employers.

In the slash-and-burn anti-union culture inspired by Margaret Thatcher and her clones, this was something of a victory. It was a special moment for me when Simon, our assistant manager at Charing Cross Road and an active union member, hired Cyril, a young black man, to be our branch accountant. We became good friends; while there were no overnight revolutions, I've been pleased to see on visits to England in the years since 1997 when I left their employ, that diversity is alive and well in the world of Waterstones today.

Other revolutions were under way and we were feeling both positive and negative effects of these in London, and in the shop. By 1990, the Velvet Revolution in Czechoslovakia in 1989 had introduced me to the poet Miroslav Holub. In 1992, the novelist and short story writer Ivan Klima had published a collection, *My Golden Trades*, fictions based on his years — like Holub — as a non-person and banned writer under the communists. Later in that year, he came to the branch to launch the book; as I'd read it and was a Klima fan, I offered to introduce him on the night.

Ivan Klima, Prague 2007.

Such events were always worth a second look: whether it was the novelist who insisted we turn off the noisy air-conditioning fans in the height of summer, so she could be heard reading; or seeing Roddy Doyle's aunts in the front row, laughing at the references to rural Irish eccentrics he'd smuggled into his fictions. It could get dangerous too: the IRA were regularly bombing London and in 1989 a fatwa was pronounced by the Ayatollah Khomeini against Salman Rushdie for alleged blasphemy against the prophet Mohammed in *The Satanic Verses*.

The Klima visit went off without any such angst, but my interest in him was definitely piqued as he signed my copy after the long line of fans had disappeared. Suddenly I found myself saying, "I'd like to come and visit you in Prague!" My schoolboyish enthusiasms and inclusion needs had not changed since I went knocking on Peter Hooper's door in 1965. Klima was not at all taken aback (he'd recently done book tours in America, after all). "I am not hidden," he declared with an air of mystery, as if, indeed he once had been. Fifteen years later, I would make good my word; in the meantime, it would take a visit to Prague the following year to whet my appetite for the spirit of Kafka.

As well as the bookshop readings, there were small music and poetry venues all over the city: *Time Out* had pages to devoted to such events. A mere ten-minute walk from our flat near Hilldrop Crescent N7 (a street infamous for including the murderous Dr Crippen's residence) was the Torriano Meeting House: a "grass roots volunteer-run arts and community organisation in Kentish Town". In 1991, I'd gone there for computer and word processing help and discovered that the next poetry reading would feature Stephen Spender, the last of the living 'Thirties Poets' from the generation of Auden and MacNiece. I'd read his memoir in 1989 while at Kenward House and was excited by the opportunity to hear this survivor of a storied era read his work. I hadn't known he was still alive, a man now in his late 80s. I got in touch with my Kiwi friend Ken, our companion on the journey in 1987, and we set off to listen to the great man.

Spender arrived late, to a small but appreciative group of listeners, shoehorned into an area not much bigger than your granny's sitting room. He was a tall, rangy figure in a tweed houndstooth trenchcoat, emerging out of the night like an elderly flâneur who'd blundered in on a church meeting. Under his arm was an exercise book and an old paperback copy of his poetry. Bedraggled and bemused as he appeared, it didn't matter to me: I knew I was in the presence of a life lived for poetry. He was an associate of those "truly great" ones he had written of in one of his best-known poems (a work I had once copied and parodied: "I think continually of those who were truly average …"). A friend of Auden and Eliot, he had known the masters in their time.

The tributes to the elder statesman were mercifully brief. When he stood up to read, Spender was incredibly modest: "Half an hour, is that all right? I can make it fifteen minutes. There might be others who want to read?" I had thought of that, but not in the presence of this man. My notes at the time continue, "I think the poem on Antarctica was best, so thick with names of place, but it is that slightly startled cast of your face that's last in my memory. I could have listened to your ideas on poetry in the questions afterwards until the cows came home, but you stood up just like that and said, 'I'm sorry, I have to go!'" He seemed agitated and mentioned something about his wife, before disappearing into the Kentish Town night.

The magic of London lay in always having the possibility of these encounters on offer. In the following year, 11 June 1992 at the Institute of Contemporary Arts, I found myself in the same room as Joseph Brodsky and Czesław Miłosz, along with the poets Adonis (Ali Ahmad Said Esber) and Derek Walcott — three Nobel Prize winners — at a poetry event entitled grandly, Towards a New Millennium. These representative survivors of totalitarian and colonial cultures were witnesses to human failure on a grand scale, living in hope for a better future in century 21 and whatever might follow. I was in awe of these titans and their example is still clear. What remains with me is this sense of lived history and its

Joseph Brodsky and Czesław Miłosz, Jagiellonian University, Krakow, 1990.
Maciej Socho

consequences, an abiding respect for the poetry of witness. The poetry remains when the poet is gone.

I found enough courage that evening to ask Joseph Brodsky to sign my copy of his essays, *Less Than One*; he obliged, smiling perhaps as he did so at my Franz Kafka T-shirt. A few days after his death on 28 February 1996, I wrote this poem after reading his 'Tristia', an echo of Mandelstam's work. I was reaching for something they both possessed, something of what he had meant when he wrote, "A writer is the tool of his language … his ethical notions are the sharper the keener his ear is".[35]

Reading Brodsky's 'Tristia'. 4.2.96

Passing the victory arches of the Raj
where iron angels bend swords in two
and smite the boar at bay, behead a stag
gone down, I hear the English of a Russian life.

They're the diesel sounds of my mother's
heartbeat, the truth I dreamed contented
in the womb: this woman, a naval officer's
wife, fed me metres to experiment with.

So now, it's past: the mothering of empire,
the soldier father and the statue, Time.
All I have is memory, like a brother
and Mandelstam's inflammatory rhyme.

My masters on their pages had done their work: metre, rhyme and stanzas. We all have our signature, our genetic code, our fingerprint, but as W.B. Yeats once observed, "All that is personal soon rots — it must be packed in ice and salt."[36] He was speaking, I believe, of form.

In pursuit of my writing dream, I enrolled at City Lit in a poetry course and later, one for crime fiction (I'd already been paying an editorial advisor to assess a bunch of short stories I wrote in those London years).

City Lit was a popular adult education college in nearby Stukeley Street — walkable from work. Our tutor was the Scots poet and novelist Alison Fell, whose tough crits could match her name at times and my class — mostly women — were pretty unsparing of chaff in the search for wheat. One unfortunate man, after a mauling, fled the class never to return. It certainly concentrated the mind. I both admired and feared Alison, but in general she was positive towards my offerings, as were the group. I'm sure this encounter had a bearing on the arrival in 1993 of what would become something of a signature poem: 'As big as a father'.

It may be true that we have one necessary poem in us and the rest are all elaborations of that knot of feelings and their triggers: events that loneliness, rage or elation might cling to, out of a need to know who we are, or might become. My mourning for my dead father, as much a keening for his inability to embrace and affirm me, as I grew in his eyes to rival him for my mother's love, had never gone away. I had written and later published a poem for him in 1973, a year after his death: it was raw and unpolished. Twenty years later, the abrasions of time and my changes of heart had left me in a new place. I wandered about in our council flat one day, thinking of something he'd told me long ago; how in the navy, wags would shake you, hungover in your hammock after one shore leave pint too many, with this: "Hey, Bill! Wanna buy a battleship?"

From that story, from goodness knows where in a stream of consciousness, I heard the words, "one of our battleships is missing", an echo of a wartime line. The ridiculous thought, the literal quibble came next: "How could you lose something as big as a battleship?" Then I had it: how could you lose something as big as a father? I fetched my pad and pen and sat down

Howick 1950: me with my father (front, centre): Mum at right, behind Eric.

as the poem began to arrive on the energy of that phrase, 'as big as a father'. Ten stanzas later, I had a poem which began:

> I lost him the first time
> before I could grasp
> who he was, what he did, where
> he fitted with her
>
> and it's always seemed so dumb:
> how to lose something
> as big as a father.

It took a few days of tinkering to find a way out, the final image troubling me, until this came:

> The last time I lost him
> I lost him for good:
> the night and the day
> the breath he was breathing
>
> and death's head torpedoes
> blew out of the water
> the skiff of my father.

In that moment I had found my father again in a way I'd never had him with me before: the void confronted, embraced and released. I had set him free. Whatever the poem might come to mean to anyone else did not matter: this was for the two of us, alone in the room. The American poet Jack Gilbert wrote the following for a series of broadcast lectures on the Voice of America in 1965: "Poetry, for me, is witnessing to magnitude. It is the art of making urgent values manifest, and of imposing them on the reader. It is of the housing of these values in poems so they will exist with maximum pressure, and for the longest time. It is the craft of doing so in structures that are a delight in themselves. And it is the mystery of fashioning poems in such a way that the form and the content are one".[37] We all need a manifesto, we all need ancestors.

Irving Weinman, 1937-2015, writer and teacher.
© Hodder & Stoughton

From my poetry tutor I learned to keep at it; from my fiction tutor, the Jewish novelist Irving Weinman, the need for a time and place to write. He was a delightful character who helped me in many ways; his best story is with me now, the one about his city office. Irving had long ago learned you needed "a room of one's own". His answer was to hire a small office in the city, jump on the Tube in the morning with the other Joe Lunchboxes, his fellow commuters, stressed and jammed together. Arriving, he would get to work on the current manuscript until he'd had enough and it was time to go home. He had learned writing was also a job, a commitment, and if you wanted to succeed, changes of mind were necessary, and practice. He enthused our group members sufficiently that after the course ended, we met for several monthly soirées until it became obvious that, keen as we were initially, I was the only one bringing any work. We met for a final time at a spaghetti place in Covent Garden and went our ways: "My work here is done," said Irving's ghost.[38] "You write as you die, alone."

'As big as a father' on a Phantom Billstickers poetry poster in Prairie Lights Bookshop, Iowa City, seen during a writing fellowship there in 2012.

'Wall' is from *Blood Ties: new and selected poems 1963–2016* Canterbury University Press (2017)

Wall

he built a wall
a special wall
a wall of torpedoes
and drowned sailors

one he could hide behind
one he could live within
one that would keep the mines away
and the burning oil

he formed a shell
an iron shell
a shell that the crabs who
fed on drowned men made

then backed the shell
in behind the wall
where the Stuka banshees
could no more reach

and with a set of Crown
and Anchor opened a bottle
of finest rum opened a vein
and disappeared

Police confronting Poll Tax rioters, London, March 1990.
Wikipedia Commons

32

Te hokinga mai

The '90s had begun in a time of flux and change. The world scene and the landscape in Britain were equally disturbed: war in the Gulf, the invasion of Kuwait, then Iraq. It was the beginning of the end for the increasingly tyrannical Margaret Thatcher as she lost touch with her support base, railroading the country with her deeply unpopular Poll Tax. Europe was in the throes of epochal transformations, the revolutions in Poland, Czechoslovakia, and the bulk of the old Iron Curtain vassal states — even in Russia itself. It was a time you couldn't ignore politics, as old regimes crumbled and the right-wing neo-liberal project in Britain slowly gave limited ground to pressures from beneath. Labour under Kinnock was hammered by the Murdoch press, and we would have to wait for the Blair revival of New Labour in 1997 to see the Tories removed.

Or so we thought. Along with others, I should have been warned when Blair expressed admiration for the Iron Lady. In 1994 he stood up against the union involvement that had given birth to his party, and would go on to embrace the Thatcherite reforms (she later claimed her greatest achievement was New Labour). The post-war accord of citizen and state, the New Jerusalem of the NHS and nationalisation my father and his fellow servicemen and women had voted for was unpicked piecemeal and consigned to history, as Rogernomics was doing in my New Zealand homeland. Not only did I feel uprooted in Britain, but also a deepening alienation from the direction its leaders were taking. The political zeitgeist might not be so much different back home, but I knew in my bones I would one day have to get out of London and return.

For the next five years I hunkered down as a bookseller, writing and reading, getting to hear as many visiting writers as I could at shop events and elsewhere. I was beginning to accept that being a writer or an artist was a normal occupation, not needing a reflexive justification of your existence on some misunderstood margin. Britons on the whole might prefer John Betjeman to Philip Larkin, but they did honour national poets and made space for them in myriad ways. The sheer weight of numbers, of history, ensured a measure of diversity and some sense of ownership of the bards. It was possible to enter the stream of writing anywhere and find living poets, the brash newbie and the all-but-forgotten elder.

John Betjeman statue, St Pancras Station, 2007.

Europe was drawing me in: in Easter 1992, we flew to Prague for an Easter break, thundering eastwards in an ancient CSA Tupolev 154, landing at Ruzyne, greeted on the tarmac by an AK47-armed soldier in military fatigues. Václav, our taxi driver to the Pension Fox B&B, was a chemical engineer, reduced since the revolution to driving for hire in a lived-in Škoda. He pointed out sites of interest as we passed — "That was the old KGB headquarters" — and as we drove out of the city into the tower blocks that passed for suburbs, the impression of being inside a John Le Carré novel was hard to resist. The people on the tram stops huddled in the spring winds, women with baskets and headscarves, men with felt hats and long raincoats — most it seemed with their eyes downcast, hunched against the chill.

That impression lifted over the next few days, but not entirely. Prague was emerging from a long night of repression as the country began a delayed journey away from 1945 and the double wounds of first Nazi, and then Russian occupation and domination, up to 1990. We stood now in the material manifestation of the inner world Miroslav Holub and Ivan Klima had unveiled for me in their poetry and fiction. These were the dark materials and the black holes émigré poets like Czesław Miłosz and Joseph Brodsky were trying to communicate to Western audiences, innocent of the reality of totalitarianism. They were writing out of a sensibility I had first encountered long ago at high school in the work of Franz Kafka; an atmosphere that hovered in Market Square under the spires of Our Lady of Tyn, where vendors on the cobbles now sold Kafka T-shirts and Good Soldier Švjek dolls. I bought one of each and the tram tickets that took us to Kafka's grave in the New Jewish Cemetery on the outskirts of the city. His remains were there with his parents, but not those of his three sisters, murdered in the Holocaust, present only in their names.

As an act of homage, we caught a train from Prague to Terezín (Theresienstadt), used by the Nazis as a holding camp for Czech Jews and others, before they were moved on to their deaths. From here the trains carried you beyond hope to Auschwitz; here also was the cell where Gavrilo Princip had been imprisoned after the assassination of Archduke Franz Ferdinand in 1914, triggering the catastrophe of the Great War and lighting a long fuse for the next. After Princip's death in 1918, in the dismantling of the old Austro-Hungarian empire, came the creation and brief flowering of the first Czech state.

It was here that teenage Ivan Klima and his parents awaited transportation to the death camps, surviving to rejoice at the sight of allied bombers high overhead on their way to Germany. He was hoping against hope that the dark Hitlerian night might soon be over, if only the end came in time to save them. On 8 May 1945, Russian troops reached the camp: in a place where 35,000 had died and 88,000 were deported to be murdered, the Klima family were among the few survivors. The sight of a tour bus full of Germans in the car park disturbed me: how could they come here? And yet, how could they not?

I would return to London meditating on this experience: Charles Bridge festooned with painted Easter eggs, the bullet holes still visible in the walls of the church of St Cyril and Methodius where the Czech fighters who had assassinated the Nazi governor, the 'Butcher', Reinhold Heydrich in June 1942, were killed by the Germans. On Hitler's orders, the SS launched a brutal wave of reprisals culminating in the massacre of the inhabitants of Lidice and the razing of the tiny village.

When I asked our landlady at the Pension Fox about visiting the site, she was visibly disturbed: "Why would you go there?" She wanted to forget the old and embrace the new. With posters for a Bruce Springsteen album *Lucky Town* appearing on walls, waves of tourists from Germany and soon, America, a new invasion of Czech lands was happening and the

Brick chimney, Lumb Bank, Yorkshire: the view from my writer's shed window at the course.

locals were embracing a future that had to be better than their 20th-century past — surely? Not everyone would be convinced: on New Year's Day, 1993, Czechoslovakia was dissolved into the Czech Republic and Slovakia.

The new year saw me digging deeper into the need to write: over the next twelve months, I wrote short stories and started a novel, since perished, and began sending out poetry to local magazines. One of these, *IRON*, based in Newcastle was offering a discounted Arvon writing course to take place over a week in April at Lumb Bank near Hebden Bridge in Yorkshire, in a house once owned by Ted Hughes and Sylvia Plath. I paid the fee and travelled by train to Brontë country. The magazine's editors, Peter and David, ran a fruitful seminar series daily, while each of us had the time and a private space to write. Everyone would share their work and discussion was always positive, tough but fair.

My moment came when I read a simple story about an incident that had happened to me in Auckland when I was a five; a kindly old man had done me a favour, making me a beautiful carved wooden boat. 'The Boat', told from a five-year-old point of view, tells of a broken promise; it was based on my father breaking his word, that he would bring us a flash toy motor torpedo boat home from Japan. That never happened: we were presented instead with the cheap toys described in Chapter Two. I felt again our disappointment, weaving his gambling habit into the story's last line where my mother speaks of a betrayal that would cost us all dearly later.

When I told David that I'd written it the week before, at one sitting, he found that hard to believe. "I write them over and over to get that effect," he said. "This is exactly the sort of consistent point of view I try to teach people. It's all seen through the child's eye, but it's what isn't said about the parents that you learn, by what happens to the child and his responses." If Peter agreed, he said, they would publish it (a promise made good in the magazine's November issue). I was glowing by that point and the feeling stayed with me for some time. Back in London a week later, I recorded

Drawing for 'The Boat' by Dylan Tempest, *IRON* 74, November 1993.

in my diary a definite change in my habitual levels of anxiety. Since my meltdown at Kenward four years earlier, they had never died away.

I wrote in the diary again: "Going to *IRON* at Arvon broke something. Having my 'Boat' story recognised and accepted as a work of art ... even though it had [only] been written at work the week before." I seemed shocked that this could happen at all. "It was the recognition of what I'd done, the acknowledgment of who and what I am. I'm a writer and if I want to, I can write — and keep writing — stories. I don't know how long this will last, but I'm not going to be anxious. I feel as if my real life is just beginning, the life I've had to wait so long for to live and nothing will take the new life away from me. I just feel quiet and pretty humble." It isn't often we feel we're in a Rubicon moment: as it was in the evening of my spiritual awakening in Runanga fifteen years earlier, something inside me was rising, like a diver returning from the depths to the light.

More inner changes arose in that same year, as my stubborn homesickness refused to leave me. The longer I stayed away from New Zealand, the more I became aware of how different we were from the English people around us — and how deeply imbued I was by the unconscious but felt presence, of things Maori in my life. I would see Maori scaffolders on a site in Soho, hear them joshing each other; I would wander into Kiwifruits Bookshop under New Zealand House in the Haymarket and come out with books on how to learn te reo; seeing *The Piano* stirred up my separation from the beaches and the bush, the rain and sea thunder; watching *Once Were Warriors* the following year drove it home. I was incomplete.

There I was, a Pakeha fish out of Maori waters. The violence of crazy Jake Heke — the terrified kids hiding under the bed while he gave Beth the bash downstairs — broke me open into sobs in the darkened West End cinema. I was repelled by the on-screen brutality I knew so well, yet I was drawn back home to be once more with his people. I went along to a couple of Ngati Ranana gatherings, a Maori cultural group for those of all iwi, living and working in London. It left me intrigued and confused; I didn't know quite I where I fitted. I wasn't Maori but I knew I wasn't an Englishman either, despite my birth at Richmond, a few miles West along the Thames. It was the beginning of a series of expatriate epiphanies.

Maori were the invisible strand in my New Zealand identity and this slow but certain awakening — shared by thousands of Pakeha New Zealanders on their OE — seemed to call for affirmation. I came to a point where I knew I could not feel myself to be authentically a New Zealander until I acknowledged what Maori had done for me — *who they had been for me* — since we had landed in 1950 in the country of my mother's birth, her whenua left behind in the earth at Wanganui in 1921. She had gone back home. I needed to follow. I had been reading how, at the age of seventeen, the Russian poet Anna Akhmatova (born Gorenko) had adopted her Tatar grandmother's surname, "in response to her father's fear that a 'decadent poetess' would shame the family name".[39] It was a seed that influenced my next move.

I decided to change my name by adding Paparoa to my identity. Bringing my West Coast world to rest between my given and my family names was an act of poetry as much as politics, but not an act of possession. Rather, it was an acknowledgement; not conferred but borrowed, a mihi to the reo I was hungry to explore. I knew by then that their migration canoe, their mountain and river were important to Maori as signifiers of belonging to

The cloud-misted Paparoa Range frames the repair of the flood-damaged Blackball Bridge, as a brave soul crosses the Mawhera (Grey) River.

My pepeha, drawn by Cecile Aubert-Jacquin, 2017.

time and place. My mountains were certainly those dark shoulders of the Paparoa Range behind my old home, Blackball. It was also true that living there for ten years to the east on the Grey Valley, Mawhera my awa, that I had also lived for another decade on the seaward side, west, in Dunollie and Runanga, Te Tai Poutini — near half my life.

After reading Janet Frame's memoir on the night train back to Kenward after my breakdown in 1989, I had felt then and often later that my internal landscape had nothing to do with the rivers and vales of Kent, nor the council house towers of Hackney E9 or Islington N7. My psychic country was completely embodied in that place of rain and floods; of brooding mists in deep valleys where miners had toiled and died; in flax bending and threshing along coasts whipped by Tasman winds. Paparoa: I chose *to be that place* named by Maori, tangata whenua, my forebears as inhabitants, as explorers. I would discover later, it was as the poet James K. Baxter had written in an essay, "Ko te Maori te tuakana, ko te Pakeha te teina — Maori are the elders, Pakeha the younger." [40] My pepeha was now clear: "Ko *Rangitiki* te waka, ko Paparoa te maunga, ko Mawhera te awa." I began signing my drafts *Jeffrey Paparoa Holman* and sending them out as waka, seeking a favourable shore.

News arrived late in the following year from my family in New Zealand that over Easter in 1995, the Blackball School would be holding its centennial, a magnet to me. After Christmas, I booked my flights and took a month's leave from Waterstones, staying with my brother in Greymouth for the duration of the celebrations. I knew this was a once-in-a-lifetime chance, the first in decades, to see the people I had grown up with — and for some, it would be the last. The weekend was a medley of recall and forgetfulness: "Ah, yes!" moments along with too many "I know the face, what's the name?" and other gaps. It was wonderful to see my mother and my siblings lapping up our return to what had been, at times, a place of sorrow and shame. Now, there was joy and redemption.

I caught up with old friends, a few old enemies, and revelled in the chance to fire off rolls of film on my trusty Canon AE-1. It would be more than just a blessing for my memories: with a telephoto lens, I was able to capture a few candid shots of old identities, including a black and white head and shoulders image of old 'Bud' Biddulph, the father of kids I'd grown up with. He was to die not long afterwards and I managed to get a copy to his widow, Lotus. She wrote and thanked me, saying that Bud hated having his picture taken and they had few good ones. It was for moments like this I had returned.

'Bud' Biddulph, Blackball School centennial, 1995.

I drove down to Okarito in a borrowed car, drinking it all in, trying with no success on the way to locate Peter Hooper's grave. Back in London, that frustrated mission would take shape in a poem. In Christchurch before leaving once more, I rediscovered Lyttelton and the Port Hills with my old friend Maurice Teen: waking up mornings in his house to the arguments of magpies in the macrocarpa, Kim Hill on the wireless and a twitter of Kiwi accents. I was halfway home in my heart and while it would take a couple more years to make the return, I was even then leaving London behind. There was too much pulling me back where I belonged. I boarded the plane to England wishing I could stay where I was.

In my Dylan Brixton '95 T-shirt: farewell to the vanishing Blackball Bridge.

Back in London, I was in the unpacking room at Waterstones and deep into union matters; I had transferred to the goods-in section to get off the counter after three years on the front line (busy retail work in London high streets had a way of wearing people down). It was easier to get away and write. As long as the boxes of books got unpacked, nobody kept an eye on you. My workmates Alan and Graeme were characters in their own stories: Graeme was training to be a homeopath and it was unwise to declare a headache in his vicinity, as he would kindly offer a remedy. Alan was a DJ paying the bills through bookshop work, a huge Man United fan, educating my ears to dub, rap, acid jazz and hip hop — I couldn't convert him to my burnt-out hippie '60s songbook. We managed to get the aircon fixed in the airless summers and have the room sealed to cut off the exhaust gases getting in from the loading bays of shops next door. By the time I left, they were union men.

There was still plenty on offer in sights and sounds, but not always enough money to pay for the concerts of the big names that came through. I did get to hear Marianne Faithfull in the old Shepherd's Bush Empire, and Dylan again in his 1995 pomp at the Brixton Academy. In a peak moment, with my daughter I saw Allen Ginsberg on stage at the Royal Albert Hall in 1995 in a performance called *The Return of the Reforgotten*, fifty years on from the first International Poetry Incarnation show at the same venue. Paul McCartney strode on stage and backed Ginsberg on bass in 'A Ballad of American Skeletons', bringing the house down. London, always a city of surprises. Just in time: Ginsberg died the following year.

London: who can exhaust you? Certainly not me, nor Dr Johnson — but by the summer of 1996 I was worn down in the heavy unpacking role, humping the cartons in which our books arrived, pallet loads of fifty-plus from WH Smith's massive depot in Swindon. I stood back one day and

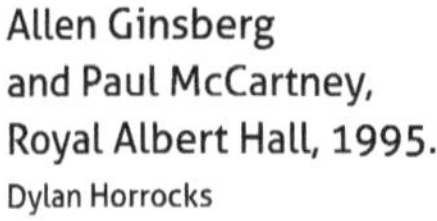

Allen Ginsberg and Paul McCartney, Royal Albert Hall, 1995.
Dylan Horrocks

Alan and Graeme, Waterstones' unpackers *extraordinaire*. Tudeley, Kent, 1997.

heard myself mutter out loud, "What am I doing here?" What was I doing, pouring out my strength, helping other writers to sell their books while I nibbled at the margins of my days: every 24 hours, a poem here, a short story there, pushing fifty? It was time to get out. Theresa — who needed to complete a degree she'd started — wasn't ready to leave. She made a suggestion: why didn't I re-enrol at university in Christchurch, go home, finish that abandoned degree and see what happened? She could follow later.

I thought about it, but not for too long; whatever nerves I might have about re-engaging with study, I was confident I could make a start. It needed some enquiries to see if I was still eligible (yes) and could I enrol from London and turn up on the day (again, yes). I began the process of withdrawal from my natal city: giving notice at work, last coffee meetings with AA friends, disengaging from that world. It was hard to leave the home we had made — a certainty of sorts — and return to stay with an old friend, becoming what is known as a "mature student". On my penultimate day, workmates from Waterstones took me to a real ale pub off Leicester Square. While I slowly sipped a Coke, they steadily anaesthetised themselves with pint after potent pint. They stood glassy-eyed and immobile as I left, unable to wave goodbye, swaying and grinning. My English friends, how could I ever forget you?

33

Te Ao Marama: an adult education

On a fraught morning in February I watched the blue Fiat Uno with its NZ sticker disappear with our goodbyes, as Theresa drove off and vanished into Kings Cross–Thameslink traffic. I struggled with my suitcases onto the Gatwick train, leaving London behind in a whirl of regrets, anxiety, excitement and relief. It was finally happening: I was going home and back to study, back to whatever might come. Boxes of books would soon be following me on the water.

In Christchurch our friend Anne Thompson was waiting to pick me up and host me as a boarder while I got on my feet. She was an ideal choice: an old family friend from the 1970s, a mature student herself who would go on to complete a PhD in French literature.

The best memory of that journey is the "Welcome home!" of the Maori immigration official and the faces of Polynesian Auckland in the airport, affirming my embrace of a place to stand. Then the flight to Christchurch, following the backbone of the land as we took off: the hills, valleys, ranges exposing their wrinkled flanks to the brilliant light. As soon as we rose over Auckland, the waters surged inside me; the cloud kingdom broke my heart with its spider's-nest-on-gorse tracery. By the time I saw breakers smashing along the Raglan coast, I was weeping all my desolation. I made a promise to myself not to forget this sense of gratitude, the meaning of this place: "If I go back on this, let me be a sheet of corrugated iron flattened by a rusty CAT D-9, driven by a backsliding alcoholic."

Hyperbole, yes, but I'm still aware of that sense of the holy I wrote of then, as we flew over the Kaikoura Range:

> Now we come to the back
> of te koura: touch him
> and he flicks his muscle!
> The land of Ruaumoko
> has food in plenty.

What I could not know then was that later the land *would* flick its flexing muscle with a vengeance, right where I was about to alight: Christchurch.

Otautahi. Once it was a childhood home and now, forty years on, a return to the life of the mind. Anne soon had me set up in her Shirley home, a room of my own and two friendly dogs. Once the jetlag had eased and I'd found my feet, it was time to enrol and become a student again. I knew I'd turned my life around. Soon it would be upside down.

I was fortunate to have other friends on campus: Tracey Hunt, daughter of a West Coast family from those Runanga revival days, was finishing off a psychology degree and kindly guided me around all the stations of the cross on enrolment day. This involved marching from one registration activity to the next; with five previous papers from 1971–72, I was halfway towards a bachelor's degree and in my first year back, enrolled in four semesterised English papers. This half-year intensive system meant I could take my first steps with two papers (Renaissance Poetry and Prose, Australian Literature) and test my mettle. I loved it: digging deep into Milton and Patrick White, I soon realised this was what I was meant for. An A and an A+ at the end of the first semester were proof of my keenness and the fact that mature students, perched in the front rows of the lecture halls, usually had fewer distractions in their lives than freshers and assorted 20-somethings.

It was a privilege to be lectured by my old English professor, David Gunby. He was delighted I had made it back from 1972, when he taught me English literature and also offered extra-curricular support as my life fell apart that year. I was introduced in the Australian paper to a couple of lecturers who would come to exert strong influences on my study and later, my writing. Rob Jackaman was a poet I'd known in the early 1970s. In 1998, in the following year, I would enrol in ENGL 231, his creative writing course in poetry. Patrick Evans— a profound thinker who would shape my future direction— sharing the teaching of the Australian material, would later teach me in New Zealand Literature and open up the world of Maori writing in English. While I couldn't take Maori language classes in my first year due to timetable clashes, I resolved to make that move in the next.

I found other outlets for the hunger that had arisen in my expatriate English decade: the University of Canterbury kapa haka group and the Anglican Maori Mission, a tikanga Maori church in Phillipstown that was the base of the South Island diocese, Te Hui Amorangi o Te Waipounamu. Here I could listen to te reo, sung in himene and waiata, prayed in karakia and recited as liturgy in Te Whakamoemiti Nui, the Great Thanksgiving. From Easter 1997 until today I have lived my faith as a Pakeha member of Te Hahi Mihinare, the Anglican church that first preached the gospel, Te

Rev Canon George Ehau with his ukulele, Tumuki Chapel, Otautahi.

Rongopai, in the Bay of Islands on Christmas Day 1814. It is a privilege to serve as a kaikarakia (lay reader), chair the vestry these days and eat my fill of rewana (unleaved) bread at the kaputi after services.

By absorption I was learning the mita (rhythm) and the whakahua (pronunciation) of Maori, both in the ranks of a kapa haka ropu and the pews of a Mountford church in Phillips Street where the whanau gathered every Sunday. The net effect was that for at least three days a week, sometimes more when kapa haka had to practise for an event, I was making relationships on a more than nodding basis with tangata whenua, all the while hearing and seeing some of what it was like for Maori as the second millennium neared its end and the first treaty settlements were signed.

Between lectures, study, kapa haka practice, writing essays, walking Anne's corgi and the whippet, life was full. I had time to visit family: my mother in Nelson and my sister Elisabeth nearby on their orchard at Appleby, my brother Eric on the West Coast and at the year's end, a trip to Masterton to see my other sister, Jill. I was experiencing a deeper level of whakawhanaungatanga: making family bonds anew through mature adult choice and commitment. Reconnecting with them, studying and reading full time, writing as often as I could and producing new poetry, I was coming back to myself. I bought a cheap bike and on freezing winter mornings with an old familiar frost, would head out to Ilam for an early lecture. In the evenings I would bike out again for kapa haka, chilled but excited that I was part of something that mattered. Standing in lines, repeating the words and movements over and over in a disciplined group that still managed to laugh and play the fool, I began to feel a member of a larger body.

It wasn't easy to start with: who was this old Pakeha guy who turned up and joined in on the first night? I was one of only two or three white faces and the feeling of being in a minority and marginal was salutary. Maori had put up with that for years in all sorts of settings, universities being a special challenge. I had to learn to get over myself. One night in a practice break, I got talking to an older man, Ted Te Hae. He was a social worker, ex-army, Vietnam; a native speaker, Tainui-Waikato, he would become a good friend over time. There was a younger man, Darcy Hata, who shared a joke one time about cartoon voices, how we heard those figures speaking in our own voice when we read the comics as children. I said I thought Donald Duck sounded like me, shocked to hear his actual cartoon voice later on. After that, to Darcy, I was Donald.

It was these small breakthroughs that mattered; through commitment and respecting the group's mana, I began to find acceptance. While it was hard to shake off that one-armed paperhanger feeling doing the moves, the surge of collective energy as we performed haka and sang in unison was compelling and uplifting. I had to be realistic: most of the kapa had been doing this since they could walk, hanging around as tamariki, joining in, copying, getting the rhythm, learning the songs, living the wairua Maori of a unique art form.

I made friends who are still friends, enjoying that signature Maori tikanga, the custom of manaakitanga, welcoming the stranger. I began to realise why the rituals of encounter that had survived the storms of colonisation were so important; not just to Maori as tangata whenua, but to us all as tangata tiriti. We are a Treaty people, a nation founded on a covenant, however much it has been trampled and sullied since its 1840 signing and 1970s resurrection. I knew the Treaty of Waitangi was back on the table and we were duty bound to respect it and live with its consequences. I soon discovered that not all New Zealanders regarded this prospect with open hearts and arms.

Watching the news one evening in April, I saw a group of Cassino veterans flying out to commemorate the 1944 battle in Italy that took so many New Zealand lives. One of the interviewees was an old man with a beard and beret, identified as Dick Moth — the old communist fruit-seller from my Blackball days. Dick had turned up at our house in 1965 after I'd written that letter about Vietnam to the paper, the one that got me razzed at the sawmill after it appeared: "Better Red than dead," I'd opined. Dick agreed with me and came knocking, hoping he'd found a willing recruit to Marxism-Leninism. Not me, I was just being bolshie, but never forgot this crusty character who would drive from his home near Takaka in a rattly old Commer truck, all the way down to the Coast, selling Golden Bay produce to the locals and distributing political tracts. I jumped for joy — I knew I had to find him.

A quick search of the phone book found a Dick Moth at Onekaka near Takaka, so I called him up. He could hardly be expected to remember me, but he was warm and encouraged me to visit. I took a bus up to Nelson to stay with my sister, borrowed a car and drove over the mountain into Golden Bay, tracking him down at his fastness — Villa Karl Marx. He'd laid a concrete path up to the house and inscribed it with sayings from the gurus of communism: Lenin, Marx and others. It was a kind of pilgrim's path and the man himself certainly had the wild and locust-eating visage of a biblical prophet — except that God, that dope dealer of proletarian delusion, was nowhere to be seen or heard.

Dick ushered me into a room filled with mementoes: posters, photographs, newspaper clippings on the walls and the incessant buzzing of swooping blowflies, later to provide loud symphonic background music on the recordings I made of him on my Walkman. He regaled me with stories of the fight to bring communism to the miners of the West Coast where he was born, in Dobson, and to the people of Golden Bay today. The hills of the area reminded him of Cassino, where he was an ambulance driver during the war. As a man with an internationalist philosophy, he had no wish to kill fellow workers who were not his enemy, but he was willing to serve to help the wounded. He told me the story of the bravest man he'd ever met as a driver: a German.

"He was shot in the stomach, no hope. But we loaded him into the ambulance with our wounded, into a bunk, along with our own man. We had to drive across a ploughed field to get out of there to the road and it was rough as guts, even driving slowly, you couldn't go too slow or you'd bog down. The Kiwi boy in there was howling with the pain of his wounds, but the Jerry didn't say a thing. When we got them back to the field hospital, the German boy was still alive but bleeding from the mouth. When they had a look at him, he'd bitten through his own tongue to stop himself from crying out. He didn't last long, poor bugger, but he was the bravest man I ever met."[41]

Dick was full of stories and it was hard to get away. He showed me around the yard, talked about the creation of the Philosopher's Walk up to the house, bewailed the drift of the country since 1984, then as a *pièce de résistance*, introduced me to the remains of his pensioned-off Commer truck. It was the same vehicle he'd loaded with fruit to ferry to the Coast where I'd met him and later, on a windy rain-swept night on

Dick Moth, 1997: communist, raconteur, local identity, with the remains of his Commer.

the Dobson Straight. I was hitching with my mate Frank after missing the last Blackball bus home from Greymouth. Here was the same truck that had given us a scary ride with a whisky-sodden Dick Moth, weaving all over the road with its one useless vacuum wiper waving away on a suicide mission to sweep the floods of rain from the windscreen.

He would straddle the centre line to keep on course; when another car approached, he'd swing wildly back to the left, just in time, as the oncoming dazzle of headlights in the rain came straight at us. Who knew whether he had even dipped his lights, and in all likelihood was blinding the approaching vehicle? As Dick mashed and smashed his merry way through the crash gearbox, its solid lever upright beside my legs, it was obvious we'd made a bad choice. We whispered to each other it was time to go and asked him let us out near Taylorville, saying we lived there, not Blackball. Sometimes you have to lie to survive. Dick Moth, I salute you, you old original Marxist renegade! And I know you won't be turning in your grave over the direction the country took after 1984; you were giving it to me both barrels right then and there as I sat in your bluebottle-crazy kitchen. You were burning alive the heretics, the slaves of Rogernomics, with a fiery contempt for their backslidden ways.

Back in Christchurch, I was writing new poetry and revising older work like never before: in a writing environment, reading and thinking

The Philosopher's Walk, Villa Karl Marx, Onekaka.

about what I was reading, writing about what I'd just read and having to work within word limits for essays and towards time constraints for completion — all of this was manna from heaven. The same skills a writer needs to produce work are those of a successful student: turning up at the coal face daily, opening yourself to new ideas in fields of art and thought that have gone before you, producing a literate and literary response. It was all there. I read somewhere about a poetry competition run by the Whitireia Polytechnic in Porirua, so looked at what I might have to send. In the end, I felt that my poem 'As big as a father' was the best I could offer; following all the rules as I'd learned to do in competitions in England, I sent off my entry and forgot about it.

Keeping in touch with Theresa in England and my adult children in France and America, I was lonely at times, so threw myself into work and kapa haka, church and AA. I made some other friends in my class: Carl, a young man who was open and warm towards me and would share a coffee and his story. I also hung out with a few of my alkie friends outside of meetings. It was a time of growth and change, of dislocation and adjustment; no matter how alienated I'd felt at times in London, for the past ten years the city and English culture had been my life. There were a few losses, especially in the realm of cultural riches. I found some gratitude at last for the way England and expatriation had changed me and broadened my world, especially in art, literature and race relations.

My old friend Maurice Teen, my flatmate and bread-round partner in the 1970s, was by now a senior Employment Court judge. Weekends spent with him and his partner Kay at their South Shore home near the beach, watching rugby tests on TV with Kay's dad helped to counterbalance the transition. Gradually I felt not just at home again, but a fresh sense of belonging. In September, out of the blue, a letter arrived from the Whitireia Polytechnic to advise me I'd won first prize in their poetry competition. It was an invitation to come to the award ceremony and collect the prize.

At the Whitireia Poetry Prize evening, 1997: Sam Hunt wins by a hair. Elizabeth Crayford (left), Trina Saxon on my left.

34

Bringing in the sheaves

I called the number and spoke to an administrator at the polytechnic; yes, it was true, the poem about my father had risen to the top of the pile and they would pay my fare to come north for the award. I was delighted — and surprised. For years in England I'd sent poems to competitions and literary magazines, with little to show. I'd concluded that my poetry wasn't that good. The lift this gave me would be temporary, but I went with the moment. A friend in Wellington, Trina — another Coaster — agreed to put me up and drive me out to Porirua on the night. The troubador Sam Hunt would be there to award the prizes, so it was pretty damn exciting all round. The evening would also be graced by the presence of Alistair Te Ariki Campbell and his wife Meg, elders in the poetry firmament and kaumatua in the Whitireia literary culture.

When we arrived I was introduced to Sam (who I'd met years ago at a Greymouth poetry reading in the 1970s, when both of us were the worse for wear). The poet James Brown, the chief organiser, told me there'd been a thousand entries; they'd whittled them down to a hundred for Sam to judge. "Your poem jumped out, even then," James said. Sam finished off the story, pumping my hand, "Bloody great poem, made me cry, made me cry, had to ring my friend and read it to him over the phone!" — all related in his signature intonation that's become a call sign in Kiwi culture. Sam asked me what I was doing, what I was writing these days? I told him I was back at university, studying English.

That flicked a switch. "University? Get away, get out of there, it'll kill the muse, get out of there and write!" I had no answer to that. Sam's path was different to mine, but I held him then — and still do — as an essential voice in the rise of post-war writing in this country. His phenomenal recall of poetry — "telling the poem", as he describes his delivery — is the mark of a true bard. He loves the sounds of language. It was a magical night, the more so to see him there with his dear friends the Campbells, a treasured memory. I'd written to Alistair from England and he had always faithfully replied, a constant encourager and friend of other writers; to see him there now with Sam Hunt was more evidence of his aroha. The icing on the cake was James Brown's offer of showing the poem to *Sport* for possible inclusion in the magazine. Fergus Barrowman took it for the Autumn 1998 issue, along with the work of another poet, Glenn Colquhoun, whose poem appeared in green on the white cover.

With exams coming up, I had to get my focus back on finishing the year with good results. I'd dug into New Zealand Literature and what was then called New Literatures (formerly Commonwealth, later, Postcolonial). I'd got my mojo back for essay writing and was studying hard. The year ended with a headful of Milton, Patrick White, Witi Ihimaera and Ngugi wa Thiong'o — along with an A and three A+'s. So far so bloody good: I was back where I'd left off in 1972, twenty-five years older, starting over.

I needed a holiday job and so took myself off to Student Job Search, finding a spot with a small owner-operated rental car company. I had a money left over and discovered a nice old Datsun 180B for sale in the paper. For a very reasonable $600 I had transport again, a chance to unwind. I would soon discover just how much had changed in the world of the New Zealand worker since the union-bashing reforms of the early 1990s: the infamous Employment Contracts Act.

1975 Datsun 180B: student wheels and the country opened up again

My career as a rental car cleaner and driver was brief and inglorious; it paid the bills, helped me run the Datsun and taught me a good deal about industrial relations in the post-Muldoon era. Taking a trip to the Employment Court in a later dispute with my employer — won with the help of my lawyer friend Maurice and his ACC-consultant partner, Kay — I got a glimpse of how the Bolger regime with its attack on trade unions and the 1991 Ruthanasia 'Mother of all Budgets' had tipped the balance of power from worker to employer. Without my friends in the legal profession the system could have screwed me too, just as it was doing to those with less recourse to support.

What the job did give me was a poem that would appear in my next book. 'I Meet Mr Hiroshima' was a version of an encounter with a Japanese tourist I'd met with a car at the airport. As I waited and bore aloft the sign for him — 'Hiroshima' — it struck me as a moment heavy with irony. Many a passerby thought so too, staring at me with my terrible sign of the times, held high.

When I finished at the rental car company, in the fortnight before university began again in 1998, I took a trip north to visit my sister in Masterton. I explored some of my old stamping grounds in the Wairarapa, especially the East Coast back country between Eketahuna and Pongaroa, driving in a borrowed Hillman Hunter back to Tiraumea and the climb to my old farm workplace, up the Pori with Doug Falconer.

A local farmer told me Doug was long dead, in Waipukurau where he'd retired. The farm had been sold and some years later, vandals had come and burned the empty house to the ground. There was a gatepost I could recognise where the driveway had been, some rotten boards and rusty scraps of iron where we'd shared a living space in 1967. In the grass, I found an old amber long-neck beer bottle, which I took away with me and still have; it reminds me of how hard the winds blow in places like that, when the people who lived on the land are gone. They blew that day and gave me another poem. In 1998 at the beginning of the first semester, enrolled in Rob Jackaman's ENGL 231 Poetry Writing course, these experiences were provoking more poetry and short stories. Once kissed, the muse was waking up.

Amber relics

(found poem, letter)

But the desolation that came over me
the empty space that greeted me
the yards, the dog kennels, the driveway
just the wind, the grass, the macrocarpas

not even a rusty pot, or a nail —
the best I could find was some broken bricks
a couple of the old long-necked beer bottles
amber relics of a lost tribe

35

Breaking up

In 1998 two entangled forces, love and poetry, took over in my life. There are times in our lives we can never fully explain, nor with respect to others should we try. That's a way of saying this was never going to be a tell-all journey and those of whom I speak now didn't ask to be on these pages — it's my story, not theirs. When they do appear, it will be brief and without elaboration. Anyone that was hurt or damaged, blessed or exalted in this time, I hope I have already made my peace with them. Let's begin with the poetry: the blood here is in the print.

The year began with a song. I'd finally begun attending Maori language lectures and was starting the poetry writing paper with Rob. I couldn't wait to get to his lectures and the weekly tutorials with Julia Allen. It was a combination of informal teaching, where each week a literary form like the sonnet, or some aspect of technique that Rob would present; in the tutorials, we would bring our work for discussion. The lectures for Maori beginners took place in large, unfriendly theatres designed for mass education, not quite so user-friendly. But we were under way: learning to think and speak in another language, and between the two classes, the juices flowed.

I was making new friends and strengthening the bonds: some of my fellow students in MAOR 115 were in the kapa haka group, and others familiar from my church. The Maori Department moved into a new home that year and we were involved in the celebrations, which meant more

Te Rita Papesch, new ta moko: one of my early kaiako in te reo Maori.

practice sessions, getting the moves and the waiata polished for the big occasion. I'm sure that the music and the movement embodied there had an effect on my writing: poetry along with all language forms is first a physical effect in experience. Oral cultures, those that privilege memory and performance, know this well; for me, the page and the stage are friends. I'd long since formed the habit of reading aloud and testing the sounds and rhythms in my writing, prose and poetry.

Rob's classes and Julia's tutorials gave me an outlet at last, sharing work with like-minded others as I'd been able to do in those courses in London. Presenting our poetry in these classes, I got to know Jeanette: we were two older students in the group and often sat and talked together. She was a lecturer in the Maori Department; she also had West Coast roots, born in Hokitika, educated at Westland High School and taught English by Peter Hooper. My old master's influence had a long reach. He'd gone there after his bookshop venture had been unable to support him; students like Jeanette had been privileged to have him in his final years of teaching.

Rob's insistence that we take our writing seriously pushed me into doing something I'd wanted to do for some time: self-publish. There were plenty of stories around during my pre-internet days in England of groups and loners who made demo tapes, sent them to a music publisher or DJ — and got a break. I started to work up a collection of poems I'd written in London during the 1990s, plus a few new ones the course was throwing up. I was writing more often with the input and the support of the class. By the middle of the year I had manuscript and a title: *Flood Damage*. With a nod to my developing reo, I created a national publisher, Kupu Books: sought out a small print company, Molten Media, and with the help of its editor Jonathan Fisher, produced a booklet.

It had a card cover, it was stapled, it was thin, but it was mine. We set up a launch at the Green Room in town. Jeanette and her two children turned up and some new friends from ENGL 231. A week or two later I loaded the unsold copies into the Datsun and took it on a spin to the Coast for a launch in the fabled Blackball Hilton. It was raining hard through the Lewis as I slipped on a soul music tape and turned it way up high: Brook Benton crooning 'Rainy Night in Georgia'. The whole car seemed to wail with him as the fingers of water drummed on the roof. On the night of the launch, friends and family turned up at the bar, along with the odd heckler. I was home at last, spinning poetry into the air of the same room where my father had flung his darts into double tops in the music of pub-roar men-talk.

Back home, I wrote a poem about *Flood Damage*, the pub, kapa haka and the journey to print, 24 years since my first and only publication thus far: *Strange Children* (in *Two Poets*). It would turn up in the next volume.

Barrelling down the Grey Valley at 90K
and Thar She Blows! Harpoon sunbeams
spear the mist to crown my lifelong
destination: Blackball squats in cold wet
skirts, my longtime mother, Paparoa. Are
you two still at it? Tear the world apart all
day, each evening lying back exhausted. The stars
are my witnesses: two lovers in mud gone

glorywrestling. I pass a truckload of spaghnum
moss, I pass the New Forest Sawmill at Ngahere
and it's almost 1957 in my Popchart.

Patrons in the Blackball Workingmen's Club and Mutual School of Arts.
Pete Bell, courtesy Nicola Bellugue

ABOVE Cover image of Blackball Bridge for *Flood Damage*.
Inkster photo

It was 18 months since I had left England and there was still no certainty about when Theresa would join me. A gap was opening up in my life as I slowly confronted the truth: my attentions were turning elsewhere. The film festival was in town and I was going to see *Mabo: Life of an Island Man*, a 1997 documentary about the Torres Strait Islander Eddie Mabo. In 1992 his challenge to the '*terra nullius*' lie changed Australian history, when a High Court ruling recognised the islanders' equality before the law and their prior occupation as conferring native title. Jeanette was keen to go and so we went together. I'd already decided to tell her my feelings had gone beyond friendship and, sharing coffee afterwards, she came clean too.

There is no easy way to end a marriage, no way that isn't cruel and selfish, that doesn't wound children and confuse friends. My reaction to falling in love and feeling my feelings, grieving losses old and new was to break down in my little flat, weeping as if somebody had died. I'd moved out of Anne's place: she was an old friend of Theresa's and loved our children, as I did her son. I had to go. I sought out a counsellor, a wise Catholic nun trained in the field of transactional analysis. She was well qualified to understand my conflicts with Christian teaching, especially the words of Jesus on marriage and divorce. She helped ferry me across that Jordan, into a sanity that left me stable enough to carry on. Within the next few months, I found myself with not just a new love, but her two children.

We began another journey into the world of the blended family — somewhere I'd been before with Lee, but with a few street smarts by now. As 1999 began we were all together in the house where I live today. I struggled through my final undergraduate year trying to keep on an even keel. You have to be some kind of machine to leave twenty years of marriage behind and build a new world at the same time. I was flesh and blood; human, all too human. Mid-life love and leaving is complex and volatile; it isn't surprising that second and third marriages and partnerings go the same way as the failed first. We're still together by grace alone, twenty years on. Along the way, I was passing my Maori language papers and studying Maori politics, as well as the sociology of ethnic identity. Something was building and by the end of that year, at long, long last, I graduated with a Bachelor of Arts.

In the following two years, 2000 to 2001, I studied for Honours with a double major in English and Maori Studies, working with Patrick Evans and John Newton. John encouraged me to go and interview my old hero Bill Pearson, the author of a ground-breaking 1960s novel set in Blackball,

Coal Flat. Shy and self-effacing, in a series of two long interviews, this deeply closeted retired English professor spoke with me about his life and writing. One session had been conducted in 1999, the second in 2001 for my Maori Honours research essay. I used some of the material I'd collected on his relationships with Maori during his time at the University of Auckland, and how he came to discover the Maori family in Blackball who were models for the publican's wife and daughter in the novel.

With a focus on the representation of Maori by Pakeha writers, I chose Lyndsay Head for my supervisor in that paper. A colleague of Jeanette's, an early student and graduate of the Department, Lyndsay had been taught by Margaret Orbell and Bill Nepia. A fine Maori linguist and historian, she was one of the few academics teaching history in this country at that time who were literate in Maori and able to read and interpret historical material — letters, newspapers — written in te reo. It was a fruitful encounter, even if Bill Pearson wasn't too happy with my conclusions when I sent him a copy of the finished article, with its "unfriendly tone". He'd begun planning the novel in the late 1940s: he didn't know as much about Maori then as he would later discover, in his relationships at the University of Auckland in the 1950s, and it showed in the writing, and revision of the manuscript.

In the same year, I'd finally got another manuscript together and with input from James Brown, the writer-in-residence at Canterbury, and Bernadette Hall, local poet and friend. At last, we had something. James suggested I send it off to Roger Steele of Steele Roberts in Wellington, a small independent publisher with a strong and growing poetry list and a commitment to writing on Maori and Pakeha relationships. I took his advice, sent off the manuscript and waited. I had plenty to occupy myself with: one reo paper demanding attention and another involving the translation of historical documents. In the world beyond these shores, on September 11 of that year, hijacked jets crashed one after the other into New York's Twin Towers; an old world burned down with them, falling, falling.

36

Why I love Jack Gilbert

Poetry, for me, is witnessing to magnitude.[42]

— Jack Gilbert 1926–2012

I've heard it said recently that memoir and autobiography tend to fizzle out and deflate as the writer winds down or runs out of puff; as life gets more settled in middle-age, it supposedly gets less exciting. My mid-50s seemed to be going in the opposite direction, much of it with no effort on my part. The world had gone crazy — or crazier — after the attack on New York, in a year when Jeanette's father had died suddenly and the pressure of finishing Honours was intense. I arrived home one day and picked up the mail: white, undistinguished envelopes that looked like bills or pleas for money. My habit was to decant my books, make a coffee and then sit down to check the post. One had my name and address handwritten so I flipped it over.

On a back was a twin dolphin-mirrored image and my heart skipped when I recognised the Steele Roberts colophon. Rejected manuscripts were usually returned in the SAE dutifully included, so a letter was a good sign. The manuscript had not been sent back. I still have that letter which began, "Kia ora Jeffrey, I think your poems are great and I'd be proud to publish them ..." I did start to shake a little, reading to the end of the page with the details about the need for Creative New Zealand support if the book was to see daylight — but that didn't dampen my joy. I was so excited, I rang Roger right away, babbling about how wonderful it was, how happy and grateful I was, how, how, how ... etc. He had to calm me down, reminding me that we needed funding. If that came through, we could go ahead and publish in 2002. I would need to get up to Wellington sometime so we could work on the manuscript. It was like a dream.

I burbled away, breathlessly, admitting, "I don't know what to say!" Roger didn't waste the opportunity, "How about 'goodbye'?" He was a busy man with many books to juggle, occasionally possessed of a straight-shooter's aim when it came to time-wasters. I hung up and glowed, alerting all and sundry to the good news, family first, giving thanks in my heart. Why all this internal drama? Those who take a long-odds bet on themselves for a decade or three understand just what it is creative artists do — singers, painters, actors, playwrights, novelists, sculptors and yes, poets — to reach that moment when a door opens.

This means no disrespect to the miners, mill hands, shearers, social workers, wharfies, rubbish collectors, posties and a million other hopefuls in other worlds of work. I've been there and done my share; but there is a difference between a steady job, regular pay, legal protections — with the chance the artist takes, the misunderstandings, the cold bath of reality with rejection as part of the job description. I'm well aware of sackings, redundancies, bankruptcies and workplace psychopaths that many workers face, as well as stupid politicians who keep making it harder for us to survive. There is no safe place, no womb-to-tomb security; but the inward adventure, to discover who we are is a risk worth taking. So now *As Big as a Father*, the book, was pregnant.

Roger secured the funding and so the book could go ahead. I travelled to Wellington, we met at last and clicked. He had a sharp beard, a sharp eye for editing and a sharper wit; as we sat side-by-side in front of his huge Mac desktop, drilling down into the poems on screen, he covered his face in his hands after a long session, looked at me sideways from between his fingers and muttered, "I hate poets, don't you?" Well met: it took a while for me to get what sort of a kidder he was. Next minute, he was on his feet, grabbing a guitar, striding around the book-canyons of his crowded office, strumming and singing a Bob Dylan song.

It was Robert Graves who, when informed there was no money in poetry, retorted, "Well, there's no poetry in money, either!" Roger knew that only too well and yet was willing to publish *and* perish, if need be. He was also a Maori speaker, friend of a New Zealand literature that would cede some stolen ground to Maori writers and those who wrote about our shared history. We could hongi together as men who supported the kaupapa of creativity with justice; it wasn't long before he was addressing me with my chosen name, Paparoa.

We would go on to publish three collections of poetry together, the first making it to the Montana New Zealand Book Awards in 2003 when *As Big as a Father* got as far as the poetry shortlist, with books by Robert Sullivan and Glenn Colquhoun (who took the honours on the night, his book also published by Roger). The book garnered some good notices along the way: Peter Bland in the *Listener* liked "a touch of the Steinbecks"; Mark Murphy in the *Press* felt "the outstanding feature of his poetry is its verbal energy"; Andrew Paul Wood in *Canta* was not so thrilled, with "poems that spraggled down the page" — referring to the collection's opener, 'The last Huron language speaker'. This poem about language loss among indigenous peoples was the one that, Roger Steele later told me, had drawn him in from the first reading. You can't win them all, but this dream beginning was the kick-start I needed, to go on.

That same year, by virtue of Roger's friendship with her, I got to meet Jacquie Baxter at a celebration in the Green Parrot restaurant, on the day she was given a long overdue honorary doctorate by Victoria University of Wellington. The widow of the poet James K. Baxter, a poet and short story writer herself who blossomed in a late career as a writer, she had been Steele Roberts' first published author when the firm began in 1996. Her collection *Dedications* deservedly won a poetry honour award at the Montana Book Awards in 1997 and it was a signal pleasure to meet her. My impression of her deep humility was instant: she deflected all my congratulations and spent the rest of our brief exchange asking me about what I was doing. She'd had years of practice in self-deprecation, living in the shadow of a legend, alive and dead. "Kaore he kumara e ki, he aha tana reka — the kumara does not boast of its sweetness."

The last Huron language speaker

The last Huron
language speaker
in the world.

(Let us weep for him)

The last Huron
language speaker
in the

(Let us weep for

The last Huron
language speaker
in

(Let us weep

The last Huron
language

(Let us

The last Huron

(Let
The last
(
The
...

The Green Parrot in Wellington, 2003: Jacquie Baxter, Jeffrey, Father Paul Bergin, Roger Steele, Christine Roberts and Robin Brew.

As the dust settled after that wonderful year, I touched on a trigger to my old West Coast life in a *Listener* review of a book about New Zealand bridges. They had used a photo of my beloved Blackball bridge, mistakenly identifying the ancestor as "the Ngahere bridge". I began to think about the part that structure had played in my early life, those ten years growing up in Blackball. I began what became a series of forty-five poems, syllabic sonnets recreating the life of the town and its people with the bridge as a portal into that vanished world. It was the usual probe into the darkness where a poem begins, a line that moves off and takes you along with its energy to whatever lies behind.

It began with a memory of finding that old abandoned spaniel, sighted at the end of the bridge one misty night as we rode in the NZR bus from Ngahere across the Grey River to the Blackball pictures (we still lived in enemy territory at that stage, before we crossed over). Sandy had become our childhood pet. I made him the star of a first poem, that triggered another. I found myself meditating on a past life in that lost world; over the next few weeks came a steady, if irregular flow of unrhymed mostly iambic sonnets. They resolved themselves in a series of glimpses: pen portraits of a community integrated by its *raison d'être*, the coal in the hills, a radical socialist history and the dead-end geography of a mountain valley where the road petered out as the mouths to the two mines opened up. Like this:

Sonnet ii

Even as a photograph you carry weight.
Even though you're roofbeams now and carry sky.

The last time I had my picture taken on your rotten
deck the gorse flowered over slabs of bitumen

where fat black NZR Bedford bus tyres and
coal train wheels rumbled come rain or shine.

I don't feel the least bit sentimental for the sunken
nineteenth century, but Brother Bridge, I do miss you.

They don't make them like that now.
Why would they? How could they?

Now, you're obsolescent planking, marking
the route to my old town's grave: but when coal

was still some kind of king, you were
the royal road to heaven for kids like me.

I had found a form to carry the freight of what I wanted to get across: the bridge of memory with its weight of the past. As well as the poem sequence, in 2002 I'd begun doctoral studies: the heavy reading of theory and finding short-cuts to untangle the nets of postmodernism was relieved in the moments I sat down to escape by writing poetry. The poem's flow came to a point where I sensed it was ebbing, that I'd said enough and needed to leave town again. I had written forty-four sonnets, so one more would give me forty-five — the name of a local card game the townspeople used to play in the evenings in the local Druids Hall: *45s Tonight* chalked up on a blackboard outside the door.

Roger liked the manuscript and took it straight away. I searched for photographs from the National Library to make the book into more than just a volume of individual poems held together by the psyche of the poet. In the process of writing, it seemed to have become an insider's social history told from experience, a search for the voice of the town and its people. The finished book was a beautiful object: with its front cover photograph of the bridge undergoing demolition, wreathed in a Grey River mist, the last span blown up with dynamite on the back cover. Steele Roberts had created a larger than usual format, with a host of black and white images depicting the life of the town. Roger had high hopes that we would again get into the running at the book awards, but no dice this time. What was better for me — in the heart, not the ego — was taking the book back to Blackball in September 2004 for a launch in the Hilton.

All my family came: Mum, my older brother Eric, sisters Jill and Elisabeth, Jeanette and her son Mark, a host of locals and my old school friend and musician Read Hudson who played some cool workingmen's ballads. It was a night to savour and cherish, as I wrote afterwards to my

The Holman clan: me, Mum, Jill in front, Elisabeth beside and Eric.

children overseas. "The sweetest thing was to see your Gran there, the old lady, a tiny matriarch, the crown of her clan with her children all around her. It will never happen again, that we go back to Blackball together, but this was enough. The Holmans came home and we could finally leave, dignity intact."

The book got some good notices and there were a few letters from Coasters, even a phone call where the caller told me he had read one of the poems to an elderly relative who knew the person I'd described — and he'd cried. Those are the best reviews. I was grateful to Roger and also to Steve Braunias, books editor for the *Listener* who had done a two-page spread of the poems early on and encouraged me to keep at it. I'd discovered I liked writing series — a long poem, if you will, in a group of related shorter pieces. I suspect it was an instinct to escape the cage of the short lyric and return to an early poetic in the tradition where poetry told stories and contained histories of a people, a group, a tribe or a nation.

Sonnet (xv)

My politics came in the daily bread: the Tories
were waiting their chances to pay back the men

who'd stood with the wharfies in 1951. Sid Holland
and his fascist gang were out there somewhere, in

the hills. My enemies were Japs, Jerries and bullies
on the school bus home, Saturday night and the slam

of the red front door: I knew first-hand that life
was war. When National closed down Roa, we knew

the Tory wolf was back for more: "Why the hell else
would they want to lock up the best metallurgical coking

coal in the world?" Revenge, if you believed the union:
"Break the miners, you can break the workers!" And all

the while the river tore at the bridge's weakest link —
that eastern bank where the Furies of the Flood bore in.

The impulse to pick up something I cared about and examine it from many different angles stirred me; along with the single poem, the isolated lyric, I found myself over the next few years writing themed collections. *Autumn Waiata*, a series reflecting life around the university campus, was begun in 2004 and finally, in an expanded form saw daylight in 2010 with

Reading a Blackball sonnet at the Blackball Workingmen's Club 2008 Crib Time Strike Centennial.
Lianne Dalziel photo

Roger Hickin's lovely Governor's Bay-based Cold Hub Press. The next year I moved on to my aviation obsession, a collection called *Wing Waka*, which never saw the light of day in that form. Roger Steele reckoned it needed a few more iterations, and eventually I cut the poems off that bore no relation to the flight sequence and refashioned as *Fly Boy*, which appeared in the same year as *Autumn Waiata*.

Richard Reeve, reviewing *Fly Boy* in *Landfall Review Online*, found many of the poems "pleasurably reverberative, imaginative, where his poise and rhythm and flair for rich language surface." He was not so thrilled in the collection as a whole, calling for more weeding out of lesser poems.[43] Harvey McQueen, on his *Stoatspring* blog a few weeks before his death on Christmas Day 2010, had found a contagious intimacy in the poetry, writing that had he known earlier of the fantail poem 'Piwakawaka', he would have included it in his final work, the anthology *These I Have Loved*.

Piwakawaka

Waka jumper, feather box of tricks on
springs, tree-hopper, handbrake-turn show-stopper,
fantastic tail-spreader, full-house tree-clown
two flits short of coming a bad cropper.
Pathetic fallacy! For one moment
my heart jumped out and into you: beyond
the window's glass you snatch up joy. Insects
actually: heaven sent by the fat
season's purblind hand smack
into your squeaky trap's sweet reflex.

He put the book down, he wrote, "enriched by Holman's enthusiasm, rapture, questioning, explanation. His volume is an example of why I like poetry and poets who make it."

When you receive a response like that, it is a reminder that we write for only one reader at a time, whoever it might be; the reception hot or cold. E te rangatira, e Harvey, haere, haere atu ra, kia okioki ai ki ou tupuna ki tua o te arai![44]

Attempting to capture my experiences on shearing gangs in a series called *Second Cuts* has never quite got over the finish line; it waits for the sheep to dry and work to start again. A series of Bob Dylan fanboy poems began in 2008, digging into the lines of 'A Hard Rain's a-Gonna Fall' as kickstarters. Weaving through a number of metamorphoses and publishers' readers, it saw the light of day in early 2017 under the auspices of the Mākaro Press as *Dylan Junkie*. Six weeks before that, *Blood Ties: New and Selected Poems: 1963–2016* had emerged from Canterbury University Press, poems from many of the above volumes included there with others. Murray Bramwell reviewed both volumes favourably in *New Zealand Books*.[45] Vaughan Rapatahana in the *Pantograph Punch* found the collection "potent and engrossing, but one that might possibly enrage."[46] It's been a season of harvest since stepping on that plane back home in 1997.

The proverb quoted earlier in relation to Jacquie Baxter, "Kaore he kumara e ki, he aha tana reka — the kumara does not boast of his own sweetness" applies here too, as a disclaimer. The above list of works is not meant to blow my own trumpet. I set it out as a record of what can happen when we take our gifts and abilities seriously and find shelter, support, critique and succour in teachers, helpers and healers. None of this would have happened had not many kaiarahi, loving guides, appeared in my life over those years. One of the greatest was now to desert me: in 2005, after a long and at times difficult and dangerous life, my dear mother Mary went to her rest on 20 June, after a night of watching her favourite TV show, *Dancing with the Stars*. She surely did: arising that morning early, she went to the kitchen, poured a glass of water and fell down dead in an instant, her tired old heart giving up at last.

She was the chief of my teachers: carrying me inside her, delivering me into the world, bringing me to language, and so, to poetry. Her Welsh forebears on both sides had given me the music and my father, the London cheek and the grit to "smile in the face of mankind" — another Dylan line with echoes. I owe it to her for all her care, and to Robert Zimmerman for all he taught me, to write it down and speak it out. I owe life a payment in kind.

Not long after we buried mother dear with her long-dead sailor husband in the RSA plot at Greymouth's Karoro cemetery, sitting quietly at home

Wedding day,
Fairfield House, Nelson,
18 December 2005.

one day, Jeanette said, "I think we should get married." Eight years on from our first meeting, I was happy to agree — and so we did.

So where is the poet Jack Gilbert in all this, and why do I love him? He turns up in the story of my poetry in that same year, 2005, with mother gone and an ache in my heart to nurse. I'd subscribed to the *Paris Review*, having — in the third year of my doctoral scholarship — more money than usual. As well as publishing poems and stories, the magazine has revelatory writer interviews. My first issue contained a conversation with an American poet, Jack Gilbert — a man I thought I'd never heard of (I discovered later he was one of the contemporary American poets David Walker had recommended over the course of our correspondence in the 1980s, and I'd never chased his work).

I started to read the interview: it wasn't long before I found myself stopping, re-reading over and over some of the things he was saying about poetry, about what it meant to him and what he felt it could do out here in the world. It was as if I'd stumbled into the lost city of the human heart: Gilbert's credo and poetics may not be for everybody, but he had me by the spine, by the marrow. In 'The Art of Poetry No. 9', I heard things articulated that I believed, that I had to some degree lived, but could hardly have expressed — there they were. Like this: "When I read the poems that matter to me, it stuns me how much the presence of the heart — in all its forms — is endlessly available there. To experience ourselves in an important way just knocks me out. It puzzles me why people have given that up for cleverness. Some of them are ingenious, more ingenious than I am, but so many of them aren't any good at being alive." [47]

It wasn't just his views on poetry in the interview, but more his attitude to life and to his own experience. He'd fled fame when lionised young after his first collection, *Views of Jeopardy* won a Yale Younger Poets Prize in 1962 and was considered for a Pulitzer that year, along with collections by Robert Frost and William Carlos Williams. His early life in the steel city of Pittsburgh where he'd worked in those monstrous and dangerous mills was right there in the sample of poems published at the end of the interview. I went out and ordered his most recent book. There I found my world again in language that reached into me, mysteriously empowered by the presence of a heart "endlessly available", as he'd spoken in the interview.

Anyone who could write —

> If the locomotive of the Lord runs us down,
> we should give thanks that the end had magnitude[48]

— had my attention. I ate him up and he entered my bloodstream, another of those chosen ancestors, whose paths we cross without intending a meeting. By a series of divine flukes, I found an old friend of his online, Bill Mayer, who had known Jack in his Berkeley days in California. He gave me the rest home address of a man now old in that city, silenced in the end by Alzheimer's. In 2012, a few days before he died, I paid Jack Gilbert a visit.

Said, 'Jack'

> Nobody knows what colour the next rainbow
> will be. We think we know, because we remember.
> What if the next bow were the colour of blood? A voice
> from space declaring, 'Your time is done'? You would lift
> your head from your book, would you not? *The Great*
> *Fires* by Jack Gilbert, source of a lifetime's jewelled wisdom.
> And that line: 'It wakes them up, baffled in the middle
> of their lives', out of 'The History of Men' — his heart applying
> itself to yours, fixing your father's bleeding negatives deep
> in a bath of potent chemicals. Now, I can feel a new kind
> of rainbow: not because the poet is dying, dying soon
> at the end of the line, the one that breathes, 'pneumonia'.
> This bow is bending my hand to the wheel — it's ploughing
> up what's left of my heart. Its colour somehow knows I love him,
> I only get there just in time, put my hand in his — say, 'Jack'.[49]

How does this happen? After all this time, I don't know: the poets, the poetry, the stream of life that delivers us into the world, into language, into the arms and the presence of others. I'm just grateful for what is, right now, whenever life conspires to deliver a poem, or conditions propitious. It was like that in 1998: full of juice in Rob Jackaman's course, studying the history of stained glass windows in another paper on 12th-century church culture, inspired by a visit of the Australian poet Les Murray where he gave a reading on campus, I was kicked into action by hearing him that night. It was a poem about birds on a dead tree in the middle of a farm dam in rural New South Wales that got me. I could see them, I could see that dam, just like those I'd seen years ago in Western Australia. Creative jealousy or creative drive: who knows? The poem that came out of this matrix, 'The Iconography of Birds', I dedicated to him, sent it to him — and still regard it as having wings.

The iconography of birds

for Les Murray

Christ the Pelican tears His own
breast in the rose window of heaven.

Across the Gothic vault of the sky
migrate the wings of faith, as waders fly

the jampacked estuary, each knot,
oystercatcher, bar-tailed godwit

feathered with the flag of Odysseus,
wings oar-dipping from parenthesis

to parenthesis of the food season's
cornucopian twin hemispheres.

Christ the Dove migrates there with them
as herds of dwindling crosses vote for a heaven

they can't see, can't touch, can't taste or smell
but know is there by scriptures from the gene pool

drummed into hearts by the wingbeat:
instinct, instinct, instinct, instinct.

37

Doctor Best

With all this versifying, in the early 2000s I had a PhD to start writing: an adventure that would send me into the heart of the Urewera. In harness with the making of poems, from 2002 until 2007 I was head down into a doctoral thesis I'd never planned to write. I'd already enjoyed five years of university life and the chance it gave me to expand my views of the world and bask in a writing environment. Whatever Sam Hunt thought about academia killing the muse, for me it was life support. I knew that James K. Baxter after his year in Dunedin as the Burns Scholar in 1966 had called the university culture "an old men's home" — but that depended a little on whether or not you were old to begin with, a seeker for security without risk. I'd met people like that everywhere and good for them, but I was wary of ennobling the opposite: risk-taking and iconoclasm for their own sake. There was plenty of that in the drug and dropout world I'd escaped to in the years I stayed parked intellectually, drunk and stoned.

Yet the student loan I'd accrued bothered me. By the end of 2001, I was looking to get out and earn some money — but how? Going back to bookselling was an option (I'd worked part-time for a couple of local shops), but I wasn't thrilled by that. It felt like going backwards. In the Maori Department towards the end of the last week in the final term, Lyndsay Head, my Honours supervisor for a paper I was writing on Bill Pearson, asked me about my plans for the next year. When I told her I was thinking of leaving, she looked at me like I was crazy. Why didn't I apply for a scholarship? I had good grades, there were Masters and PhD awards available — why not try? I had no project in mind, but she said that wasn't a problem; we could find one, surely? We sat down and cobbled together something capacious, on the representation of Maori in fiction and film in the 20th century.

We had to get the proposal lodged in a hurry; this was on a Monday or Tuesday and applications closed on Friday. I spirited the document over to the appropriate authority in the Faculty of Arts and waited. We'd gone for the doctor: Lyndsay thought I had the ability to step straight into a PhD project without doing a Masters first — the scholarship paid more, too. It all seems daring at this distance (you could not do this today), but we took a risk and it paid off. I was granted a doctoral scholarship for three years, with my fees paid and $15,000 per annum. That may not sound a fortune now, but back then, it was way ahead of whatever was in second place. For the next five years, I would undergo a radical refashioning of my ideas; a deepening experience of Te Ao Marama, the Maori world of light enmeshed with my own, yet so different — and with a sting in the tale.

Lyndsay agreed to be my principal supervisor and John Newton from English would co-supervise. I was given an office and my own hand-me-down E-Mac desktop computer that looked like a space capsule. I loaded the shelves with books acquired since my return in 1997 and sat there trying to look like I knew what I was doing. I had to create a bibliography and write a proposal, which meant hours of reading around in postcolonial theory. The original back-of-an-envelope proposal was scrapped, the focus narrowed down from films to books and eventually, the writing of Maori history in the 19th and early 20th centuries by the two most prolific Pakeha authors: Elsdon Best and James Cowan. It was soon obvious that Best was by far the more significant figure and his work became the subject of the thesis.

Effective research, I learned over this time, should at the very least change the mind of the seeker from where they begin — if you already know the answers, why bother? In certain fields, like those which touch upon Maori-Pakeha relationships past and present, research can rewrite your life. It was certainly true for me: the more I dug into this man, one I would come to characterise as a frontier intellectual (self-taught, ornery, tough and smart), the more I was drawn to the world of the Tuhoe iwi in the Bay of Plenty. Best lived among them for fifteen years, from 1895 to 1910, seeking as a budding ethnologist to track down the secrets of "the Maori mind" and "the old-time Maori".

The journey would take me out of that cosy office and into the Urewera itself where Best did his fieldwork: to meetings with Tuhoe men and women there, descendants of his informants and also his enemies, those who disputed his findings then and now, those who revered him while he wrote their histories in that era and those who, in a different day, still do. In the process, I was to encounter — first on paper, in letters written in the early 1900s — his principal informant, his ruanuku (wise man), the Tamaikaimoana chief, Tutakangahau of Maungapohatu. Later I would meet the old man's descendants, men like Tipene Ohlson of Kaingaroa, becoming firm friends with him after he played the part of his ancestor in a film made about Best and Tuhoe, by one of their own, Hemana Waaka.

This came about after my first visit to the area in 2004 when Hemana, a documentary filmmaker from Ruatoki, heard about my research and came looking for me. He took away chapters I had written, and later made a film. Tipene played Tutakangahau in the docu-drama that emerged from this encounter, shown later on Maori Television and TV One. With Tipene's help I would eventually get to visit the sacred site of Maungapohatu itself, deep in the Urewera where Best had worked and lived. I even got involved in an online auction for a trove of the ethnographer's books, signed copies of the tomes that were his intellectual storehouses, his pataka of overseas 'authorities'. My bid failed, but the buyer, a secondhand book dealer I tracked down, kindly allowed me to visit his shop and create a bibliography of Best's fiery annotations.

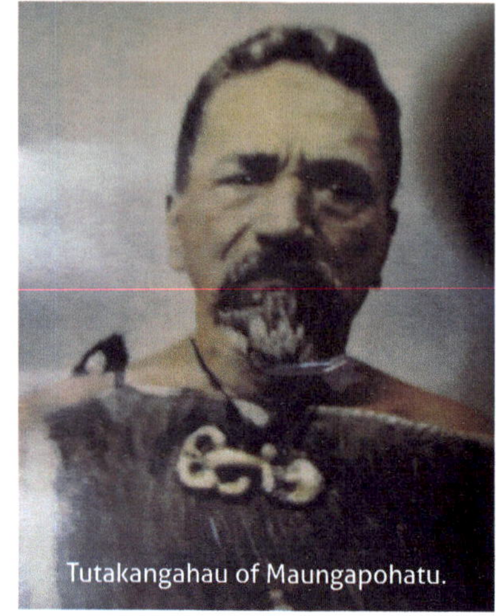
Tutakangahau of Maungapohatu.

With Lyndsay beside me, reading successive chapter drafts and sending them back for revising, spattered with red ink, and the same again to the altered drafts, we dug for gold. Slowly, the picture of Best's work, its sources and its long-term influence in the literature of this country became clearer, his primacy as an interlocutor of pre-contact Maori society was obvious. The place of Tutakangahau in this story also began to unfold and deepen. I was hooked.

My luck leapt when Jeanette — translating letters in Maori, written to the government by Tuhoe leaders over land issues in the early 20th century — handed me a copy of one written to Tutakangahau in August 1906 by a secretary from the Native Affairs Department. This informed him that, in view of Tutakangahau's support for the prophet Rua Kenana, his pension had been reduced and the mail run from Ruatahuna had been given to another leader, Te Whenuanui. This began a whole new focus for the thesis, a more fully rounded human figure emerging from those Urewera mists. I would devote a whole chapter to Tutakangahau's presence in the available literature and primary sources: letters he wrote to government officials and to the Maori language newspapers that flourished in the 19th century.

This is what makes research exhilarating: the unexpected, the epiphany that comes after hours of groundwork. The same cannot be said for a parallel, difficult and protracted human resources issue at the university which cannot be reprised here. This resulted in a flight from my perch in Maori Studies to a refuge in the English Department, rescued by Professor Patrick Evans. He'd seen his share of university office politics and opened the door to me. I would remain there to the work's completion: my progress was just as the writer Daniel Mendelsohn has described such ventures, in an interview with *Listener* journalist Diana Wichtel: "Insert yourself into the stream of history, you'll be amazed what happens." [50]

My space was little smaller than before: I shared the office with another post-graduate student, Sam Lister, finishing his master's. A dyed-in-the-wool Bob Dylan fan, we enjoyed each other's company and pushed on up the hill like Sisyphus, praying our fat documents wouldn't roll backwards in the night and disappear into the university's servers. Finally, the big day came: it was done, finished, the draft copies off to the examiners. By the end of 2006 I had no more thesis hanging over me and could concentrate on poetry. My fate was now in the hands of the academy, and I carried on with my part-time job at a community care home for one-time psychopaedic patients from the former Templeton Hospital.

When the day rolled around for my viva — the oral test where I had to defend the thesis — I took with me as whanau support my Tuhoe friend and co-religionist in the Maori church, Here Wilson (Heremahoe Hauwaho-Wilson, of Ruatoki). She enjoyed it more than me: after the karakia, after the grilling and the presentation of the overseas examiner's comments, after leaving the room and coming back twenty minutes later to be congratulated — I'd passed. This was Here's moment too: not an academic herself, but a woman who took no prisoners and feared no man, all five-foot-five of her, cancer patient's oxygen supply in tow, she regaled the assembled professors with her own perspective on Te Peehi (Best) and had them hanging on every word. Sighing with relief — the other members of our war party having departed — she and I drove to the local mall and shared a Chinese meal together in the surreal babble of that postmodern psychodrama, the Food Court. It seemed apt, and she loved it.

All that remained was for me to do the corrections, make the changes suggested by the examiners (par for the course with theses) — and then it was all over. I could graduate in 2007, as Doctor J. Far out: a member of the academy, a way away from the dope smoking chip-on-my-shoulder burned-out rebel of the 1970s. I wasn't too sure what it all meant, but I was proud of what I'd got through in the past ten years and only wished my mother — and yes, my father — could have lived to see it and rejoice with me.

While I was waiting for that day and having a superb korowai tailor-made for the moment when we would all cross the stage in the Town Hall on Graduation Day, I made a few notes; some chapter headings for a possible book that might come out of the thesis material. By this time the university had begun uploading theses to the library, so the work would have a permanent, accessible online presence. This meant that in New Zealand — a domain with few academic publishers and a small market for specialist books — there was no real point in revamping the doctorate in that form.

'Best of Both Worlds: Elsdon Best and the metamorphosis of Maori Spirituality: Te Painga Rawa o Nga Ao Tokorua: Te Peehi me te Putanga ke o te wairua Maori' — was going to have to find another life somewhere. That came about almost casually when my colleague, Paul Millar, a Baxter scholar and Bill Pearson's biographer, asked me what I was going to do with the thesis. I mentioned the outline I'd written and he asked to see it. I emailed him the one-page document of chapter topics and without telling me, he kindly fired it off to Geoff Walker, the managing editor of Penguin Books (NZ), suggesting he get in touch with me. Geoff was a well-known champion of New Zealand historical writing, editor and close friend of the historian, Michael King.

An email out of the blue arrived from Geoff, asking if I'd like to talk about a possible book on Best and Tutakangahau. I jumped at this and we had a conversation over the phone. He told me if I could write a proper proposal and send a sample of my writing, he'd look seriously at preparing a contract. I did just that and without much ado, we signed up for a book to be called *Best of Both Worlds: the story of Elsdon Best and Tutakangahau.* It happened so quickly, it was hard to keep up. I'd also heard about an award given each year by the Copyright Licensing Fund: $35,000 dollars for a work of non-fiction. I made out an application and once again found myself supplied with manna from heaven. At graduation soon after, enjoying that moment when the new doctors donned robes and bonnet to walk across the stage, I knew all I needed to do now was write the book. Scary.

The icing on the graduation cake was another invitation that mattered to me deeply: the event for Maori graduates, He Hui Whakahonore, held in conjunction each year with what Maori students called "the Pakeha graduation". This hui honours graduating Maori students, and it is a discretionary decision by Te Akatoki — the Maori Students Association — to invite Pakeha students they want to join them. For me, this was a deeply moving moment. My brother Eric and his wife Nancy came along

Jeanette, Jeffrey and Here Wilson, at the hui whakahonore for Maori graduates, 2007.

as a contingent from the Holman clan of old. I treasure both celebrations: carrying my Nanny Airey's old walking stick — carved anew by John Rua (the prophet Rua Kenana's mokopuna) — and swathed in my new korowai with its Blackball rugby league colours, I walked with the past into the future, facing backwards as Maori say.

The Best book now came to rule my writing life, although poetry still ran alongside him. All the next year, 2008 and into 2009, I sweated over the work, trying to find a register, a voice not academic yet one that rested on the research base of the thesis. I wanted to craft a book that found its own way of reaching the intelligent committed reader of New Zealand history, especially Tuhoe and other Maori who would be interested in the relationships and the times the book sought to unfold. As it took shape and a final draft was delivered on time, I now found myself in the skilled hands of Mike Wagg, the copy editor hired by Penguin to sweep the book clean of errors, large or small. Here was a man who could turn straw into gold, helped in the first instance if the gold was nearer the surface; we clicked together right away and he later told me I'd made his work easier by writing well in the first place.

In 2009, with the help of my friend Tipene Ohlson, we'd made contact with Richard Tumarae, the chairman of the marae committee at Maungapohatu and requested the opportunity of coming to meet the people of Tamakaimoana, Tutakangahau's whanau, with a view to launching the finished book there in March the following year. When the invitation came, I took a bound copy of the as-yet unpublished manuscript as a koha. It was an emotional moment when we were called on at the powhiri: it was here in 1916 that police had raided the community, shot and killed Rua's son Toko and his uncle Te Maipi, arresting the prophet, manacling him and some of his followers in a deliberate act of humiliation (whakaiti), on the pretext that he was spreading sedition in his opposition

Te Rau Tau (centennial) of the police raid on Rua's community.
Te Ururoa Flavell challenged by Tamakaimoana, Maungapohatu, 2.4.2016.

to conscription. These people owed me precisely nothing; the debt was all the other way.

The welcome was warm, the whaikorero spine-tingling and the hakari, the feast, fit for a king. They sent me away rejoicing, with the promise the committee would let me know in due course if I could bring them the book to launch. Within a few weeks, Richard had sent confirmation: yes, we could come, and he gave us some dates. I was elated: the book simply had to go there, to where it belonged. Busy with poetry book events as the year ended, my heart was overflowing. We looked for elders to come with us on the day, inviting Wharekawa Kaa, our Ngati Porou kaumatua from Te Hahi Mihinare, and Rangihau Te Moana, a Tuhoe elder resident in Christchurch. They both agreed to join us and our ope began forming for the walk up the mountain.

With family, publisher Geoff Walker, the elders and others who wanted to come, we assembled a team for the powhiri. Then we got the bad news: Tipene had suffered a massive heart attack. He was in Waikato Hospital undergoing a triple by-pass. Sadly, that meant this man who had done so much in getting me into Maungapohatu and past its gatekeepers, could not be there. We swallowed that disappointment and set out. Flying to Rotorua, we met Geoff and carried on to an overnight stay at Oputao marae at Ruatahuna;

Tipene Ohlson, Maungapohatu, 2009.

the powhiri at Maungapohatu was not due to start until 1 p.m., and we couldn't make it in a single day. The next morning, fortified by Tuhoe hospitality and regaled with stories, we packed up for the drive deep into Urewera country, where the seal ends and Pakeha dominion seems to evaporate.

It was only after arriving, and finding our other guests — Best's relatives, the Mackey family — who had been waiting for two hours after not hearing of the later start time, that we turned around and saw another four-wheel drive pull up at the gate. It was Tipene, fresh out of his hospital bed and hardly able to stand. "I wasn't going to miss this, my brother," he wheezed, as his son stood behind him, shaking his head. He'd refused to drive his father, fearing he would die en route, so Tipene said to him, "You drive me or I'll drive myself!" It was shaping to be a day I would never forget.

KI RUNGA: Tanenuiarangi meeting house and Te Maunga, Maungapohatu.
MATAU: Oputao 2010: Wharekawa Kaa, Rangihau Te Moana and Jeffrey.

Te Mapou marae, Maungapohatu.

38

The word made flesh

As we turned and looked up the rise from the gate to the marae atea, there they were on the porch of the meeting house, waiting for us: the ancestors. All the photographs of the tupuna had been taken from inside the wharenui and arranged in a line to look out at the manuhiri approaching with Tutakangahau's story as koha. There they were, the dead with the living, brought back to the life once more outside the body of the ancestor. Flanking them on either side were the black-clad kuia with their green pare kawakawa garlands; in a line on the right were the elders on the paepae waiting for their moment to stand and speak.

Anyone who has ever stood waiting to be called on knows that this is a significant moment of spiritual warfare. This is when your intentions are made clear, when you hear the challenge and the welcome, when you have a chance to respond and, in the process, become one with tangata whenua for the duration of the hui. When I saw those images, I trembled a little, my mouth was just that bit drier; this was no ordinary welcome. Tutakangahau was there, all of the hapu, all of the iwi, even Best himself, on the porch to acknowledge what was happening: the recognition of Tuhoe mana. The karanga rang out and we walked on, slowly, reverently. We took our seats, surrounded in the open air by the watching maunga — and waited. Tamakaimoana rose and spoke: one by one, their men regaled us. I could hardly think. Across the dry-grassed hill, flanked by a flowering camellia bush, outlined by mountain and cloud, Te Mapou spoke.

When our turn came to reply, Tipene rose unsteadily to his feet, the wind all but blowing away his words. Weak as he was from massive surgical intervention in his body, he stood there and replied. Later, he would whisper to me, "That's the first time I've ever done a whaikorero, my brother. I did it for you." This man — who, as a seven-year-old boy, alone in the bush with his dogs and a huge .303, shot and killed his first pig — now slew the monster of fear and ancient feelings of whakama. There were times as a child when his taha Pakeha, the Norwegian ancestry of his grandfather's whaler genes, had led others to question his whakapapa, his rights. No more. That day he stood tall and established forever his mana on his ancestor's ground: Rangi tu te Maungaroa Tipene Ohlson, tihei mauri ora!

Tipene Ohlson and his maunga, 2008.

The day unfolded as if the script were written on high: the hariru, the hongi, the kai, the korero, the giving of the books, the hakari that evening and the haunting sound of the Ringatu prayers in the evening as the believers chanted their liturgy from memory, keeping alive a world of oral transmission now under siege, inherited from Te Ao Nehera, the ancient world. In the middle of the night as most slept, I woke to hear one of the men chanting a karakia in the darkness. I knew I was in the presence of a unique gift, a privilege not granted many: a river that runs on through the world beyond, unsourced, its music and wisdom unheeded. This was the voice of the stars. I went outside and saw above in the bowl of the sky, the Milky Way unsullied. As I stared, a shooting star swept across my vision and vanished. Taking my cue from Father Abraham, I knelt down in the night, kissed the earth and prayed. There was no going back from here.

With Anipeka and her copy of the book at the launch.

Poem from the Blackball Bridge sonnets on the wall of the old miners' bath-house in Blackball.

39

The library is burning now

The libraries are burning now: fires of memory, pyres of happenings and encounters, the weaving of time and currents of feeling, leaving us as we breathe. What we remember is conditioned by what others do: the stories of our elders, of a time before we were born, times when we were too young to know and times when we began to call back time and tell our own version of events. They become as if true, histories beyond dispute, as if they had happened the way we become accustomed to telling them. Memories have their own polished truth like well-rubbed prayer beads, which in themselves contain faith and little else. When you sit down to retrace your life, one thing is true — the book is already written in your body.

This means my mother who bore me; my father's life, his war; my life as their son; my journeys around the day and the night to find him when he had gone, and her too now she has joined him. It means the people I met along the way, all manner of faces with all kinds of tales to tell; memories that burn impressions in, that time then burns away. Our libraries cannot be preserved for long but stories matter, so we keep on telling them. I'm grateful for every tale I've been told.

Deliverance

for Ken

Today I went back to Blackball
with Ken Oliver, entered
my old house and drank
tea with the new owner.

He's chopped out half the walls
in the kitchen and made it his.
I was more than a mite dumbfounded
at what little hold the memories had.

It was like I'd died and a curious
ghost had called in my place.
Steve, our host, showed us a scar
from massive heart surgery

and asked Ken was he living
pure, still walking the Jesus Road?
We drove to the bombed-out bath-house
where grass grows in the showers.

We tried to explain the Freudian impact
of showering with our fathers: going
into the high priest's chamber
and meeting your god, butt-naked.

He took shots of the empty Anglican church
on a crazy angle; I sang cowboy songs
made up on the spur of the moment.
We sat on the rim of the League field

as the wind waved tides of grass.
Was this the Blackball versus Ngahere
grudge match, played with no players,
no result, and a crowd of spooks?

We left before the whistle blew.
We couldn't stand the suspense.

Rugby league field, Blackball Domain;
seats from the old miner's bath house.

Te Mapou Marae, Maungapohatu 2009.
Jeanette King photo

Mihimihi — acknowledgments

While every effort has been made to trace and contact the owners of copyright material reproduced in this book, we would be pleased to hear from any copyright holder we have been unable to contact. Full details of permitted sources appear in the endnotes that follow.

Whanau: I acknowledge my family and close relatives, the living and the dead. To my grandmother, Eunice Winfred Airey; my parents William Thomas (Bill) Holman and my mother, Mary Elisabeth Holman (née Woollam); my brother Eric Holman and my sisters, Jill Clarke and Elisabeth Richards — arohanui.

To Theresa Newcombe and her mother Alice Noble; to Lee (née Gosden); to our children Timothy, Lex and Raine; to my wife Jeanette King, to Adele and Mark; and to our tamariki mokopuna — arohanui.

Writers: Thanks to Jennifer Blackburn and the family of Peter Hooper for approval to use material from my personal correspondence with her late brother.

The estate of James K. Baxter, 1972, for permission to reproduce selections from the poet's verse, and to Paul Millar.

Photographs: Thanks to Doreen Adams for the photo of the Ngahere gold dredge.

Thanks to Nicola Bellugue, Pete Bell's sister, for his photo of the Blackball Workingmen's Club.

Thanks also to Peter Tremayne, ex-RNZAF, for photos of the C-124 Globemaster at Wigram, 1957 and the Bristol Freighter in Malaya, 1960.

Artists: Special thanks for permission to use their work here: Jan Fitzgerald, Earl Tutty, John Madden, Les Holmes Germanicus, Dylan Horrocks and Sharon Murdoch. I acknowledge the Hotere Trust for the use of Ralph Hotere's cover images on books by Hone Tuwhare and James K. Baxter.

Publishers: Special thanks to Rachel Scott, Otago University Press, for assistance with obtaining permissions.

Endnotes

1 Arthur Charles Venus (formerly Chief Visual Instructor RNZN), with interviewer Kelly Ana Morey, Oral History Project, Navy Museum, Devonport, http://rnzncomms.org/memories/venus/
2 Auckland City Libraries, Ref/ 7-A14286A.
3 See Paul McBride, *The West Coast Farming Times,* February 2015, pp 3-6.
4 'Ngahere railway lovin' blues, 1958', in *As Big as a Father*, Steele Roberts, 2002, p 37.
5 Babette Deutsch, 'Marseillaise', *Honey out of the Rock*, D. Appleton & Co, Michigan: 1925.
6 *The Lost Pilot*, Penguin New Zealand, 2013, pp 33-34.
7 *'Sonnet xxx, The late great Blackball Bridge sonnets*, Steele Roberts Aotearoa, Wellington, 2004, p 49.
8 *Modern World Book of Flying*, R. Haddon, C. Harvey, E. Wolff, Sampson Low, Marston, London: 1955, p 45.
9 Copyright @ 1965 by Warner Bros Inc, renewed by Special Rider Music.
10 nzhistory.govt.nz/people/wilfrid-clouston
11 In *Fly Boy*, Steele Roberts, Wellington: 2010, p24.
12 Inesis Feldmanis & Karlis Kangeris, "The Volunteer SS Legion in Latvia". Ministry of Foreign Affairs of Latvia.
13 For more information on this period, see, *Beautiful Balts: from Displaced Persons to New Australians*, Jayne Persian, New South Publishing, Sydney, 2017.
14 Read more: www.bobdylan.com/us/songs#ixzz3bUEKfAY9Copyright © 1962, 1968 by Warner Bros. Inc.; renewed 1990, 1996 by Special Rider Music
15 By kind permission of Jenny Blackburn, Peter Hooper's sister, 2018.
16 Jack Gilbert, 'Steel Guitars', from *The Great Fires: Poems 1982-1992*, Alfred A. Knopf, New York: 2008. © 1994 by Jack Gilbert, whose work is used by permission of Alfred A. Knopf, an imprint of the Knopf Doubleday Publishing Group, a division of Penguin Random House. All rights reserved.
17 W.H. Auden, 'As I Walked Out One Evening', in *Another Time*, Random House, New York, 1940.
18 Theodore Roethke, 'The Far Field', in *The Far Field*, Doubleday, New York, 1964.
19 www.educarchile.cl/ech/pro/app/detalle?GUID=123.456.789.000&ID=101109
20 From *Selected Poems* by Pablo Neruda, edited by Nathaniel Tarn, translated by Anthony Kerrigan, W.S. Merwin, Alastair Reid and Nathaniel Tarn, published by Jonathan Cape. Reproduced by permission of the Random House Group Ltd, ©1970.
21 *ibid*, *Algunas Bestias/Some Beasts*, translator Anthony Kerrigan.
22 D.C. Walker, 'Baxter's Notebook.' *Landfall 97,* March 1971, pp 20-24.
23 James Keir Baxter, Sonnet 34, *Jerusalem Sonnets, poems for Colin Durning*, Bibliography Room, University of Otago, Dunedin: 1970. Reproduced with the permission of the estate of James K. Baxter, 1972.
24 James K. Baxter, *Ode to Auckland and other poems*, Caveman Press, Dunedin, 1972. Reproduced with the permission of the Estate of James K. Baxter, 1972.
25 *ibid.*

26 See Eric Beardsley, *Sliding Down the Hypotenuse: a memoir*, Canterbury University Press, 2011, Chapter 11, 'Ink on my fingers', pp 133-55.
27 Janet Frame, *An Angel at my Table*, Women's Press, London, 1984, p 127.
28 'In My Craft Or Sullen Art', Dylan Thomas, from *Deaths and Entrances*, Dent, London, 1946.
29 V.S. Naipaul, *The Enigma of Arrival*, Penguin, London, 1988.
30 L.S. Lowry — www.iwm.org.uk/collections/item/object/17026, Public Domain, https://commons.wikipedia.org/w/index.php?curid=42129163.
31 Letter to the Colossians, Chapter 1, verse 27.
32 See *The Lost Pilot*, Penguin, Auckland, 2013.
33 Miroslav Holub, *Vanishing Lung Syndrome*, Faber & Faber, 1990.
34 *ibid.*
35 Joseph Brodsky, 'On "September 1, 1939" by W.H. Auden', in *Less Than One: Selected Essays*, King Penguin, London, 1987, p 347.
36 W. B. Yeats, *Essays and Introductions*, Macmillan, New York, 1961, p 522.
37 Jack Gilbert, "Jack Gilbert and the Landscape of American Poetry in 1965", in *Contemporary American Poetry: Voice of America Forum Lectures*, Washington, 1965, pp 133-44.
38 Irving Weinman, writer, teacher, voice for justice; born Boston, 1937, died Lewes, England 2015.
39 *Harvard Book Review*, 2008, Justine Nagurney, *Reinventing a Good Thing: Anderson Fails to Improve on Older Translations of Akhmatova".* Reviewed*: The Word That Causes Death's Defeat: Akhmatova's Poems of Memory,* Nancy Anderson; Yale University Press, 2004.
40 See John Dennison, 'Ko te pakeha te teina — Baxter's cross-cultural poetry', *JNZL No. 23: 2* (2005), English Department, University of Waikato, pp 36-44.
41 Dick Moth remembered the soldier as Karl Kraus: "We picked him up in early 1944, on the Sangro/Rubicone rivers." There is a Karl Kraus (died 13.05.1944) buried at the German military cemetery in Cassino, Block 9/Grave 433.
42 Jack Gilbert, 'Jack Gilbert and the Landscape of American Poetry', in *Contemporary American Poetry*, Howard Nemerov (editor), Voice of America Forum Lectures (undated), p 133.
43 www.landfallreview.com/who-remembers-the-barouder-se-5000/
44 www.stoatspring.blogspot.co.nz/2010/11/fly-boy.html
45 https://nzbooks.org.nz/2017/literature/jewels-and-binoculars-murray-bramwell/
46 http://pantograph-punch.com/post/blood-ties
47 www.theparisreview.org/interviews/5583/jack-gilbert-the-art-of-poetry-no-91-jack-gilbert
48 Jack Gilbert, 'A brief for the defense', in *Refusing Heaven, Poems*, Albert Knopf, New York. © 2005 by Jack Gilbert. Used by permission of Alfred A. Knopf, an imprint of the Knopf Doubleday Publishing Group, a division of Penguin Random House LLC. Any third-party use of this material, outside of this publication is prohibited. Interested parties must apply directly to Penguin Random House LLC for permission.
49 Jeffrey Paparoa Holman, 'Said, 'Jack'', in *Blood Ties, New and Selected Poems: 1963–2016,* Canterbury University Press, 2017, p 61.
50 Daniel Mendelsohn, interviewed by Diana Wichtel for the *NZ Listener*, 2015, cited in *Driving to Treblinka*, Awa Press, Wellington, 2017, p 4.

Index

D

E

F

G

H

I

J

K

L

M

N

O

P

Q

R

S

T

U

V

W

Y

Z

(xxiii)

In the house of my body I carry that river.
In the depths of my being I'm water. My

body's the home of a wandering miner
too old to go down and too tired to go on.

When I stand on the world and look over
what's living, what's left, I'm the bridge

to the past and the road still unfolding.
Wheels and water, tracks and steam, all

the footprints beside the river, thousands
of hours spent double in blackness, a light

on my head to remind me I'm human. In
the shape of my bones I'm an NZR sleeper

and when my last shift comes, my Dog Watch
boys, lay me like coal by the sea at Karoro.

The late great Blackball Bridge Sonnets, Steele Roberts 2004